Brand from the Inside

Eight Essentials to Emotionally Connect Your Employees to Your Business

Libby Sartain

Mark Schumann

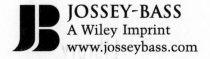

JOSSEY-BASS
A Wiley Imprint
www.josseybass.com

Published by Jossey-Bass
A Wiley Imprint
989 Market Street, San Francisco, CA 94103-1741   www.josseybass.com

Jossey-Bass books and products are available through most bookstores. To contact Jossey-Bass directly
call our Customer Care Department within the U.S. at 800-956-7739, outside the U.S. at 317-572-3986,
or fax 317-572-4002.

Jossey-Bass also publishes its books in a variety of electronic formats. Some content that appears in
print may not be available in electronic books.

Library of Congress Cataloging-in-Publication Data
Sartain, Libby, 1954-
  Brand from the inside : eight essentials to emotionally connect your employees to your business /
Libby Sartain, Mark Schumann—1st ed.
    p. cm.
  Includes bibliographical references and index.
  ISBN-13: 978-0-7879-8189-1
  ISBN-10: 0-7879-8189-3
  1. Employee motivation. 2. Brand name products. I. Schumann, Mark, 1955- II. Title.
  HF5549.5.M63S27 2006
  658.3'14—dc22
                              2006001081
Printed in the United States of America
FIRST EDITION
HB Printing 10 9 8 7 6 5 4 3 2 1

CONTENTS

For our spouses,
David Sartain and Leann Schumann,
for living with our work for all these years
and living their own "best brands"
of nurturing and support

INTRODUCTION

If it doesn't happen inside, it can't happen outside.

If the brand doesn't live on the inside, it can't thrive on the outside.

And if the brand isn't built from the inside, few may believe it on the outside.

That's why we wrote this book.

To show you, as a leader in business—whether in human resources or corporate communications or marketing or some other area—how to create an emotional connection with employees on the inside of your business so that they, in turn, deliver to your customers on the outside.

If you don't bring it to life on the inside, it can't live on the outside.

You may be thinking *That's a nice idea, but is it essential?*

Fact is, businesses in every corner of the world look for a "secret sauce" to accomplish many things. How to outsmart competitors. How to stay out of trouble. How to make more money and increase shareholder value. A lot of what businesses need to do boils down, simply, to how to engage employees. How to recruit, retain, and motivate the right employees in the right jobs, to do the right things at the right time, to deliver what customers expect. And that boils down to how to emotionally connect employees to the business so that, as a result, the business succeeds.

At the same time, in every corner of the world, businesses look for new ways to clearly and directly address issues related to talent, to people. To skip through the presentations to get to the core of what needs to happen so the business succeeds.

And in every corner of the world, businesses look for solutions to the ever-growing problems of silo thinking and working. Wanting to break through the internal barriers so well-intentioned people can connect the dots rather than work in isolation. So the business succeeds.

The essentials to these and other critical issues for business can be found in the brand a business takes to its publics, outside and inside. And that's what this book is all about.

For over twenty-five years, we have found ourselves in the middle of businesses struggling with formidable people issues. Along the way we have learned how so many issues boil down to the emotional connection a business builds with employees so that they in turn commit to the business as a place to buy and a place to work, deliver what the business promises to customers, and nurture what the business promises to employees. Our work—through trial and error, success and miss, enlightened efforts and less enlightened ones—has shown us what may be the secret sauce that business seeks.

We call it <u>employer brand</u>: how a business builds and packages its identity, from its origins and values, what it promises to deliver to emotionally connect employees so that they in turn deliver what the business promises to customers.

Building the employer brand from *inside* the business—with a consistent substance, voice, and authenticity throughout the employment relationship—may be the most powerful tool a business can use to emotionally engage employees.

That's what employer brand is all about. And why we wrote this book.

Brand is a language and a process of thought that is, ultimately, simple. Business, in every corner of the world, begs for simplicity.

At every business, the issues can be so complex, solutions so involved, and working teams so spread out that it's easy to lose sight of what it takes to get something done.

Based on our years of doing this work, we believe employer brand may be the secret to simplifying how business can approach many issues.

Now, you may say, "Oh, I've heard of that employer brand stuff, and it's only an HR thing" or "Yes, I went to a seminar on that employer brand stuff, and it's a communication thing."

Wrong.

Even though we are from HR and communication, our point of view extends beyond these immediate worlds to how to solve business issues.

We see, every day, that well-intentioned people in business can easily get mired in silos and complexity and, as a result, let themselves be less than completely effective.

We believe that, by using employer brand as a framework, you can cut through what gets in the way of your business getting things done. Because brands are, at their core, simple.

And business begs for simplicity.

We share parallel passions about what employees can contribute when emotionally connected to a business. Libby has worked the internal hallways of human resources; Mark has worked as a consultant in corporate, employee, and HR communications. We joined forces, as client and consultant, to help build employer brands at two legendary businesses: Southwest Airlines and Yahoo!

When we started working together, at Southwest in the late 1980s, we first collaborated to communicate a new flexible benefits plan. We quickly realized this could be a prime opportunity to deepen the sense of relationship between the business and its people. Rather than produce conventional benefit communications, we got to the heart of the emotional connection through a multimedia campaign that could have emerged from an advertising agency to promote a product to customers—using every creative way we could imagine to market the plan *and* the company. We discovered that to get people to pay attention, we had to approach them emotionally, to connect with them emotionally. And motivate them to connect the dots to discover why benefits, in addition to being personally important, symbolized their relationship with the company. Little did we know this would be the start of what is now considered a legendary employer brand at Southwest.

Then we communicated another benefits program. And another. We moved into other topics and, within a few years, had created a total picture of the work experience at Southwest that reached out to prospective, new, current, and departing employees. With every opportunity we contributed to a fabric that would later be articulated as the Southwest employer brand. With every opportunity we planted seeds that, when nurtured, would become the emotional connection between the company and its employees and customers. We did it with common sense, hard work, and a desire to do the smart thing for the business and the right thing for people each step of the way. When all the pieces came together, we had created a marvelous employer brand that the business has successfully sustained. And along the way we coined a few lasting phrases, such as "color outside the lines" and "we are serious about having fun."

A few years ago, Libby began applying the lessons of Southwest to a business just starting to address its employer brand: a new, vibrant business fully committed to connecting its customer and employer brands in a seamless way. The Yahoo! experience reveals what a business can accomplish inside when it leverages the magic it creates outside.

We approach employer brand from two perspectives. Libby works in the world of human resources, with deep experience in building programs that define a place to work. Mark's world of communications is all about articulating the employee experience. Libby sees employer brand through the lens of HR, in which the best programs are built on an authentic foundation of corporate identity and values. Mark sees employer brand from the employee perspective of how real people think about where they work.

We learned most of our lessons together. Even when we worked on separate efforts, we constantly shared ideas and experiences. And although we never viewed our collaboration as unique, we certainly see what a difference HR and communications people can make when working together rather than pursuing isolated strategies. In workplaces, whereas HR often focuses on strategies and processes, Corporate Communications frequently takes on internal and external messaging, and Marketing focuses on a brand that must be delivered outside. The three never seem to meet—or worse, they compete.

Building a great brand from the inside of a business takes more than one corporate function. It can't be done by Marketing alone or HR alone or Corporate Communications alone. Though each well-meaning silo may create its own programs to build a brand, reinforce a culture, or communicate a message, such programmatic efforts cannot change the way people think and act. Only when people work together, seamlessly, can there be hope for authenticity in the employer brand. This book provides a way for these groups to work together, and the methodology we suggest transcends the traditional work of Marketing, Corporate Communications, or HR. Focusing on the employer brand can help your business overcome the common stumbling blocks of bureaucracy, egos, territorialism, fiefdoms, matrix structures, and misaligned goals.

That's why we call employer brand the secret sauce that, when properly prepared, can create real results for business. And we're among the first to tell this story. Although many books talk about brands and customers, few focus on how to build a legendary employer brand from within. This may in fact be the first book to focus on what must happen inside a business for an employer brand to create not only positive buzz about a business as a place to work but also a commitment from people that produces extraordinary results.

That, in a nutshell, is what we've learned along the road to employer brand. What it can accomplish for a business. What it can mean to an employee. Why it's critical to any business strategy. And how it should connect what happens inside a business to the customer experience on the outside. We've learned what works and what doesn't. What succeeds and what bombs. How the best intentions can get trapped in silos within a business. How some brands understand who they are, offering a real essence and spirit, while others remain hollow.

The key to attracting, retaining, and engaging employees is the creative, holistic use of what the business believes from its core, as articulated in its employer brand. It's securing the right people with the right skills in the right jobs and, once in place, establishing a relationship of trust that engages them to deliver the right behaviors so that, ultimately, the business executes on strategy and delivers its promise to customers. And it all begins inside. Just as a brand makes promises to customers on the outside, that business makes promises to its employees on the inside. And for that internal experience to be authentic, it must build what it is and what it believes from inside the business. So that leaders in the business deliver on the promise to the employees, who deliver on the promise to customers. So the business captures a share of the heart of the employee, who in turn captures a share of the heart of customers, which ultimately results in success for the business. The essence of this emotional connection is the same core of a business that is at the core of the brand the business takes to its public.

Any business, in any corner of the world, must create an experience to engage its employees *before* it can expect those employees to deliver the brand to customers. The key to employer brand is tapping the emotional essence of the company and its brand and using that emotional essence to frame and articulate the employee experience. It takes a collaboration of many in a company to nurture the employer brand that will make a difference.

This book is your guidebook on an important journey for your business: to create this connection. Although the lessons we have learned frame our point of view, this is essentially a how-to guide for any business leader who wants to engage people. And wants to find the essential ingredients of the secret sauce.

We share the shortcuts we wish we had taken. Material we used that may be helpful. Questions we asked (and wish we had asked). And things we hope you remember that we hope we never forget. Practical tips and methods rooted in business fundamentals and common sense to ensure that every employee understands what it takes, each day from each person, for a business to become a great place to work *and* a great brand to buy.

For years we have planned to write this book. We have discussed it over lunch, over drinks, on the golf course, when preparing and delivering presentations, and after our most productive business meetings. The pace of business evolution compels us to write it now. Business leaders have long known the need to differentiate products and services. Today it's critical for business to differentiate the strategy for people—to get the right people in the right jobs at the right time and to emotionally connect employees to the business so they commit to what the business promises to customers.

This book describes, in detail, the eight essentials for you to build your employer brand for your business—from the inside—to create the emotional connection with employees.

Our goal is to inspire you to champion brand transformation from within your business, working together instead of in silos, to create a seamless, consistent, authentic experience for employees and customers.

We believe in the power of employer brand.

Thanks for joining us.

February 2006
San Carlos, California   LIBBY SARTAIN
Ridgefield, Connecticut   MARK SCHUMANN

PART ONE

GET SMART!

Chapter One

Essential #1: Discover

We, the authors, are brand dependent.

And we admit it. We love to discover brands.

We each begin each day sipping or gulping a certain brand of coffee, showering with a specific brand of soap, eating a particular brand of yogurt topped with a selected brand of naturally healthy cereal. Nothing gets between us and our brands.

We are emotionally connected to our brands. And we come by this brand dependence naturally.

Our childhood memories are filled with brand images. The smiling face of a cold pitcher of Kool-Aid. The roar of Tony the Tiger. Our sadness at learning that Trix are for kids, not for rabbits. Mark running down a suburban street wearing Keds and a Davy Crockett coonskin cap. Libby playing with a Barbie doll.

Our mothers were classic brand consumers of the 1950s and 1960s. Mark's mother would serve only vegetables by Del Monte, catsup by Heinz, and soft drinks by Coca-Cola. Libby's mother would emerge for the day with makeup by Frances Denney, a permanent by Toni, and nail polish by Revlon. Our fathers got into the brand act, too. Mark's family only drove Chevrolets; Libby's family, only her father's Oldsmobile.

We were lucky to grow up in an era of great brands that instantly commanded respect and passion. Imagining the grand images of air travel of Pan Am and TWA. Trusting the family car to the men who wore the Texaco star. Watching a fatherly Walt Disney on television (before cable) introducing his *Wonderful World of Color* and telling us about the latest rides at Disneyland.

Laughing at Lucy and Ricky as they smoked their favorite cigarettes (provided, coincidentally, by the sponsors of the show) while chatting with Ethel and Fred. Hearing Dinah Shore sing that we should "see the USA in your Chevrolet." Wondering if we needed an application to join the Pepsi Generation or if we really could teach the world to sing in perfect harmony by drinking Coca-Cola. Watching McDonald's dot the nation with fast food, Sears and JC Penney becoming gateways to anything a consumer could want, and Macy's putting on a parade long before businesses plastered their names on stadiums. We defined our lives through our brands. And we learned, first hand, how to emotionally connect to everything a brand represents.

With such branded beginnings, it's no surprise we would land in branded experiences in our early professional work. Libby would spend her early HR years in the hallways of the legendary Mary Kay, two words that instantly evoke images of pink Cadillacs and successful saleswomen. Mark would write copy and stage new product events for, among others, Minute Maid and Quaker Oats—where he came up with the idea to introduce a new cereal to employees *before* the debut for customers. After all, he reasoned, "If we want customers to eat the new cereal we should first let employees experience the taste."

We learned from these early years, as brand users and workers, just what a brand can do. How people react to brands. How brands provide emotional connection. How brands simplify. And we picked up valuable lessons that, years later, would help us capitalize on the power of this most intense business tool to create emotional connections.

So for you—someone interested in what an employer brand can do for your business—your first essential is to focus on your observations, in general, of what brand can do. The power. The language. The simplicity. Starting with the brand will help you apply its mystery to the realities of your business. So you can first absorb the fundamentals of how brands work and what brands can do, so you fully realize the potential of brands to create emotional connections with the people who make a difference to your business. Your employees.

Here is the short course: fifteen key lessons we have learned over the years for you to keep in mind as you build your employer brand from the inside.

FIFTEEN THINGS TO LEARN ABOUT BRANDS

1. BRANDS ARE ELUSIVE, MYSTERIOUS REALITIES OF BUSINESS.

Brands make people do things. They command people to think and buy, to want and do. They motivate people to consider and choose. They push people to do everything from pull levers in voting booths to fill shopping carts in a bricks-and-mortar store and on line. Their power is the target of billions of marketing dollars spent each year. A brand's influential power may be its most seductive feature. The feelings a brand generates. The personal experience of connecting with a favorite brand. The commitment to a longer-term relationship with a brand, filled with loyalty and trust. Why else would you, as a brand-driven customer, spend money at a retail location for a cup of coffee you could easily brew at home? Or go out for ice cream you could simply store in the freezer?

2. BRANDS SIMPLIFY THE VALUE, OPPORTUNITY, AND RESULTS YOU EXPECT.

Brands boil down choice to what is ultimately simple.

They crystallize what you, the customer, need and want. They articulate what you anticipate and experience. They simplify what you receive and remember. Every day, as a consumer, you make buying decisions based on the reputation sealed in a company's brand. You consider whether you trust a brand, believe in a brand, agree with a brand. And you remember what you choose.

Of course, this brand memory reaches beyond the items you purchase to the places you first choose to work. That's what we found. For Mark, the first branded stop was flipping hamburgers and dipping ice cream cones at the well-branded Dairy Queen just as it was introducing its now-famous Brazier Burger. For Libby, it was working at a coffee shop at Marriott, a hotel chain that had already learned the importance of employees in delivering a consistent customer experience. Something about the brands helped us make these initial choices. Just as if we were consumers buying products. They also help us remember why we were there. Is it the same for you?

3. EVERY BUSINESS HAS A BRAND.

There's no "get out of brand free" card. Every business has one.

Or, we should say, every business that wants to be known by someone for something.

Every business, no matter its size, no matter what it does, has customers. Although some may have more visible marketing to customers—because of what the business does—every business is known for something. As a result, every product has something in the market it needs to be known for—to sell more products. And that is the job of a brand.

At the same time, some businesses with many products or services may brand each product or service separately. The business overall may want to be known for one thing that captures the essence of all the consumer brands. That may be why Procter & Gamble, while branding specific products with particular labels, states on its internet site that "two billion times a day, P&G brands touch the lives of people around the world."[1] "We want to be in touch, in the lead, and improving lives every day," says Diana Shaheen of Procter & Gamble.[2] Or why Kraft, through its many branded products, makes an overall brand claim of "helping people around the world eat and live better."[3] And when Anheuser-Busch, while marketing its distinct products in distinct ways, places everything under an umbrella of "making friends is our business."[4]

4. BRANDS ARE ULTIMATELY COMMERCIAL.

Businesses do not have brands just to have brands. They have brands because brands help them sell.

A brand is the shortcut to your process, as a customer, of choosing. To make it easy for you to base that choice on a sense of experience, reliability, reputation. To limit other choices you might consider. To move you directly to action.

As you consider the lessons of brand, you need to look at brand as shorthand for choice. A shortcut to action. A brand that does *not* lead to choice—the right choice—may entertain but it will not succeed. It will not make a difference to the business. And brand is all about a customer making the choice a business needs.

Brands are not passive. They do not merely appear. They are about action. Doing something. Choosing something. Believing something. They motivate people to buy. To choose. To vote. To commit. To recommend. To connect. Looking at any issue through the prism of brand forces us to think commercially.

So a well-branded company, like Hallmark, realizing the importance of keeping its brand alive and relevant, says to employees in a company publication, "The Hallmark brand sets our company apart from the others. As Hallmarkers, we enhance the value of our brand each time we uphold our brand promise of enriching lives. The action doesn't have to be complicated or even plum colored. What if we simply focus on enriching lives every day? Think what a difference we can make."[5]

5. BRANDS INFLUENCE CUSTOMER CHOICES AT EACH TOUCH POINT.

Every customer experience is a series of touch points.

A brand promises a specific experience at each touch point that you, as a customer, have with a product, service, or message a business delivers. A touch point occurs every time you come in contact with what a business offers. And at each touch point the brand can comfort or irritate, assure or frighten, satisfy or disappoint.

As a consumer you see this every day. You view brands through the touch points you experience. The foods you select. The restaurants and hotels you choose. The airlines you endure. The places you visit. The products you rely on. Brands assure you that a product or service you select will be functionally reliable to get the job done as well as to deliver an emotionally satisfying experience.

At each touch point you test the authenticity of the brand promise. Every time you touch a brand, you ask, "Am I getting what it promised?" And if you experience disappointment, you may wonder, "What other brands may be available that may deliver the same thing?" As UPS announces to its employees in a special brand publication, "living out the brand doesn't come solely from mission statements. Or product differentiation. Or lower prices. Or snappy logos. It flows from the intersection of culture and people. It flows from the living, breathing brand."[6] This lives every day at UPS. "Our promise," says Tom Pizutti, corporate employee communications manager, UPS, "is that we will make each customer feel as if they are our only customer."[7]

6. BRANDS DEFINE YOUR CUSTOMER EXPERIENCE.

Brands paint the picture a customer steps into.

Every day, in every corner of the world, customers make choices. Some choose to buy. Others to avoid. Some recommend a particular brand. Others complain. Some complete a transaction; others engage in a relationship with the business that produces the product or service.

As a consumer you look to the brand to define the experience you choose. You expect Ritz-Carlton to offer luxury because that's what the brand promises. You expect to "have it your way" at Burger King because that's what you repeatedly hear. You look for the friendly skies because the brand says that's a fair expectation. "The consumer is boss," says P&G's Diana Shaheen. "Our purpose is to improve lives in small but meaningful ways every day."

The brand promise frames what you expect and defines what the product or service—and the business—should deliver. As you use what you purchase, you ask yourself if the product or service lives up to its promise. If the promise foretells the experience. If the experience ultimately lives up to the expectations the brand sets.

Brands adapt as customer experiences change. Take, for example, what's happening today on the Internet. This new dimension of the customer connection intensifies the experiences a brand defines. For example, as a customer, you can sit in front of a computer to shop for a car. Once upon a time, you would go from dealer to dealer to kick tires and consider options. Now it can all be done online, transforming the car-buying experience from potentially confrontational to fully informational. You can use a myriad of consumer reports and reviews, sites like Yahoo! Autos, to compare *before* starting to shop. You call the shots with the click of a mouse. It's no surprise that, in response, the automaker must dramatically change how it presents its brand. No longer is the televised image the only way to convey the look and feel.

7. BRANDS CONNECT CUSTOMERS TO A "BIG IDEA."

Brands do not simply sell. They capture the essence of a mission.

The power of brand doesn't stop with a specific choice or transaction. It doesn't end with *functional* and *emotional* connections.

The potential for brand can create a "halo effect" for the entire business *if* it delivers more.

A brand is at its most powerful when it reaches beyond the product to represent an idea emerging from the soul of the business. When purpose reaches beyond the sale to advance the relationship—to engage you, first on a *functional* level for being reliable and then on an *emotional* level that will touch your feelings. Real brand power occurs when the brand reaches you *inspirationally;* when you connect with the "big idea" the business and brand stand for. When the brand reveals what happens *inside* the core of a business, giving you a glimpse of what makes a business tick. What the business believes in. Its values. Its heritage. Its icons. And a bit of its soul.

Why else would Apple, so brilliantly, make you believe you participate in a cause, not simply that you buy a product? Or Disney make you feel, as parents, that childhood without a visit to the Magic Kingdom will not be complete? Or Whole Foods make you feel, as you buy organic peanut butter, that you are somehow helping to keep the world healthy? Consider the "creative impulses of young storytellers" that are "bits of magic stored in Crayola brand crayons, markers, paints and colored pencils, or unleashed in the pliable potential of Silly Putty." Or how, "for nearly 100 years Hallmark has believed in the very best of human nature" and how that belief stirs a passion "you see and feel in everything that bears the Hallmark name—in a store, in your mailbox, on the internet, on your television." As CEO Don Hall remarks, "We are invited to give voice to people's feelings—of joy and grief, of compassion and healing. We provide ways for people to express themselves" and "help them reach out with words of hope and encouragement every day. These are enduring human needs, which is why I have such confidence in the future of our company."[8]

A brand can connect a customer to what a business is all about—its character, personality, and values. To be remembered, a brand can give a face to a business. And to be revered, a brand can create a sense of comfort, a degree of security, a spirit of hope. It can symbolize the larger meaning of what a business stands for—the idea, experience, or relationship. The way Disney "is dedicated to making the dreams of families and children a reality"[9] or how the Body Shop is committed to "passionately campaign for the protection of the environment, human and civil rights, and against animal testing within the cosmetics and toiletries industry."[10]

8. A GREAT BRAND WILL STAND THE TEST OF TIME.

The power of brand is not simply for the short term. A great brand is in this for the long haul. It will last through fads and fashion, trends and styles, economic ups and downs. Articulating a core that will not change with the times, even as products and services adapt. Standing on values, not just current offerings. Think Coca-Cola. Pepsi. General Electric. Wells Fargo. Great brands become (and remain) essential to what you need, not only through products and services, but through value systems. What would you do without Starbucks coffee? Or Kleenex? Or GE light bulbs? Or Colgate, with its claim to "offer products that allow global consumers to improve quality of life for themselves and the ones they love"?[11] These brands are relevant not only for what they do but for the business ideas and experience they represent.

To stand the test of time, a brand must stand for something. And for most that something has to be more than simply selling more. The brand can provide a glimpse into what thrives at the core of a business, why it must exist, why a customer must emotionally invest in its success. So it's no surprise that brands often commit to big ideas, such as Pfizer's commitment to "improve the quality of life of people around the world and help them enjoy longer, healthier and more productive lives."[12] Or Wrigley's claim that its brands of chewing gum "have been a refreshing part of everyday life for more than 100 years."[13]

To stand the test of time, a brand must project a personality of a business beyond the marketing. That personality, more than the color of the product or packaging, projects what differentiates the business from its competitors. Marc Gobé puts it this way: "To realize their full potential, brands must recognize from the outset that their emotional identity is not only a result of ads and products but also corporate policy and stances."[14] So it's no surprise that, to create this link, real and imagined characters are cast in the brand drama, even after they die. Try to imagine Wendy's without the image of Dave or Disneyland without Walt or fried chicken without Colonel Sanders. They continue to be the most surprising icons, proving that brand power is not hampered by logistics. No wonder that Kellogg's, perhaps with an image of Tony the Tiger in the background, claims "you can't beat being part of a company that's like a family."[15]

To stand the test of time, a brand must celebrate its heritage and honor its heroes. Salute its legends as a business passes the core of the brand from generation to generation. Think of Herb Kelleher creating the first route map for Southwest Airlines on a cocktail napkin. Hewlett and Packard inventing in their garage. Estée Lauder or Mrs. Fields creating in their kitchens. Michael Dell dreaming in his dorm room. David Filo and Jerry Yang starting Yahoo! from a trailer on the Stanford campus, procrastinating to avoid completing their dissertations. Stories that live in the hearts and minds for generations and emotionally connect customers to the origins of the business. "We are proud of our heritage," says P&G's Diana Shaheen, "and the consistency from generation to generation helps drive pride."

9. BRANDS CREATE EMOTIONAL CONNECTIONS.

At their heart, brands touch the soul, excite the mind, satisfy the need, and motivate the action.

Emotion is at the core of a brand's power when a brand represents what you, a customer, *aspire* to be and *can* be by connecting with the products, services, and experience the brand represents. Advertisers paint pictures of what it can mean to experience the product or service the brand delivers. They connect with your aspiration of what your life can be if you follow the impulse to choose and buy. They show happy, fulfilled people using a product or service. Spokespersons who positively describe an experience. Words and images that connect what the brand can deliver with what you picture for yourself. Whether that is sitting in the driver's seat of a car, dining at a restaurant, taking a vacation or using a type of medication. Marc Gobé suggests that such emotional branding "focuses on the most compelling aspect of the human character: the desire to transcend material satisfaction, and experience emotional fulfillment." The brand achieves such an emotional connection when "it can tap into aspirational drives which underlie human motivation."[16]

Smart brands base this emotional connection on what a consumer looks for: a personal impact. They paint the picture of a lifestyle. They enable a customer to consider more than just the relevance of the product or service. They try to make customers revel in every difference. Especially if it makes sense to you, the customer—appeals to you, taps into you. As you consider any brand, you set the requirements a product or service must meet before you will take steps to seriously evaluate a purchase. You look closer only if it makes sense in terms of what you want and what you need. And if you are satisfied, you may come back. As Hallmark remarks to employees, "brands succeed because they establish powerful emotional connections with consumers. In an intensely competitive marketplace that offers a wide array of choices—people buy brands."[17]

10. THIS EMOTIONAL CONNECTION IS AT THE HEART OF A CONSUMER'S RELATIONSHIP WITH A BRAND.

A brand is only as strong as the emotions it generates.

The emotional connection with the brand is the foundation for a relationship with that brand. And like *any* relationship, this connection has many dimensions. If you trust the brand, you may want to tell others about the business, brand, products, and services. You may feel a part of what the business is all about. That is what makes Disney more than theme parks or mouse ears. Nike more than shoes. Starbucks more than coffee.

"I believe that it is the emotional aspects of products and their distribution systems that will be the key difference between consumers' ultimate choice and the price that they will pay," writes Marc Gobé. "By emotional I mean how a brand engages consumers on the level of senses and emotions; how a brand comes to life for people and forges a deeper, lasting connection."[18]

Your relationship with the specific product or service is the first step to a sense of relationship with the business. You may become loyal, devoted, committed to the business behind the brand. And you may be willing to experiment with new products and services from the same source because you believe in the overall brand. Why else would Hallmark say it pursues a mission "to enrich lives" as it expands its product line?[19] And why else would those loyal customers of Harley-Davidson, who join the company-sponsored Harley Owners Group, celebrate their loyalty to the brand at events across the United States?[20]

As Jeff Swystun and Larry Oakner remark, "building a distinctive brand is at the heart of long-term relationships between company and customer."[21] Such an overall relationship extends to many products. Like Estée Lauder's claim to bring "the best to everyone we touch"[22] and Nissan's declaration of its "passion for making driving, and life itself, a little more enjoyable." Carl Sewell and his "Customers for Life," which transformed a Cadillac dealership into a national legend by setting a standard for customer service in the auto industry.[23] Krispy Kreme's promise to "create magic moments."[24] And Washington Mutual's pledge to "make things better for customers, employees and neighbors" while offering the most entertaining of all ATMs.[25]

11. BRAND LOYALTY IS "THE HOLY GRAIL" OF ANY CONSUMER'S RELATIONSHIP.

Anyone who manages any brand dreams of brand loyalty—that magical experience when a customer simply follows the lead.

Achieving brand loyalty frees the business to introduce new things, experiment with new ideas, and develop new products, with the assurance that you, the loyal customer, will give the new offering a fair shot. And if you like what you experience, if it meets an unmet need or enhances your life in some way, you may try to influence others to try it out.

True brand loyalty occurs when the brand transfers ownership to you, the customer, to make you feel the brand is your own. Perhaps that's why the Gap promises to "create emotional connections with customers around the world through inspiring product design, unique store experiences and compelling marketing."[26] IKEA claims to be all about creating "a better everyday life for many people."[27] PepsiCo issues customers an invitation to "taste the success."[28] These brands simply become part of people's lives. As Gobé puts it, "Consumers today expect their brands to know them, intimately and individually."[29]

This magical connection may be what makes a customer looking for healthy food choose Kashi, products of a business with a mission "to provide great tasting, all natural and innovative foods that enable people to achieve optimal health, wellness and weight management goals."[30] Brand loyalty is the emotional pull that makes people pick one brand of soft drink over another, schedule a hotel stay at one brand instead of the other, or decide to go to work at one business and not another. It's why Intel describes itself as "the preeminent building block supplier to the worldwide digital economy"[31] or McDonald's as "our customers' favorite place and way to eat."[32] Brand loyalty defines how a brand attracts. Captivates. Stimulates. Motivates. Connects. As Pam Danzinger, president of Unity Marketing, comments, "In today's hyper-emotional marketplace, where marketers use every trick in the book to push consumers' hot buttons and stimulate an emotional reaction, brands have become the medium and the message."[33]

As FedEx articulates its "purple promise," it clarifies that "FedEx is a lot more than moving packages or freight, it's about serving people."[34] And its competitor UPS also maintains "Our brand is the promise we make to our customers. And customers see that promise every day."[35] But brand loyalty can affect a new product launch. You don't like it when your favorite brands violate expectations. Just think *New Coke*. Customers revolted against the product because it violated a perceived brand promise. The failure of the product did not tarnish the overall brand of the business, and in fact Coca-Cola remains a brand powerhouse. It was the number-one brand for 2005, according to the *BusinessWeek/Interbrand* annual ranking of the 100 Top Global Brands.[36]

Despite such challenges, brand loyalty is critical to a business because of the competitive landscape any business confronts. Every business—no matter its product, service, or experience—must attract new customers. It's not enough to simply keep the current ones happy. Customers die. Or go away. Perhaps change their minds. Or simply choose something else. To replace the ones who leave, the brand must actively attract new people to "try out" what it promises. The brand appeals to customers to "try it out" based on the merits of the product or service as well as the emotional appeal of the overall brand, which has everything to do with what the business stands for. It's as if the customer evaluates and decides, "If I am OK with what the business is all about, what the brand is all about, then I am willing to try the product."

But you, the customer, may not have room in your life for more brands. So something *must* catch your attention. Perhaps it will be an advertisement for a product or service. Or what others say about the offering or, perhaps, the overall brand itself. Eventually you determine what the brand promises. And begin to consider whether it could be relevant to you. The brand *engages* you in this experience, moving you from initial consideration to steadfast loyalty, ultimately creating its own *evangelists*—people who, on behalf of the brand and the business, create the buzz.

12. A BRAND IS AN ADHESIVE.

A brand has an amazing ability to store memories.

Every experience you have with a brand, product, and service will stick. The good, the bad, and the ugly. In fact, you hang on to the negative much longer than you remember the positive. The soap that doesn't clean. The blouse that falls apart after the first washing. The restaurant that disappoints. The airline that disengages. One negative experience is all it takes to undermine all the dollars spent to promote the brand. One unenthusiastic employee can counter all the positive advertisements. Brands create strong memories.

A brand collects all the experiences you have. "We have the opportunity to win at the first moment of truth, in the store, and the second moment of truth, when the consumer uses the product," according to P&G's Diana Shaheen. For any business, the brand reflects how you store memories of products and services in your own consumer bank. And this memory addresses more than just the brand name of the product. The adhesive extends to the overall brand of the business that creates the products. A brand simply never loses the memories you have attached to it. That's why a business goes to a lot of trouble to create the *intentional* brand it intends to imprint, through promotions and advertising, even as it recognizes that a significant part of brand memory consists of what may be *unintentional*—that which the business *cannot* control. As Hallmark remarks to employees, "collectively the millions of positive impressions we've made in the past serve as the underpinning of our brand today."[37]

"As organizations' offerings become increasingly similar," writes Clare Dowdy, "the brand is sometimes the only differentiator. Which means it's down to experience. If customers don't enjoy the experience of purchasing or interacting with a brand, they won't come back."[38]

13. BRAND IS A LANGUAGE THAT SIMPLIFIES THE EXCHANGE BETWEEN YOU, THE CUSTOMER, AND THE BUSINESS.

A brand is beyond a strategy—it is a language all its own, rooted in customer choice.

Brands train you to buy. They teach you what to buy, how to buy, when to buy. From an early age, you identify with the brands you choose, from your clothes to your ice cream to your toothpaste. All you have to do is look for a label on a piece of clothing or a nameplate on a car or the name of a hotel. No matter the specifics of the product or service, you know what the brand will deliver. Imagine the possibilities when Restoration Hardware says, "We want to surround ourselves with what we love. We want to inspire laughter as well as thought."[39] Or when The Body Shop says it wants to help customers "feel good—naturally."[40] That's how "leading brands communicate their promise to the market," writes Chuck Brymer, "encouraging customers to purchase the product or service."[41] Again, as Hallmark describes to employees, "To understand the power of a card, just think of the day's mail and how you feel when you discover an envelope with a familiar name on the return address and the Hallmark logo embossed on the flap."[42]

As a result of this commercial focus, brands naturally crystallize the meaning of an entire business into a few words. They paint a detailed picture of what it means to connect. To buy the products, endorse the services, believe in the big idea, and perhaps invest in the stock. The brand communicates everything a business needs to tell—its mission, vision, values, offerings, promises, results—in a small number of words and images. Who can forget the power of such phrases as "Imagination at work" or "there are some things money can't buy, for everything else there's MasterCard." Brand gives business a way to communicate, and differentiate, in a way that is relevant, compelling, and consistent. "A lasting connection with the customer requires much more than a name and a logo," says Deborah Kania. "Customers must know the brand so well that they can recite in their own words what the brand means—brand attributes, brand promise, value proposition, etc."[43]

Buzz is an ultimate result of brand—that magical experience when people talk about a brand in a "must have" manner. The way people in the 1960s had to drive a Mustang or, in the 1970s, had to own a Pet Rock or, today, have to listen to a certain personal music player. Buzz occurs when a brand reaches beyond the attributes of the product to celebrate a need that the product fills. And more often than not, buzz happens when a brand fills a need you never knew you had. Imagine. How many of you realized, before purchasing your first iPod, that you needed all your CDs stored on one device? Or knew, before DIRECTV created the NFL Sunday Ticket, that you had to be able to watch all the NFL games on a Sunday? Or felt, before TiVo, that you had to be able to access recorded copies of your favorite television shows without suffering through the commercials?

But buzz is never a substitute for a real emotional connection with a brand. For buzz may come and go just like the Pet Rock, but a real connection will last through the fads and trends. Ultimately, "brands are about choice," Brymer continues in *Marketing;* they force a business to reach beyond the buzz to "continually work out what makes them special to so many people and discover how they can continue to innovate and meet their needs."[44]

14. A BUSINESS HAS A BRAND AS A PLACE TO WORK, TOO.

Brands live inside the business, too.

And every lesson you learn, as a consumer, directly applies to your work in employer brand. The essentials of brand are the same, inside or outside a business.

Ninety percent of people online looking for jobs consider it very important or important to be able to support a company's brand and products. That's what Yahoo! Hot Jobs learned in a 2005 poll of its users.[45]

Consider how UPS explains to employees how its brand "defines how we want to be perceived by internal and external audiences" and is "supported by four core attributes that differentiate UPS and form the basis of our brand personality: human spirit, operational excellence, intelligence and innovation." And how it wants "customers to see us as one company striving toward a single vision of providing complete, integrated solutions. We also have to think of ourselves and how we interact with employees in the same way."[46] Tom Pizutti of UPS explains, "We strongly believe in doing what's right for the employee."

Every business has a brand as a place to work, just as it has a brand as a place to buy. If for no other reason, then because every business is known for something as a place to work. Perhaps it has a reputation for fun. Or job security. Or career development. Or hard work. The business could be known for grooming future CEOs. Or for offering excellent pay. Or likable coworkers. Maybe its good working conditions create the buzz. All of these attributes add up to what you, as an employee, expect to experience, in the same way the attributes of a customer brand add up to those expectations. And that is precisely what a brand, as a place to work, is all about. When you, as a consumer, bring your retail mindset to the workplace. *Your* brand dependency teaches you how to evaluate what you experience. And you do that on the work floor as well as the store floor. Brands teach you how to judge a business as a place to work. And you judge what you experience *with* each experience.

As GE's Linda Boff remarks, "Without an employer brand, some organizations could succeed. But great brands and great organizations can't succeed without great employer brands."[47] And Eric Jackson—vice president of worldwide corporate communications for FedEx Corporation—observes, "When done right, and consistently delivered, an employer brand elicits an emotional response from customers that's very powerful. For us, this emotional response feeds our employees' desire to do whatever it takes to satisfy our customers."[48]

Just as you do on the outside, on the inside you experience a touch point each time you access something the business offers, hear a message the business sends, use a product or service the business delivers. And at each touch point you ask yourself, as an employee, "Am I receiving all that the brand promised?" If disappointed, you may wonder, "What other brands may be available to deliver the same thing?"

Just as on the outside, the brand of a business promises what you should experience on the inside. You expect working at Southwest to be fun because the brand says so. You expect Nike to empower employees to "Just do it!" because the brand is so encouraging. You expect Disney to be a magic kingdom because Mickey says so. And Donald.

And, just as on the outside, more and more people look for businesses they can believe in and proudly tell others they work for. You respond to values and traditions. No surprise that, inside many businesses, stories about legends of the business pass from person to person as if to preserve the humanity of the legend. And what the brand stands for. Imagine how it must feel to read these words from BMW: "If you love mobility in all of its many guises and want to get ahead, then the BMW group is just the place for you."[49] Or these from Dell: "Winning is in our DNA."[50] What we learn as consumers can direct what we create in a business for employees.

Everything you learn as a consumer, on the outside, can teach you what employees on the inside will expect, the choices employees make. Any employee creating an emotional connection with a business will be more willing to understand what the business is about, believe in what the business is trying to do, and do what it takes to help the business advance. And the brand can help. Any employees will be willing to trust until something happens to undermine that trust; until they are somehow clued in that everything the brand communicates may not be so. Although one business or another may become "the place to work" for a period of time, if that business doesn't do what it takes to create a real emotional connection with employees and sustain that relationship of trust through business upturns and downturns, brand preference will be just about impossible to sustain.

15. BRAND IS A PROCESS THAT CAN SIMPLIFY HOW BUSINESS ADDRESSES PEOPLE ISSUES.

The power of brand, the simplicity of brand, is not just in what people experience. It's in the simplicity with which it can frame how people work through issues.

So what is your business facing? No matter the issue, looking at what you must confront through the lens of your brand can simplify the steps you take to address the challenge. That's because approaching an issue through your brand forces you to consider the commercial realities of your business as well as to simplify what you consider. Brand is all about choice. Working through your issues, as you keep in mind the choices people will ultimately make, can save you a lot of unnecessary steps that lead nowhere. Brand can keep a business focused on what really matters: how to emotionally connect with the people who determine the business's destiny.

Little did our mothers know, when they pointed out the name brands on the grocery shelves, how we would ultimately use such lessons from young life in our, well, older life. But few other lessons compare to the lessons of brand.

And, today, the stakes are too high for any business to leave brand delivery to chance—especially businesses who find themselves fighting for market share, introducing new products or services, trying to turn a business around, or pursuing a merger or acquisition. They must exceed customer expectations on the outside. And that means they must look on the inside, at the experience they create to motivate employees to deliver the brand.

We believe in the emotional connections brands can create. That power comes right from the core of who the business is and what the business believes in. Because what goes around, comes around.

Our mothers probably taught us that, too.

Five Essential Steps

1. List your earliest brand memories. What do you remember? What is your favorite brand? What does it promise? What big idea does it represent? What customer experience does it promise?
2. Remember some of the lessons you have learned about brand over the years. What have you learned that can help you use the power of brand to create a positive reputation about your business as a place to work? What have you learned about the emotional connections of brand?
3. Consider the relationship of your business with your customers. How do your customers perceive the reliability of your products and services and the authenticity of your brand and the ideas your business stands for? What clues can this relationship provide for how to create a positive reputation for your business as a place to work?
4. Think about how your business can try to maximize the brand loyalty of your customers. Is it by distinguishing the products and services you offer? Or articulating the "big idea" that the brand of your business stands for? Or creating a sense of intimacy with your customers?
5. Imagine how the brand of your business can emotionally engage your customers—what it is about the core of your business that your customers are attracted to. And what clues this offers on how to engage your employees, too.

CHAPTER TWO

ESSENTIAL #2: COMMIT

You have learned that, on the outside of a business, *brand* is shorthand for the emotional connection with customers.

But brand begins at home.

Every day your employees make choices.

They get up, get moving, and choose to go to work or stay home. If they go to work, they choose to connect or not. Commit or not. Contribute or not. Engage or not. Serve your customers or not.

And through all these choices they ask the same questions your customers ask: "Am I getting what the brand promises?" "What's in it for me to choose to work here?" "Why should I choose to engage?" Any employer brand must answer these questions, to simplify the choices employees make—so they in turn serve customers. The only way your business can successfully connect with your customers is if, first of all, you connect with your employees. On the inside. From the inside. That's what employer brand is all about.

"It's critical that what we do internally mirrors what we do externally," says GE's Linda Boff. "We can't drive things outside the company that don't have their own life and authenticity as they relate to employees."[1] Linda Clark-Santos, senior vice president, Talent & Organizational Ability at Washington Mutual, agrees. "The brand must live inside employees. It must be compatible with how they are treated in the workplace—it cannot contradict their real experiences as employees."[2]

More than 50 percent of human resources professionals around the world view the employer brand as "the essence of our offering as an employer that is communicated internally and externally," according to a Global Employer Brand study conducted in 13 countries in 2005 by Hodes Research. At the same time, 60 percent say their organizations formally support an employer brand effort. Looking forward, some 66 percent of these HR professionals envision a formal employer brand effort at their organization within five years. According to Annette Browdy, SVP of Marcom at Bernard Hodes Group, "When we conducted our survey, we found a high level of interest in employer branding in the U.S., U.K., New Zealand, and Australia, but not as much in Germany and Brazil. There is emerging interest in India. Employer branding is catching on globally, but there is more focus on communication of the brand than on creating the emotional value that can trickle throughout the organization."[3]

On the inside of your business, your employer brand is shorthand for the emotional connection with employees. It frames how you motivate employees to deliver what your business promises to customers and how you nurture a working environment that prospective employees will want to join.

So as you continue your exploration of employer brand, your second essential is actually all about employer brand. What results it can create. How it can be the glue that binds a business. And how you can make it happen. You need to absorb the ins and outs of employer brand—based on what you just learned about brand in general—*before* you start to build from within.

Here is the short course—the fundamentals you need to learn about employer brand.

> People always ask, what makes Southwest, Southwest? How do they continue to sustain perhaps the most legendary employer brand? Well, on-brand behavior begins at the top with senior leadership who live the values. The customer focus is intense. And the company genuinely tries to do the right thing for its people. Southwest lives a golden rule for business: do the right thing for your employees and they'll do the right thing for your customers.
>
> **—Libby**

Every day, hundreds of millions of people around the world connect to their world by logging in to Yahoo! No longer a novelty, Yahoo! has become a necessity for people in every arena. The essential way to connect with everything they want to do in their lives. This happens for people on the outside only because of the environment the company carefully creates and nurtures on the inside. This internal-external parallel is essential to any customer's having any type of positive experience when interacting with any company.

—Libby

FIFTEEN THINGS TO LEARN ABOUT EMPLOYER BRAND

1. YOUR EMPLOYER BRAND MUST ARTICULATE YOUR PROMISE TO YOUR EMPLOYEES.

Just as every business has a customer brand, every business has an employer brand, too. Whether or not your business has ever spent any time developing it.

That's because every business needs employees. And as it recruits and retains and motivates, your business needs to clarify what it stands for. Why it must exist. What difference it can make. What it believes in. How its offerings align with its values. And if your business doesn't define your employer brand, just ask the recruiters. They will tell the story based on their own experience. In fact, more than 90 percent of people on line looking for jobs say they must very closely or closely understand the value of working for a company, according to the 2005 poll by Yahoo! Hot Jobs.[4]

Your employer brand is your promise to your employees to provide an experience that, in return, will motivate their commitment to deliver your customer brand. The real spirit of your employer brand is a combination of what your business may promise and deliver, inside and outside. Essentially, it's about a relationship, between your business and your people. "Anywhere in the world," says Tom Pizutti of UPS, "I can identify with all UPSers, simply because we hold the same values. This includes realizing that the importance of relationships, with colleagues and customers, is at the heart of what it means to be a UPS partner." As Washington Mutual's Linda Clark-Santos observes, "The brand is what you show to the world, whether to a customer or a candidate. Values and culture are how you treat each other internally. They must sync up or there will be a disconnect. They must be compatible." At P&G, according to materials distributed to employees, the company shows "respect for all individuals, the interests of the company and the individual are inseparable, we are strategically focused in our work, innovation is the cornerstone of our success, we are externally focused, we value personal mastery, we seek to be the best, mutual interdependency is a way of life."

How business generally approaches people, or talent, has actually changed a bit over the years. We can remember when business viewed employees as followers in a campaign—people who simply did as they were told. Then, as time passed, business progressed to considering employees as partners in the implementation of strategies. This led, in recent years, to a consideration of the exchange between employees and business—sort of a "you do this in exchange for this"—to express the relationship. But that was primarily a financial transaction. And over time the old ways of framing the relationship *functionally* became outdated. Employees began to demand a relationship that reached for something more: an emotional connection.

That's where employer brand makes a difference.

"It seems cliché, but at FedEx it's true, our people are our most important resource," says Eric Jackson of FedEx. "For any organization the people component is the key success factor and if organizations can get their people issues right they ultimately compete more effectively."

Your employer brand can be a magical combination of what your business values, offers, and rewards—marrying what your brand promises outside with what your experience demands inside; what your business believes in and how you fundamentally respect the people who deliver your brand.

For a hotel company that kept one eye focused on customers, the other focused on employees, the essential word was *care,* to help the team realize the key to customer satisfaction is employee satisfaction. One senior person told me, "This business is simple, for the key to delighting the customer who pays is by delighting the employee who works." Part of the thinking was that if they teach employees how it feels to experience care, they will be more familiar and comfortable with what it takes to provide care.

And this company that believed in care did a lot to make sure it took care of any say/do gaps. Twice a year it would survey all employees in every location on, essentially, what care they experienced and what care they delivered. This included how they were treated by supervisors and what environment hotel managers created. Results formed the basis for training and communications as well as provided input for manager incentive. The key word was *care.* To customers, the company worked to create an atmosphere in which guests felt cared for. And it did the same for employees, creating an atmosphere of care so they in turn would want to care for guests. From hot meals for employees to clean uniforms to on-site classes in English as a second language. And they simplified this commitment as "We care for you so you will care for guests"— a simple declaration of what the business believes in, stands for, and is committed to deliver.

—Mark

2. YOUR EMPLOYER BRAND MUST SUPPORT YOUR BUSINESS STRATEGY.

But you can't just build an employer brand because everyone else does. It's too important. There's too much it must accomplish. The need *must* come from your business strategy.

"The key to a successful employer brand is alignment with the business strategy," says Yvonne Larkin of Diageo. "You have to have a clear business strategy that shapes the organization strategy. Together the business and organization strategies give the employer brand a reason for being."[5] Diana Shaheen at P&G agrees. "An employer brand must be based on business strategy," she says. "If you don't focus on the business, the employer brand won't work." Results from the Yahoo! Hot Jobs poll support this. More than 94 percent of people on line looking for jobs say they must very closely or closely understand and believe in what a company they might work for does, according to the 2005 poll results.

The power of employer brand is how it connects the internal experience to the external business need. How it grounds the necessity for this internal experience in the economic realities of the buying decisions your customers make. As Jeff Swystun and Larry Oakner comment, "Companies are learning their brands stand or fall on the internal relationship with their employees as much as the external promise to customers."[6]

So, what *is* your business strategy? For example, is your business in a phase of rapid growth? An employer brand is essential to your growth strategy. That's because growth will demand that your business continue to hire the right people in the right jobs at the right time. And keep the people you currently have. This constant effort to recruit and rerecruit demands that your business enjoy a reputation in the marketplace that will support your ambitions for growth. Your employer brand can help your business clarify what will and will not change as you grow. And what growth means to the people who choose to work for you.

Or is your business shrinking? An employer brand is essential to your strategy for stability. It can, simply, give your employees something to hold on to during periods of significant turbulence. Your emotional connection with employees will be tested as your business faces challenges, such as reducing your size without cutting out your heart, or shifting your direction from what employees may consider sacred.

And is your business changing? Considering or pursuing new strategies? Your employer brand is essential to any change strategy simply because it provides a focal point for your employees. Your employer brand is a touchstone for your employees, as their willingness to emotionally connect may be tested with each action each day. The essence of effective change management is effective stability management, giving people things to protect as they adjust to things that change. Your employer brand can give people that emotional anchor as they may emotionally react to how they are expected to change. It can help people sing off the same page and embrace a common vision.

Long before I joined Southwest, the company discovered their differentiation came from spirit of our people. I mean, every airline had airplanes. Some airlines had meals—but who has ever chosen an airline based on the meals? And all airlines flew from point A to point B. But not every airline had the compassionate, customer-service-delivering, fun-loving employees of Southwest. So when we started, and coined our first brand—"The Love Airline"—attracting and retaining the right kind of employees became our secret weapon. Our first flight attendants wore go-go boots and hot pants. Our employment ads solicited Raquel Welch look-alikes. Our consumer ads asked "How Do We Love You?" or touted "We're Spreading Love," stemming from our desire to continue to base our operations from Love Field, the inner-city airport in Dallas. Then, after we won the battle to fly there, we began to use the word *love* to emphasize our mission, which was dedication to customer service "delivered with a sense of warmth, friendliness, individual pride, and company spirit." Over the years our branding evolved from the "Love" airline to the "Company Plane" to the "Low Fare Airline," then it was "Fun, Fun, Fun" as our advertising communicated our strategy of low fares, frequent flights, point-to-point service, and fun.

—Libby

3. Your employer brand must define, for your employees, what your customers experience.

Your employer brand will never thrive if it's only an HR thing or a Communications thing. If its only purpose is to "make people feel better." It will only thrive if it makes a difference in results by making a difference to customers. If it supports every touch point your customers have with your business.

Yahoo! Hot Jobs' poll results indicate how important this is. More than 89 percent of people online looking for jobs say they must very closely or closely experience as an employee what the company promises to customers according to the 2005 poll results.

Such importance is a key reason why Hallmark, as part of its internal efforts to excite employees about its consumer brand, annually gives each employee a "card pack" as "a friendly way to tell others of sending greeting cards." The card pack is just that—an attractive folder with three greeting cards inside, along with a note to the employee suggesting that they share this pack with someone outside Hallmark and their immediate family, such as "a new neighbor, the person sitting next to them on an airplane or bus, or the helpful sacker at the grocery story." The approach clearly connects employees to consumer touch points "to help share Hallmark's mission of enriching lives." Says Dean Rodenbough, Hallmark's corporate communication director, "The response has been tremendous, with nearly two-thirds of our employees giving out their card packs last year."[7] According to materials distributed to P&G employees, "Every time we interact with consumers, customers, business partners and one another, we create an experience that either strengthens or erodes P&G's equity," and "Every experience is an opportunity to demonstrate that P&G is in touch; that P&G is a leader in everything it does; that P&G—through our Brands and our People—is genuinely improving lives every day."

Again, a touch point occurs every time a customer comes in contact with the product, service, or a business overall. And every business, no matter what its business, has many customer touch points. Online. In person. Drive-by. Times when someone comes in contact with something your business does and forms an impression that, with the adhesive quality of a brand, may last a long time.

A customer who has a positive experience will be more likely to return. With money. To buy more. But that positive experience doesn't simply happen. People make it happen. And most of these are employees of your business. A customer's experience, regardless of the product or service a business offers, is a series of reactions and observations at each touch point: how people notice, observe, hear, experience, talk. How your business, through its employees, makes the most of each touch point can differentiate your business from your competition and, ultimately, help you gain market share. This becomes more important as price competitiveness and commoditization erode traditional concepts of brand loyalty and place more pressure on staff to deliver easy-to-differentiate products or services.

Touch points are everywhere. And at each touch point customers test the authenticity of the brand promises. "Every time a customer experiences a brand, he or she asks, 'Am I getting what they promised?' What employees deliver and the experience the customer takes away, determines a company's reputation in that person's view. Because our people are our product, getting it right with our workforce has always been the key to our success," says Eric Jackson of FedEx. "Getting it right is all about setting expectations to get the desired behavior from your employees so the promise we make to the customer is met or exceeded every time."

Your employer brand must support these touch points. Employees inside your business influence the brand at each touch point, whether or not they actually come in contact with a customer. There is a difference, at each touch point, between someone who is simply doing a job and someone who delivers the brand. Your employer brand must influence employees to make the most of each opportunity.

| NOTICE | OBSERVE | HEAR | EXPERIENCE | TALK |

First, your customers notice.

Perhaps it's an advertisement. Maybe a news story. Or a comment from a friend. For every brand, there is that moment when the customer hears about it for the first time. Think back. The first time you heard about or noticed someone using an iPod. Or before that, a Discman. Or before that, a Walkman. Or before that, a transistor radio. Held up to the ear.

This first impression, of course, lasts only a moment. And it may or may not be remembered. A lot of that opportunity to be memorable is a product of how the product or service is branded. And the importance of the first impression places a lot of pressure on the brand. To get it right. The first time.

Next, your customers observe.

At a retail outlet, you observe the outside of a store before walking in. You see employees, wearing the logo, in many places. You read about the business in the newspaper, or see a story on television.

You quickly size up what a brand and a business are all about— what the business could be as a place to buy and, possibly, as a place to work. Certainly you consider what it could mean to those employees to work at that place.

Every employee in a business has the opportunity to positively or negatively influence how a customer perceives your business and its brand. As a place to buy *and* as a place to work. Every customer who enters a store or restaurant or hotel observes how employees act, are treated, react to each other. You notice the cleanliness of a store. The consistency of the packaging. The appearance of the product.

Picture, for a moment, images that ring true of strong brands. How pillows are arranged on a heavenly bed at a Westin. How pastries are arranged to be tempting at Starbucks. How the Yahoo! home page is organized. How the dealer showroom at Carmax is set up. How the produce appears at a Whole Foods. How clean the outside of a Chili's restaurant is. How up-to-date or, perhaps, beat up the lobby of a hotel can look. How fully stocked the shelves appear at a retail store. How the employees smile, even if they say very little.

Employees create every visual image a brand conveys. And it's not just observation through visuals. Think of other senses. The temptation of walking through an airport and smelling a Cinnabon. Or the aroma on entering a Krispy Kreme or Mrs. Fields location. Or the ever-tempting smell of the McDonald's french fry. You sense. You want. You remember.

Then, your customers hear.

To a customer, this may be the sound of a friendly voice. On a manufacturing floor, it's the sound of an efficient machine.

The initial sound of a positive brand experience is the sound of efficiency, reliability, and, in the case of customer-facing employees, comfort and interest and a sense of friendliness. The first sounds can make or break the brand. The tone of a customer service representative. The operator at a hotel. Or the receptionist at an office. The warmth of a voice can speak volumes. Likewise, a cold, insincere voice speaks louder than any words in any advertisement. After all, when was the last time you were pleased with service from Directory Assistance?

You also hear things others say. You hear actual stories others may share about their experiences with your business and the brand. Of course, you are more apt to listen if you trust the source.

So when you hear someone you know and trust talk about a place to buy or to work, you pay attention. Just as you do when someone you trust tells you about a good meal or a bad meal or when you hear a film critic you trust recommend a movie to see or warn you away.

And your customers experience—and talk.

Every brand experience has a defining moment. When you use the product or service and your reaction is positive or negative. When you are pleased or disappointed. An authentic brand experience will be consistent from one person to the next because employees internalize what they must accomplish at each customer touch point. And ultimately you will tell others what you think based on what you experience.

Commitment to the brand is just as important for an employee who touches customers as for an employee who never sees a customer. People who work with customers must "live the brand" in every interaction they conduct. Others, at the same time, work behind the scenes to make sure customer-facing employees have the tools and support they need for a positive interaction. *Any* business has people who never see a customer but who, in every interaction, represent the brand.

Regardless of where an employee works, the commitment to deliver the brand involves internalizing the *promise* the brand makes, developing the *skills* necessary to deliver the promise, and displaying the *behavior* necessary when implementing those skills. At every touch point.

4. YOUR EMPLOYER BRAND MUST DEFINE WHAT YOUR BUSINESS NEEDS FROM YOUR EMPLOYEES.

All the magical things that can happen when a brand connects with customers don't simply happen. Your employees make them happen.

"It's the people behind the brand who make the brand," says Diana Shaheen of P&G. "We work very hard to bring our brand to life so our people can feel it, no matter where in the world they may work or what specific product brand they may work on."

Your employer brand is more than simply articulating what the customer brand is all about. Your employer brand must define what your business needs from employees to deliver the brand

Any business would like to believe its people would be supportive during a trying time. And if it came right down to it, that employees would even picket to save the business. Well, that's what happened when employees of a health care organization so believed in its mission, they actually carried picket signs. This private non-profit health care organization was reinventing how it communicated with employees when, all of a sudden, a public for-profit health care company announced it wanted to absorb them.

Our new approach to communication with employees was all about the brand, the values, the mission, and having the communication vehicles in place to quickly inform employees of what was going on. The new communication system included regular message briefings for opinion leaders (specifically, the doctors and nurses) as well as new uses of electronic billboards and other media to quickly reach other employees. This situation certainly put this new system to the test, as the hospital used every possible means to organize employees and other supports, with a focus on the values and the mission. It turned out these employees were so in tune with the organization they were sincerely frightened about it going away. So they organized a groundswell of support. They engaged community leaders. They contacted the news media. And they carried picket signs. All because they believed in the mission and brand of the organization. And it worked. The organization avoided the takeover and is thriving today. Simply because of the strength of what we now call the employer brand.

—Mark

promise to customers. At most, an advertisement defines an expectation. No matter how clever, it does not actually deliver anything. People who understand and believe in the brand deliver the experience the advertisement promises. The employee must do the work, acquire the skills, and demonstrate the behavior that, in turn, delivers the brand. As James Trusty comments, "If your internal and external branding messages aren't aligned, the front line will not deliver on the promises."[8]

For FedEx, the employer brand is expressed as "the Purple Promise," which, as Eric Jackson describes, embodies the discretionary effort the business needs from its workforce to meet customers' expectations. "The Purple Promise is our willingness to make every FedEx experience outstanding, with equal commitment to deliver on that promise inside and outside of the organization."[9] Your business may, through its marketing, present campaign after campaign to lure customers. But what is the parallel effort, inside, to connect the staff to the promise? What is created to help employees see, moment by moment, how they deliver the promise to customers? What is the internal dimension of the brand promise? What motivates employees to fulfill their connection to the brand? What's inside the brand? Who delivers the brand? What are the specific brand behaviors? Who actually delivers the promise?

Every day, companies spend millions to build brand identity. They use every type of advertising and marketing approach to promote an experience, product, or service the brand promises. They use the brand to connect. But advertising has nothing to do with delivering the brand promise to customers. It's all up to employees. Just as it uses its brand to connect with customers, a business can use its brand to connect with employees.

Two things must happen for any employee of any business— from the smallest gas station on the corner to the largest global business—to live the brand.

First, the employee must understand what the brand is all about.

This doesn't just mean the employee simply understands the products and services your business offers, although that's important, too.

The employee must understand and internalize the essence of what your business is about—how that essence authentically applies to the products and services and experiences your business offers, and how the customer brand articulates this essence.

What the brand stands for. The employee must understand the meaning of the brand behind the product or service. The idea the brand conveys. What the brand says about your business and why it exists, not just about the product and why it is for sale. As Hallmark's Dean Rodenbough comments, "When we ask consumers, they tell us what the brand is all about: caring, emotion, connections, and relationships. We connect with our customers at intimate times of their lives."

What personality the brand projects. The employee must understand what the personality of the brand says about your business and the brand. For Washington Mutual, according to Libby Hutchison, "It is intentional that our brand *not* feel like a bank."[10]

What heritage the brand celebrates. If legendary brands tell the stories of legendary people and events, the employee must understand the heritage of your business. And the folklore in its fabric. As Libby Hutchison continues, "Our brand says we are in this for the long term. We have 115 years behind us already. We realize the power of delivering on our brand."

What customers expect. To successfully deliver the brand promise to customers, the employee must understand the difference your business makes to customers—through its brands as well as what employees are expected to deliver. Which is the difference between doing the job and delivering the brand.

Second, the employee must believe how the brand differentiates from what else is available on the market.
It's not enough for the employee to believe the product, service, or business is a better choice. The employee must seriously believe it is the *only* choice.

How the brand is aspirational. The employee must believe in the authenticity of the pictures the brand can create. The idea the brand promotes. How the brand reaches beyond a single product or service to articulate the cumulative purpose of your business behind the brand and how it connects to what people aspire to be.

How the brand is inspirational. The employee must believe in the authenticity of the brand. What your business stands for. How it differentiates from others, not just in products and services, but in fundamental integrity. How its business proposition stands apart. What is unique in how your business inspires people to connect.

How the brand is emotional. The employee must feel a sense of ownership in the brand, how the brand represents your business and anyone who works for your business. As if each employee wears the brand on his or her sleeve. And it certainly involves more than wearing a logo on a shirt. This has everything to do with the values of your business. It's as if, to strongly believe in the brand, the employee must believe there is something at this business they simply cannot find anywhere else. This has everything to do with how the employee's values align with the values of your business. And if everyone in your business shares and aligns with these values, the brand will grow stronger.

How the brand is functional. Finally, the employee must believe the products and services your business produces will actually work. They must believe in the functional integrity of what your business delivers.

As Swystun and Oakner remark, "your employees are the critical link between your company and your customer, actively delivering your unique brand promise every day . . . perhaps the benefit of internal brand alignment can be summed up in a simple equation: engaged, productive and focused employees equal delighted, loyal customers, equal business/shareholder value."[11]

Years ago, a global company experienced a disaster witnessed around the world. How it reacted defined, for many years, its reputation as a place to buy and a place to work. Unfortunately, the business was widely criticized for how it handled the situation. Years later, long after the company had done everything it could to address the problems associated with the disaster, prospective employees still remembered the accident. And the employees remembered. And they wondered, seriously, what to think about the company. As one told me, "I am not sure I could work for a company that let something like this happen." Fair or not, it became a part of the adhesive of the company's employer brand. Only time, and many positive actions, could help the company shake it off. Even today, the memory lingers.

—**Mark**

5. YOUR EMPLOYER BRAND MUST DEFINE ON-BRAND BEHAVIOR.

On-brand behavior is what brand is all about.

Any business needs specific behaviors from employees to deliver its brand promise to customers. This on-brand behavior occurs when an employee acts (or delivers) in a way that is consistent with what the brand is all about. And it's important because customers experience the brand *only* when employees deliver the characteristics the brand promises—when the behavior of employees supports the promise of the brand. The key to *delivery* of the brand is the on-brand behavior of employees at each touch point. As Chuck Brymer remarks, "the true test of a leading brand is whether employees' commitment to the brand is high, because that will keep customer commitment high. Those who live the brand will deliver the brand."[12]

FedEx, in its description of the Purple Promise for employees, specifies the behaviors needed to support the brand: "An act that exceeds normal job requirements, working above and beyond for the customer to deliver outstanding customer service, including demonstrating initiative in providing outstanding customer service; demonstrating appropriate problem-solving behavior; creating exceptional ideas for delighting the customer and enhancing the total customer experience; and building customer trust and loyalty that, in turn, establishes the foundation for long-term business relationships."[13]

P&G carefully outlines the principles for creating exciting, memorable P&G experiences—in short, a summary of on-brand behavior. In materials distributed to employees, the company says,

> To make the experience personal for a consumer, the employee is encouraged, for example, to anticipate, appreciate, and respond to diverse styles, needs, and motivations. To put the guest in the center of the experience, the employee is encouraged to be genuine and authentic in actions and behavior. To deliberately build a consistent delightful experience for the consumer, the employee is encouraged to define and execute a total experience from the very first moment the guest is made aware through the final follow-up. To make the guest's experience comfortable and seemingly simple, the employee is suggested to put the guest at ease. And to respond generously and selflessly to delight, and go beyond what is expected, the employee is encouraged to always look for ways to improve an experience.

To define the behaviors you need, your business must first define the experience it wants to create for customers. Because each business may have different customer touch points, each business will have its own definition of on-brand behavior. The role of the employee to deliver the brand will differ from one business to another, simply because of the differences in what businesses offer. On-brand behavior is just as important in businesses whose employees never see a customer. Employees create what your business sells to customers. And customers experience the brand.

6. YOUR EMPLOYER BRAND MUST CONNECT WHAT HAPPENS OUTSIDE TO WHAT HAPPENS INSIDE.

Your business has a customer brand as a place to buy—and an employer brand as a place to work.

While your customer brand focuses on specific products or services available externally, your employer brand may highlight distinct experiences or opportunities available internally.

As I was interviewing for a new senior role in HR, a headhunter asked me a very interesting and thought-provoking question. "What are the things you have to do in HR no matter where you are?" My first inclination was to answer that I had no agenda; every company was different, and I would assess the need before crafting my agenda. But suddenly I knew the answer. I absolutely could not join a new company without having an opportunity to help build a legendary employer brand.

It was evident during my first visit to Yahoo! that this was a company with a unique culture and brand. Everything was painted brightly in purple and yellow. The chairs were purple and yellow. The flowers were purple and yellow. Even the dumpsters and sprinkler heads were purple. There was a big purple cow in the lobby. And just sitting in a big purple chair while waiting for my first interview, I observed the energy. Early in the morning, people were running up and down, cheerfully greeting each other and all abuzz. Later I learned that I was observing everyone going in and out of the free latté and espresso bar, and that most were hyped on caffeine.

—Libby

Your employer brand, on the inside, frames the experience your business creates for employees, so they in turn deliver the brand promises to customers.

In fact, the *only* way your employer brand can authentically reflect your business is if it articulates your identity, mission and values. That can happen only if your employer brand builds from the inside—to incorporate your essential identity, mission, and values. If you search the inner soul of your business before you package that soul for your employees. As Hallmark's Dean Rodenbough observes, "You have to be true to who you are."

But it's not just about what happens inside your business. To fully picture the potential of your employer brand, you must focus on what happens outside—and what your employees must deliver.

What motivates people to buy products or services, or develop a relationship with a business, parallels what motivates an employee to join, stay with, and commit to a business. The brand is the same. The face is different. Just as a customer brand does, an employer brand makes a promise to current, future, and past employees. Your employer brand reflects the employee experience that will motivate employees to deliver. According to James Trusty, "Your employee and your customer are really the same person, so why not use the same techniques that are used to sell product to customers to get employees aligned with the company vision? If the internal and external branding messages aren't aligned, then the front line will not deliver on the promises made to the customer in the marketing campaign, leading to frustrated consumers."[14]

Any business that wants to exceed the expectations of external customers *must* pay attention to what it takes to make that happen on the inside. For your business to successfully deliver an authentic brand experience to your customers, you must first deliver an authentic experience to your employees—you must *brand from within* to secure an emotional connection with employees. So they will willingly help your business secure an emotional connection with customers. Your employer brand frames the experience for your internal customers so they in turn deliver to your external customers. And like your customer brand, your employer brand promises a specific functional and emotional experience at each touch point with the programs, resources, and rewards your business offers.

At the time I joined Yahoo! it was one of the top fifty most recognized brands in the world. Although our brand was widely known, we hadn't done much to attach a deeper meaning to the brand. I asked our founders and leaders why we had selected purple and yellow, and no one could answer. Finally, David Filo admitted that these colors were his high school colors, but he assured me there was no correlation. He later told a crowd of our employees on our tenth anniversary that he had asked a group of the original employees to help paint the first Yahoo! offices. David, known for his frugality, was sent out to buy paint. He returned with several gallons of what was thought to be gray paint. However, once everyone had painted most of a large wall under dim fluorescent lighting, it became obvious that the paint was lavender. Left with gallons of purple paint, they decided that between the sunk costs and their efforts on the already-painted wall, it was just easiest to stick with purple. Some speculate that purple subsequently became associated with the brand as a result of this mishap.

—**Libby**

7. YOUR EMPLOYER BRAND MUST FOCUS ON EMPLOYEE CHOICE.

Every day, employees make choices about where and how to work. They view each stage of their relationship with a business as a brand experience that your business delivers. Some may consider new opportunities they believe may better meet their personal expectations. Some may wonder "What's in it for me?" if they contribute to the demands of the job and your business. Some may decide to depart a business about which they hold memories of what they experience—and they likely will share those experiences with others still actively connected to or certainly considering your business as an employer.

That's why a business needs to use its employer brand no matter what it is doing or what it needs to accomplish. Employees will influence how any stakeholder reacts to what your business is trying to do.

Your employer brand can help you think through your business from the perspective of the choices your employees make. To view your business—what you promise, offer, expect—through their eyes. To simplify your business. Brands are inherently simple. Chuck Brymer points out, "Leading brands understand that an internal culture supportive of the brand strategy has a far better chance of delivering a consistent yet differentiated experience. The internal values are aligned with brand values to shape the organization's culture and embed the core purpose."[15]

Part of this potential of employer brand is perception. How you want others to recognize you. What you want others to say about you as a place to work. What reputation you want to build. Part of the potential is tactical. How you want your employer brand to positively influence how you attract, retain, and engage employees.

Part of the potential is practical. What experience you want your business to create. And how this experience may need to vary by audience segment. How your employer brand can and should mean different things to different people. And part of this potential is strategic. To determine what niche in the employer marketplace your brand needs to play to, to reach your objectives. How you should position. How you can differentiate. Allen Steinmetz, writing in *B to B*, suggests, "align your brand externally and internally. Let your inside be like your outside. What you say externally should be the same thing you say or do internally."[16]

8. YOUR EMPLOYER BRAND MUST DEFINE "WHAT'S IN IT FOR ME?" FOR EMPLOYEES TO WORK THERE.

To connect with your business, your employer brand must answer, for the employee, the fundamental question "What's in it for me?"

"What makes the employer brand stick," according to P&G's Diana Shaheen, "is when employees can clearly see the benefit of working for the company—what's in it for them. This is similar to the approach we use to ensure that our brands delight and deliver consumers' needs."

This includes what it means to employees to understand what the brand promises to customers and what role they play to help your business deliver the brand—and why their contribution is essential to what your business achieves. It also covers what your business offers in return for employee commitment to deliver the

For Yahoo! the key to securing employee engagement in the customer brand is creating an employee experience that mirrors the customer brand. As we look to the outside, and how Yahoo! is the life engine for customers, we look to the inside at how to make sure employees (simply called Yahoos) realize they are the engine behind what the company delivers to customers. Yahoos have an emotional and a functional connection with the company. As employees focus on the emotions of life they can easily see the ways Yahoo! embraces who people are and supports what they can be, personally and professionally. And, as employees focus on the practicality of our product for customers they can easily see how Yahoo! helps them get things done—professionally at work with the very best tools and resources as well as personally on their own time. At the end of the day, Yahoos live on the inside what the company delivers on the outside. And that's the essence of an employer brand

—Libby

brand to customers. How they are rewarded. The essence of employer brand is the experience your business delivers to employees so they in turn deliver the experience your business promises to customers.

"If you take care of your people," says Eric Jackson of FedEx, "set expectations, incent, respect, and reward them, they will be aware and willingly provide the discretionary effort to deliver service levels customers want, which will in turn allow the company to deliver premium returns to shareholders, as well as reinvest in your workforce's changing needs. This philosophy has been central to our culture and core to our success."

Just as a customer brand simplifies choices for a customer, an employer brand articulates, in shorthand, what it means to work inside your business to be a part of what your business promises to the outside.

Purpose. An employer brand begins with the sense of identity of your business—the simple matter of who we are and what we do.

What difference your business makes to its customers. Why you exist and how your business creates a relationship with its customers.

Purpose + Values. Your employer brand continues with what you believe in, your values, what stakes you put in the ground.

Purpose + Values + Rewards. But this is a business, not an art colony, and any business carries expectations. Your employer brand then must clarify what your business expects.

The value of your employer brand is only as strong as its support for what your business needs to achieve. Your employer brand must support the customer strategy. Your employer brand must support your business. And the brand must support the talent strategy—that's at the heart of getting the right people, doing the right jobs, to deliver the brand. And your employer brand must support the people themselves by giving them purpose and meaning, helping them understand what is expected, and making them feel valued and appreciated.

When we were preparing to articulate the employer brand at Yahoo! we conducted employee research to ask Yahoos to tell us, in priority order, what is uniquely Yahoo! that motivates people to join Yahoo! And stay at Yahoo! We heard a lot about the "cocktail-party-effect"—how it feels to Yahoos to tell people, such as at a cocktail party, they work for Yahoo! And this was in fact a major motivator for people to join Yahoo! To be able to tell others they worked at Yahoo! And a strong tie to keep people at Yahoo! And we realized, from their responses, that to secure that cocktail party effect we had to satisfy employees two ways—functionally, so they felt they could get things done at Yahoo! and emotionally, so they felt connected to the company and to their coworkers. That's what bragging at a cocktail party is all about.

—Libby and Mark

9. Your employer brand must define your business as a place to work.

Your employer brand articulates the experience your business promises to create for employees so they in turn deliver what customers expect. This touches every dimension of the employee's relationship with the organization. What the employee must touch and feel to be willing to deliver to the customer at each touch point. What opportunities must be accessible. What rewards must be offered. What expectations must be met.

Your employer brand frames the systems your business must put in place to support employees. This includes such things such as training, performance management, and compensation—everything in the hands of Human Resources to frame the employee experience. It also includes the system your business follows to keep employees informed, as well as to explain your business to employees, which is usually coordinated by Corporate Communications. And how these efforts align with how your business promotes itself through advertisements and promotions, which is usually the job of, yes, the Marketing side of the house.

So how does a business translate the brand used to motivate customers to buy—the *customer* brand—into a brand used to articulate a place for people to work—your employer brand? The same way your business develops the customer brand in the first place: by focusing on the essential dimensions, elements, and steps. Leveraging the personality of your business: its culture, identity, and unique attributes.

Many of the most powerful brands are also known as great places to work. Think Southwest, Starbucks, Yahoo!, Hallmark, FedEx, UPS, P&G, Whole Foods. Each of these businesses, in addition to success with customers, has developed an employer brand as a place to work. Each has learned that, if customer brand loyalty is key to the relationship with customers, employer brand is central to the relationship with employees. And the only way to develop an employer brand that sticks is to begin on the inside. Each of these companies has learned that, to deliver what external customers expect, a business must develop what internal customers need.

This employer brand, as a place to work, must touch every dimension of the employee's experience, from before the first day to after the last. It must engage the heart and mind of the employee in every dimension of the employee's relationship with your business. And it must reflect the collective experience your business creates for employees—so that they in turn deliver the brand to customers. External promotional efforts will fail or, at best, achieve minimal success unless your business invests in nurturing its employer brand—unless it focuses as much effort to bring out the best of its internal talent to deliver the best to its external customers.

Only when a business translates its customer brand promise into its employer brand experience can it create an emotional and functional connection with employees.

Only when a business acknowledges that its internal customers are essential to deliver the brand to external customers can it maximize the potential of that brand.

Only when a business builds this employer brand from within can it maximize the potential of its brand on the outside.

Only when a business creates an *experience* for employees that will support the skills and behavior needed to deliver the customer brand, offers *opportunity* for the employee to experience personal and professional growth while delivering the brand, and delivers *rewards* to recognize employee contributions and results can employees, in turn, positively answer "What's in it for me?" to work there.

An employer brand can be a magnet to attract and retain the people a business needs. It can in fact be a way to differentiate what it means to work at your business compared to others. A way for your people to value what you offer.

10. YOUR EMPLOYER BRAND MUST ARTICULATE YOUR DESIRED REPUTATION AS A PLACE TO WORK.

Each year businesses work hard to establish a reputation as a best employer brand. Through recruitment advertising, community events and sponsorships, presentations at conferences and seminars, or public relations outreach they try to raise awareness and build a reputation.

When we started to work together our first challenge was how to introduce flexible benefits to Southwest employees. And if you think back to 1989 and 1990, most companies, when they introduced Flex, simply gave the facts. This is what it is. This is the choice. But we felt we could tell a larger story. And needed to tell a larger story because we needed to lure people from an old plan that was provided on a noncontributory basis into this new program, which included employee cost-sharing.

So we placed the story of BenefitsPlus in a retail setting, with messages addressed to customers who would make real choices with real money. A story about how this benefit program offered something substantive to employees so they in turn would offer something substantive to customers. It was as much the story of Southwest and customers as the facts about Flex and benefits. Oh, it had everything. In our newspaper, *BenefitsPlusToday*, we told the story through advertisements, editorials, crossword puzzles, a horoscope, a soap opera review, even a personals column. One of our favorite personals ads was "Flight attendant with incomplete enrollment form seeks soul mate with functioning writing element."

Little did we know we were planting the seeds for Southwest's employer brand. We were just trying to do the right thing for employees. The key to BenefitsPlus was putting benefits into a retail context for employees to choose, just as they made choices as consumers. Perhaps all those brand lessons paid off after all.

—Libby and Mark

Some 79 percent of human resources professionals say an employer brand can help the organization be recognized as an employer of choice, according to the Hodes Global Employer Brand study. At the same time, 38 percent believe it can increase the number of unsolicited responses from prospective employees. Of employer brand attributes, reputation is the most important in attracting new hires. Corporate culture, work environment, ethical reputation and career path closely follow. The Yahoo! Hot Jobs poll results reinforce the importance. More than 82 percent of people on line looking for jobs consider it very important or important how others perceive a company they might work for according to the 2005 results.

And each year, to be named a best place to work, companies spend many hours putting together many required exhibits just so they can beat many others to be included on one of the many lists of best places to work. Because they want others to *hear* about what the work experience at their company can be. And because they want the world to know theirs is a great place to work.

After all, people making choices about where to work can be influenced by a business's reputation as a place to work.

Your employer brand is a key to develop this reputation.

This reputation as a place to work is the result of many things—just like the reputation of a brand with customers and investors. And this reputation means something different to each business. What gives one business its reputation as a great place to work has absolutely nothing to do with a list or what can work at any other business. It has everything to do with who your business is and what your business is trying to be and how this authentically extends to the experience your business creates.

Your employer brand as a place to work requires more than simply telling people what it's like to work for your business. Your employer brand must consolidate the reasons an employee comes to work and, once at work, engages in the work. For the potential employee, your employer brand as a place to work can positively motivate the decision to join. For the current employee, it's all about brand engagement. For the former employee, your employer brand can stimulate a positive memory. For an employee in, say, a less-than-traditional relationship, such as a contractor or outsource partner, your employer brand can represent the expectations and rewards related to how your business delivers to customers. And for a vendor or consultant, your employer brand can clarify expectations.

However, a strong employer brand as a place to work is not just a matter of lists, creative messaging, or community outreach.

Everything every person experiences as they encounter your business will land in this reputation. Everything people hear, observe, and experience. Over time this reputation will become a lens through which every person interested in or connected to your business will view every experience they have with your business, no matter how insignificant it may be, no matter how brief or seemingly unrelated. Especially the bad experiences.

An employer brand becomes the filter through which employees look at everything they hear, observe, and experience about your business, the lens through which they look at the facts. And if people feel good about the brand, they will wear the brand. Just like you wear your favorite brands. Your favorite consumer brands say something about your identity and personality. That's why so many people, especially younger people, wear their brands.

The place where you work often defines you in the eyes of others. When you meet people, the first question often asked is "Where do you work?" Or "What do you do?" We call this the cocktail-party effect—that sense of pride that magically occurs when someone asks you where you work and you can proudly say, "I work at [insert name of company]!" Because any place you work, for any period of time, becomes part of your overall identity. As Eric Jackson of FedEx observes, "the cocktail-party effect really happens here. You experience it anywhere employees go, from the backyard barbecue to the soccer game. Our people are proud to tell others they work at FedEx and be a part of something larger than themselves."

History is important. Our Yahoo! origins are telling. Two Ph.D.s. Trying to write their dissertations. As they procrastinate, they explore the internet. They are addicted. They are spending all their time finding cool sites (instead of working on their dissertations) until they think, hey, let's catalog all the cool sites we find on the Internet for our friends. And then the idea grows until they have the most comprehensive directory of what's on the Internet in one place. And Yahoo! is born.

At Southwest, we cherished our history. The legendary moment Herb Kelleher drew on a cocktail napkin the triangle of the first route map. How we needed customers to accept, for the first time, cash register receipts for tickets, plastic boarding passes, and boarding groups A through C. We needed community leaders to fight for us. Flight attendants to wear hot pants. And employees to look beyond a paycheck to a total work experience.

—Libby

11. YOUR EMPLOYER BRAND MUST DEFINE WHAT YOUR BUSINESS BELIEVES IN.

Your employer brand is an organic way to articulate what your business offers, believes in, and stands for. Why your business must exist. What difference your business can make. And how its systems, programs, and infrastructure align with its values. Your employer brand marries what the organization values, offers, and rewards. Joining what the brand promises outside with what the experience demands inside. Linking what the organization believes to how it fundamentally respects the people who deliver its brand.

This is important to employees. According to the Yahoo! Hot Jobs poll results, more than 93 percent of people looking for jobs consider it very important to important to be able to support a company's values. And according to the 2005 Hodes research, 81 percent of human resources professionals around the world say an employer brand can help an organization deliver its vision and values.

At the heart of your employer brand is trust.

Your employer brand must be authentic. It must reflect the values of your business. It must accurately portray what people actually experience. It must reflect your business's personality. "Employees can sniff out if they are given platitudes and pie in the sky," says WaMu's Libby Hutchison. And Diageo's Yvonne Larkin observes, "The strength of an employer brand is determined by the level of authenticity experienced by people—that is, whether we deliver on the promises we make, whether that relates to our products, our employees, or our shareholders."

Your employer brand must be more than a marketing effort. It must be, in fact, the collaboration of all internal forces, from marketing to HR to operations, to create the emotional and functional employer brand. It is the sum of value, experience, opportunity, rewards, and results. It must reach beyond the hype of Marketing, the spin of Corporate Communications, the programs of HR.

Your employer brand must motivate employees to emotionally internalize what your business offers and demands and values. To satisfy this requirement, it must exceed the employee's expectations. It is a product of anticipation, expectation, and reputation.

Your employer brand must be the collective representation of all that your business stands for, fights for, and believes in—consolidated in one statement of purpose. What you hear, observe, and experience is based on trust. Trusting what someone says about your business, or what you observe, or an experience you have. An employer brand as a place to work develops in the same way. You come to conclusions based on what you hear, observe, and experience. And there's a thin line between a reputation as a place to do business and a place to work. It hasn't always been this way. But recent deterioration of trust in business and other institutions places new pressure on any business's employer brand as a place to work.

Years ago, we entered the workforce without thinking about a business's reputation. There was, simply, less risk. We knew going to work for just about any business would yield a stable experience. Some companies might be more challenging. Others might be friendlier. Each would essentially offer a job, benefits, and opportunity. There was little risk to consider, simply because the institution of business had such a strong reputation.

By the mid-1980s, however, things began to change. In the wake of the oil and financial collapse in the Southwest, we saw first-hand how companies pulled out of commitments they had once made to employees. We saw "retirees" leaving, perhaps before they had intended to depart. Images of those days stay with us. The day an energy giant escorted hundreds of people out the door, each to a new black limousine. They were executives being rewarded with new business cars while hundreds of their colleagues collected pink slips and had to walk past the new cars on their final walks to the parking lot.

Now, as a result of these and similar incidents, people are more careful. People don't immediately trust any longer. People rely on others to determine whether it's safe to trust. And that's why people rely on employer brand. You want to do business with companies and people you trust. You want to buy products from companies you trust. Invest in companies you trust. Work for businesses you trust. Customers trust Southwest to get them from point A to point B on time and, most important, without incident. You trust the reliability of the equipment, competence of the pilot, efficiency of the operation. Trust is based on the soundness of what it delivers: safe, reliable transportation at a fair price. Singing flight attendants, even those with hand puppets, don't fly the plane. Likewise, customers trust Yahoo! as an internet destination and gateway. You trust the security of the financial transactions or the personal connections. You trust that Yahoo! will never misuse a credit card number or any personal data it gathers online.

Managing an employer brand as a place to work is all about managing risk. You are afraid—as an employee, customer, investor—to make a wrong decision. You have been cheated, deceived, wronged too many times. When you choose, you are simply more careful. So you rely on reputation. You *hear* late-night talk-show hosts tell jokes about companies. Or you carefully *observe* news stories showing how products can fail and, in some cases, kill. You believe if you closely watch a business's reputation as a place to work—through what you hear, observe, and experience—you can minimize your risk. At FedEx, the Purple Promise helps them set expectations with their workforce for what excellence looks like. "Since the beginning our commitment to excellence has defined who we are and helped separate us from the competition. The Purple Promise is core to our culture and by keeping this promise we meet the world's expectations one person at a time."[17]

None of us likes to be disappointed. We don't want to be let down. And reputation can be a bit of a safety net. But it's only as reliable as a business's commitment to invest.

12. Your employer brand must define your desired emotional connection with your employees.

Your employer brand frees you to describe an emotional connection with your employees. What it means to your employees to be a part of what you are trying to accomplish. How it feels to tell others where they work. Why they will want to choose to work and commit. How it can feel at the end of the day to go home and say, "I did my job."

Over the years at Southwest, our marketing strategy proved so effective that Southwest became a major national airline in the mid-1990s. We needed a more powerful brand. So our executive and marketers, working with our ad agency, selected our new brand: "Symbol of Freedom." Southwest's mission to deliver low-cost air travel had given Americans the freedom to fly. We knew we needed our employees to catch the passion and power behind this vision of opening up travel to everyday Americans. We embarked on an employer branding campaign designed to make the freedom message first come to life for employees, so they could deliver on this promise.

First, our marketing department produced a stellar marketing campaign for employees, with a video and parchment declaration of freedom arriving at employees' homes. Although most understood the new branding, few internalized the message. Then our internal culture committee took a stab at communicating the brand inside. They came up with the great idea of sending a "freedom" steamer trunk in the belly of an airplane from city to city. Each location added their own unique "symbol of freedom" to the trunk as it passed through our system, with the final destination a "freedom" display at Love Field. That was fun, and nice, but it didn't compel our employees to live the brand either.

Finally, our EVP for customers convinced HR and Marketing to work together to help the brand catch on in the hearts of employees. We wanted to message that working for Southwest was unique. Our challenge was to figure out a way of making this message real, not just another one-dimensional piece of propaganda. And we fulfilled that challenge by declaring a brand promise, "At Southwest Freedom Begins With Me," and articulating the eight freedoms of working for Southwest: The freedom to pursue good health, create financial security, learn and grow, make a positive difference, travel, work hard and have fun, work and innovate, and stay connected.

—**Libby**

It is difficult for business to talk about such things. Language can get sappy. Emotions can feel artificial. But because brand is an emotional language, with employer brand the messages can ring true. And be clear.

In the not-too-distant past, as most of us entered the workforce, the employment decision was primarily *functional*. There was a job, I needed a job, I could get ahead if I worked hard, it offered a pay-check, and—cool!—it had a retirement savings plan my dad said I needed. And medical, too. You didn't necessarily stop and think about reputation. You had no reason to question whether your business would actually deliver what it promised. It was a business. People trusted businesses. As long as you had heard of it, you felt safe. There was no risk. Of course, that was before we experienced all the business incidents that threatened our trust.

With risk comes emotion, and over time employment decisions have become *emotional*. Instead of simply asking "What is the job?" the prospective employee may ask, "What does your business stand for?" Instead of asking about pay, prospective employees may ask how executive compensation is governed. They may ask about lead-ers and managers; they may want to meet their coworkers before joining. Instead of only asking about career, the prospective employee may ask about balancing work and life. Ultimately the prospective and current employee asks "What's in it for me?" if she or he were to work there. How your business can begin to answer that question is a big part of its reputation as a place to work.

Your employer brand must create this *emotional* connection between the employee and the product or service and the business. It's the emotional connection you create with your employees, on the inside, so they in turn connect with people on the outside. Your employer brand is the experience a business *should* carefully build to create the emotional connection with employees so they in turn connect with customers and other key stakeholders. Every experi-ence an employee has, for better or for worse, will contribute to the reputation they carry of your business, which your employer brand articulates. Your employees are at the core of how your busi-ness connects with every possible stakeholder. The customers. The vendors. The people in communities where you have locations. The investors. The news media. The financial community. Your employees represent your business to each of these stakeholders.

Your employer brand, for example, can be key to how your business works with any number of vendors, including independent third-party contractors. While on site or at work for your business, these independents essentially represent the brand, just as actual employees do. Your employer brand can frame such working relationships. Today, in fact, many companies depend on vendors to deliver products and supplies to customers. Many supply chains rely on contractors. Many businesses outsource elements of their customer service. Much of what customers experience depends on people a business does not employ. So a business's reputation as a place to work extends to every vendor it works with.

Securing the emotional connection—to secure the commitment to deliver the brand—is essential to building a successful brand. This can happen only if your employees and, as needed, your vendors believe the brand is a cause, well above the simple completion of the tasks of the job.

Your employer brand must project what an employee *aspires* to be and can be by connecting with your business. It must paint a picture of what life can be if the employee works at that business. The brand must *inspire* the employee to become an advocate of the brand and your business—and to emotionally invest in its mission. For an employer brand to create such aspirations and to inspire, it must create an *emotional* connection. This connection must make the employee feel good about the work experience.

At Southwest we struggled with a new provider of our Employee Assistance Program. We were having so much trouble, in fact, getting them to work with our employees in the way we promised our employees they would experience, that we put the EAP staff through the culture and customer service (internal and external) aspects of our new employee orientation. This was so successful that we ended up putting all the vendors who worked with our employees through the training, resulting in their delivering the right service to our employees. This is a real lesson to any business that is outsourcing any aspects of its employee experience.

—Libby

For your employer brand to successfully create this emotional connection, your business must achieve certain standards in every dimension of the employee experience. Otherwise it risks offering a less than satisfying experience that in turn can undermine other aspects of the connection. Before an employee is willing to feel *intimacy* with a brand the employee must first feel *comfortable*.

An employer brand must be easy for an employee to emotionally recognize. The employee must feel it is within reach, as if "this is something I can experience, I can permit myself to connect with." Otherwise the relationship with your business can feel merely transactional. And that is not a step to engagement.

In the wake of the Hurricane Katrina disaster of September 2005, Yahoo! jumped in to help people cope with the tragedy, find access to vital information, communicate with loved ones, and lend support to those who faced the challenge of rebuilding lives, homes, and livelihoods. Not only did we quickly replace advertisements with Hurricane Katrina coverage and links for donations, but we also opened a Yahoo! Store that raised over $55 million for the Red Cross. With a company match, our employees raised $250,000 in just a few days. Most impressive were the Yahoos who quickly volunteered to forfeit their Labor Day holiday weekend to fly to Texas and assist the evacuees in Dallas and Houston. Within ninety minutes of issuing a call for volunteers on our company intranet, we had to pull the story down because the response was so overwhelming. Yahoos set up computers, helped people search for loved ones, posted and responded on message boards, and actively reunited families, couples, and friends. One of our founders led a team that created a metasearch tool that searches multiple missing-persons sites simultaneously and a more effective alert system for evacuees who couldn't find one another in the large stadiums. There were many stories in the press about the efforts of Yahoo, but we made those efforts because it was the right thing to do, as a place to buy and a place to work.

—Libby

13. YOUR EMPLOYER BRAND CAN HELP YOU RECRUIT EMPLOYEES.

Your employer brand can create demand among prospective employees. It can help a business compete for talent. It can create the positive buzz. It can be a framework for how your business communicates its value proposition. And it can articulate what your business believes in and stands for.

According to the 2005 Hodes research, 81 percent of human resources professionals around the world say an employer brand can help attract candidates. Some 51 percent believe it can shorten the time to fill, and 44 percent believe it can lead to a higher job acceptance rate.

By describing, for example, what your business offers on a web site for a prospective employee. Populating the recruitment materials with key messages. Facilitating a recruitment process that is respectful as well as stimulating. As JetBlue says on its internet site, "Imagine how you would create an airline if you were building it from scratch."[18] And as Intel asks, "Are you ready to make the most of your mind?"[19] When Nike says, "If you have a body, you are an athlete," it speaks to its prospective employees, who likely are also its potential or current customers.[20]

"We tend to hire people who are aligned with our brand," Washington Mutual's Libby Hutchison observes, "and we pay special attention during the hiring process so we are certain someone we hire is aligned with what we value."

14. YOUR EMPLOYER BRAND CAN HELP YOU RERECRUIT EMPLOYEES.

When an employee joins your business, your employer brand becomes a guideline for what we can expect. Just as with the customer brand, your employer brand promise frames what the experience should mean.

The 2005 Hodes research shows that 63 percent of human resources professionals around the world say an employer brand can help increase the retention rate. And as people who work for your business, just as they use the product or service as customers,

A company was having real trouble in the marketplace. Its customers were being attracted by flashy new competitors. To get their attention back, the company decided to retool the brand and marketing. Now, it would take some time to prepare to launch the retooled brand. So in the meantime as the company took steps to recapture the good will of customers, a group of employees came up with an idea: how about if we let the world (and our customers) know how much we care for this company and how much we want to keep it alive? We put together a massive volunteer effort of employees—who believed in the brand and the business—who blanketed the company outlets to reach out to customers, thank them for their support, and explain what the business was trying to do. The key message was simple: "We believe in why this company exists, why it should continue, what difference it makes. And we hope you do, too." This personal effort by employees, to tell the world of their pride, made a difference to the efforts to rebrand and renew. And this helped the company show its public that brand strength starts from the inside.

—Mark

employees ask themselves if what they experience as employees lives up to the promise. And they ask themselves what they will tell others. Will they recommend the business as a place to work, or will they suggest the friend keep looking? Just as with customers, employer brands guide people through the user experience and give them something to hold on to—while reminding them of why they made the choice in the first place. Consider how Gap Inc. claims "our brands have a simple, common purpose: to make it easy for people to express their personal style"[21]—and how so many leading companies describe their commitments to social responsibility on their web sites, such as Coca-Cola's statement that it is "committed to becoming the world's most inclusive business."[22] P&G's Diana Shaheen states, "P&G's purpose is to improve the lives of the world's consumers. This includes our employees."

Just as with customers, a business can use its employer brand to create evangelists for the brand—to reinforce word-of-mouth recommendations that effectively attract new employees, retain current employees, and continue to engage former employees. In fact, former employees can have a big influence on the market perception of the brand—specifically, your employer brand as a place to work—and they can reinforce the appeal of the brand to employees. Like Mercedes-Benz, for example, which says its success is "due to its people whose ideas and abilities have translated consumer needs and experiences into relevant products and services."[23] Or Nike, as it states, "We aren't looking for workers; we're looking for people who can contribute, grow, think, dream and create."[24] As Swystun and Oakner remark, "the challenge is ensuring your employees deliver on the promises your brand makes to the market. And that means making employees the first to know."[25]

A side benefit of a strong employer brand is the "halo effect" it can have in the community—the spontaneous word of mouth that a positive reputation can create. Just consider the things you hear, and remember, about the businesses that make positive contributions following natural disasters. Or those who appear to go above and beyond the expectations of a good corporate citizen. Some positive deeds are large. But the same can occur in small moments, such as when people in a community drive by a location every day or see a story about your business on television or see employees at work. Your employer brand can influence how these people view your business as a member of the community—beyond the value of the products and services. Think of eBay: "We've created a place where people can come together."[26] Or Diageo—the parent of Smirnoff and Cuervo, among other products—saying "we believe communities should benefit from our presence" and also conceding, "we know that, treated irresponsibly, our products can have consequences for individual health, safety and community life and so we have made social responsibility towards alcohol our primary focus."[27]

15. YOUR EMPLOYER BRAND IS *NOT* HYPE.

How employees treat customers makes a difference to what customers experience. And how employees feel they are treated makes a difference to what they are willing to do. That's what employer

A car retailer trying to carve out space in the crowded automobile retail space realized that on-brand behavior would take more than motivating messages from leadership. Especially when the behavior would be counter (in a positive way) to customer expectations. So it looked to its employer brand for guidance. And it made the commitment to change with some real teeth. The company redesigned its compensation program to eliminate what was once the ultimate sacred cow in that business: the commission. Imagine a car dealer without a commission! This subtle but significant change, consistent with the company's brand, reinvented its relationships with its customers. And it made a difference to the bottom line as well as had the desired effect on employee morale and results. And it preserved and rewarded on-brand behavior. A living example of what a business can accomplish when it follows its employer brand.

—Mark

brand is all about. But there's more to an employer brand than meets the eye. It's not a matter of simply repeating the same story delivered to customers. Nor as simple as turning the customer brand to the inside or slapping a logo on a collection of internal programs. Your employer brand is *not* simply marketing. It's not a logo or a tag line only. It is a matter of *being*.

"Our values are at the core of our employer brand," says Libby Hutchison of WaMu, "to be fair, caring, human and dynamic." Yvonne Larkin of Diageo says, "It is important to make the values meaningful. They have to become more than words on office walls and corporate brochures," and Eric Jackson of FedEx observes, "An organization's DNA cuts through the complexity and resonates with all stakeholders." At P&G, according to materials distributed to employees, the DNA is a combination of "best of the best" and "caring cultivator" and the positive tension between the two creates a "demanding yet caring" culture.

Over the years many theories have emerged about employer brands, along with a lack of consistency in what people think it is, what they think it can do, and how they think it needs to be managed. Some of the theories have become myths.

Certainly there is a marketing dimension to your employer brand. And your employer brand is an effective way to market your business to prospective and current employees. But like a certain superhero, people have x-ray vision when it comes to places they work. And they quickly see through an employer brand that promises one thing and delivers another.

Communication *is* important to your employer brand. How a business positions and messages, educates and persuades. But employer brand involves more than how a business communicates. It's all about what a business *is* and how a business applies this identity and purpose to the experience it creates for employees.

Any business wants its people to *live* the brand. Employer brand is about internalizing the brand promise. What it means, what it stands for, what's required for its effective delivery, and what connects with customers. It's about what happens every day: how bosses interact with employees, how employees interact with each other. Whether people feel personally valued and appreciated. The experience someone has at work is affected primarily by the person they work for and the people they work with. All the branding and messaging in the world can't fix bad relationships on the job.

The programs created and administered by HR define fundamental aspects of an employee's life and work at a business. They reflect the brand of your business as an employer. But there's more to employer brand than the programs. Even if these programs are on point.

The culture of a business will certainly impact its employer brand. Just imagine how the Southwest culture of fun and freedom contributes to its brand as an employer. But employer brand is *not* limited to the culture. Neither is buzz. At the same time your employer brand looks inside at the employee experience, it must look outside to the customer experience that employees must deliver. Ruth Mortimer remarks, "there was a time when 'brand' was a logo on packaging or the message in an advert. But this is no longer enough. Companies are turning to internal branding strategies and asking their employees to 'live the brand.'"[28]

Five Essential Steps

1. Articulate, inside your business, the experience you create for employees so they in turn deliver your brand to customers. Define how your employer brand supports your business strategies. Describe how your business parallels the experiences for customers on the outside and employees on the inside. How your customer and employer brands compare. How they differ.

2. Define your customer touch points and how your employees potentially influence each of these touch points. Define how your employer brand clarifies what your business needs from employees.

3. Describe how employees of your business understand what your brand is all about. And believe in what your brand promises to your customers. Consider how freely you talk in your business about the emotional dimensions of your brand. And what that can mean to employees.

4. Consider what you would say is your employer brand of your business. Is it a clear, accessible picture of an employee experience? Or something more subtle? Is it distinctive from your competitors? Or something more common? And what does it say about your business and what you stand for?

5. State how your employees would answer the question "What is the purpose of our business?" Consider how many actually understand the core value of your business.

PART TWO

GET READY!

CHAPTER THREE

ESSENTIAL #3: DIAGNOSE

Your business has an employer brand. That's not a question. It's a fact.

So you *don't* need to spend any time wondering *if* you have an employer brand. You have one—if anyone, anywhere, talks about you, writes about you, thinks about you, remembers you as a place to work or a place to buy. It's a given. Your employer brand is as much a part of your business fabric as bad eggnog at holiday parties.

There's no question that you have an employer brand. So the question is whether your employer brand is working for or against your business. Whether your employer brand helps your business recruit, retain, and motivate employees. So they in turn deliver what your customers expect.

Now that you know the essentials of brand and employer brand, it's time to check out the health of your employer brand even if you have not formally started to develop one. In fact, according to the 2005 Hodes research, 48 percent of human resources professionals around the world say their organizations have undertaken *informal* employer brand initiatives.

What about you? Start by diagnosing whether your employer brand—formal or informal—is working for you.

During the height of the dot-com boom, many companies were hiring like crazy because they had to move fast and their equity had a lot of appeal. And startups and mature companies threw a lot of money to employees in the form of long-term incentives without really thinking of the long view. They didn't think about employees who ultimately would want to know more about what a company stood for beyond the obvious financials. At that time, most Silicon Valley companies had not considered the concept of creating a talent organization focused on attracting the right talent, developing the right talent, keeping the right talent. But that's precisely what we did at Yahoo! We reinvented HR to be more than an order-processing center for job requisitions. We created an integrated talent function. As a result, talent has become a part of the fabric, and a talent mindset is beginning to permeate the company. In fact, every staff meeting includes a talent report, not only of open positions, but of what we call "green, yellow, and red flags": who is joining, hitting it out of the park, leaving, or on the fence, and where there are issues.

—Libby

DIAGNOSE YOUR EMPLOYER BRAND

We aren't doctors and we don't play them on television.

But we know your first step should be to *diagnose* the health of the employer brand of your business.

Why is this important?

Your employer brand may have evolved on its own, naturally, without any direct effort of anyone in your business. You need to know whether this *unintentional* employer brand is working for you or against you. Or you may have what we call an *intentional* employer brand—one you have put a great deal of effort into developing. If so, you need to know the direct result of your work. Or your employer brand may be in between. Regardless of its origin, you need to know its health. Otherwise you won't know what to do next.

You can find out the health of your employer brand by completing a quick diagnostic check.

Over the years, we have looked at many ways to assess the health of an employer brand. Some approaches address the clarity of the message. Or the reach of the appeal. Or perhaps the potential impact on the business. The fact is, to realistically assess the health of your employer brand, you need to measure from the inside—just as you will work to ultimately build (or rebuild) your employer brand. Ultimately, the success of your employer brand will rest on how your employees *understand, believe in,* and *do* what it takes to deliver.

That's why we have developed a simple, practical checklist of conditions to determine how well your employer brand is working. We call this your *employer brand health check.*

You can complete this health check by answering a series of questions. And by leading a discussion session with some of your peers. Some questions may be simple. Others more difficult. For some you can collect data from existing metrics for your business, including employee surveys and focus group reports. For others you may need to talk with some of your employees.

We remember when Southwest was growing so fast we experienced real growing pains. And the company realized the operation's reliability was becoming questionable. We needed to break down silos that had unintentionally developed as we grew into a major airline. Our customer feedback showed a rise in the number of lost bags, late flights, and other issues resulting from a lack of cross-departmental teamwork. Like when a customer calls an 800 number to ask about a lost bag. They just want the bag back and really don't care to hear that the bag was lost by ground operations and the 800 number rang to reservations. It all boiled down to a significant gap in the connection between employee commitment and the customer experience. So we decided to reorient all employees to the fundamentals of the customer brand. Everyone was required to attend. We called it Mind the Gap. Each class had people from all the work groups. The class was designed to help people discover how, when they do not keep the focus on the customer and the brand, they actually let *each other* down—not just the customer. The highlight was an exercise in which people from each department made a list of all the problems other departments cause when they slip up. It was a real eye-opener. People committed to make real change in their behavior. And the brand was strengthened.

—Libby and Mark

THE TEN-QUESTION EMPLOYER BRAND HEALTH CHECK

Answer each of the following ten questions on your own or use the tools we provide for discussion with your peers. Regardless of your approach, take time to think through each question.

1. HAS YOUR BUSINESS DONE SOME WORK TO BUILD AN EMPLOYER BRAND?

You may have developed an employer brand for your business. Or you may have done a lot of work that, when added up, creates the essence of an employer brand.

And your employer brand actually evolves as your business goes through the paces of hiring, engaging, and terminating employees. With each program and process a business chooses, it introduces expectations of what employees may understand and believe, how they may act, and how the business commits to value its employees. A business plants seeds for the employer brand with every program, message, and dimension of the employee experience, as well the employee input to each customer touch point. As well as any way in which the business connects with prospective, current, and former employees.

Have you embarked on efforts to define and implement your employer brand? If so, how recently? What impact did it have on the business and employees? And what change did it create?

If not, how would you initially describe the employer brand that has evolved on its own?

Regardless of its origins, how would you describe the employer brand your business currently has? And how would your employees describe it?

How would you describe your work to intentionally develop an employer brand? _____

What resulted from that work? _____

How does this employer brand help or hurt you in attracting, retaining, and engaging employees? _____

How would your employees describe your business as a place to work? _____

How does this compare with an unintentional employer brand that may have developed on its own? _____

Your answers to these initial questions will help you get started with a close look at your employer brand—to see what you can do *intentionally* to develop and nurture your brand as well as what may occur *unintentionally* to influence your reputation.

2. ARE YOU SATISFIED WITH HOW YOUR EMPLOYEES UNDERSTAND WHAT THE CUSTOMER BRAND OF YOUR BUSINESS PROMISES?

Your employees *must* understand the basics of your customer brand to bring that brand inside. That means you need to find out if they "get" what your customer brand is all about. If you can, simply ask your employees if they can repeat your brand promise. Or if they can describe, in as few words as possible, what your brand is all about. Or if they can imagine words a customer might use to recall your brand and what that can mean to a customer. Your assessment of your employee understanding of your brand will help you determine

A company was experiencing increased pressure from competitors, suppliers, and customers. Competitors were thinking faster, suppliers were moving slower, and customers were demanding more. Caught in the middle were employees, who were starting, more and more, to ask what was in it for them to continue to work here.

We talked with one employee. She said she used to love her job. But, now, since the company had taken away so many things it used to offer customers, the work was not much fun. She felt her primary job was to listen to customers complain. "It's a vicious circle," she explained. "I feel bad because we can't offer the service we once offered; they feel bad because they don't get the service they feel we promise; then I feel bad because they complain to me; then I in turn make the next customer feel bad because I simply don't enjoy what I do anymore." By asking employees what was at the heart of the issue, the company was able to address the issues from the inside. And they're doing just that.

—**Mark**

whether the employer brand that exists for your business naturally supports what the business promises to customers. Ask yourself these questions:

What does your business promise to your customers? _____

How does this promise differ from what your competitors promise?
_____

Why should your customers choose your brand over your competitors'?
_____

How well do your employees understand and believe in and contribute to this differentiation? _____

How committed are they to deliver on the promise? _____

If your employees "get" your brand, then this will give you a good place to begin to build your employer brand. If they don't understand your customer brand, repairing this will be the first thing on your brand to-do list.

Stop any person on the street and ask him to name a company where people like to work, and the likelihood is that Southwest will be mentioned by many. But there was a time, when we were first expanding beyond our Texas comfort zone, that we were having real trouble finding the people we needed. All of a sudden people were not flocking to apply. And although nothing had changed internally, the external conditions simply would not support our previous hiring methods. Fact was, we were trying to hire new employees all over the country at starting salaries equivalent to those offered by fast-food restaurants and retail stores. And because pay was established by labor agreements, we couldn't arbitrarily raise it without opening a can of worms. The market for talent had changed overnight. Before the employee's market of the dot-com boom, we could take the time to screen and prequalify candidates who would wait for the next openings. Now we needed to put someone to work on the day they agreed to join, lest they chose to move on to another opportunity. We had to get creative about how to brand ourselves during the hiring and onboarding process.

—Libby

3. ARE YOU SATISFIED WITH THE DEGREE TO WHICH YOUR EMPLOYEES BELIEVE IN WHAT YOUR CUSTOMER BRAND PROMISES TO CUSTOMERS?

It's one thing for employees to understand, but connection with your customer brand will happen only if your employees believe in its promise. In how you differentiate from your competition. In the roles they must play to successfully deliver your brand to customers. Ask yourself these questions:

How effectively do your employees believe in their roles to deliver your brand promise to customers? _____

How consistently do they see the opportunities to deliver this brand promise at each touch point? _____

How thoroughly do they believe they make a difference—even those without customer contact? _____

How accountable do they believe they are to make the connection between the brand and their work? _____

How invested are they in the success of your brand in the marketplace?

_____

Your assessment of what employees believe about your brand will help you determine whether your employer brand is "sticking" with employees. Because if they don't believe, they will not act. This assessment will help you determine whether your current employer brand is helping employees "connect the dots" between what they do every day and what customers expect and experience every day. And if it's not, what may be standing in the way.

4. ARE YOU SATISFIED WITH THE STEPS EMPLOYEES TAKE TO DO WHAT IT TAKES TO DELIVER THE BRAND TO YOUR CUSTOMERS?

In the end, all the understanding and belief won't make a difference if employees do not take the action to deliver the brand. If employees do not commit to the difference between doing the job and delivering the brand. A passive understanding without active commitment will make it challenging to actually deliver—the same is true if the business does not support the development of needed

At Yahoo!, as we were developing our employer brand, we used tools similar to those that marketers use to evaluate success. Internally, we worked with Towers Perrin to craft a survey to specifically address elements of our employee experience, such as compensation, corporate profile, stimulating work, career opportunities, likable coworkers, learning and development, work/life benefits, paid time off, facilities, and amenities. We asked which of these elements attracted them to work at Yahoo! initially and which ones had the most influence on retention. We asked our outside advertising agency to help us with focus groups and surveys of our target technical candidates so we could find out what they thought about us as an employer. The data was helpful in identifying what to work on in making improvements and what to message as employer brand attributes. Using similar employee opinion tools every twelve to eighteen months, we can measure our progress and determine whether our targeted efforts are effective. Although employee opinion is the best gauge of employer brand strength, we also look at metrics such as retention and turnover, reasons for leaving, number of candidates applying, time to hire, percentage of candidates who accept job offers, reasons why candidates do not accept, and so on. Other measurements related to brand are customer-satisfaction metrics, productivity measures, and overall profitability of the business.

—Libby

skills or the adoption of on-brand behavior. Ask yourself these questions:

How consistently do your employees have the skills the business needs to deliver your brand? _____

How easily can employees access tools and resources to strengthen those skills? _____

How effective is the fundamental infrastructure to support skill development? _____

How aware and committed are your employees to the behaviors needed to deliver your brand? _____

How easily can they observe and experience role models of these behaviors, including leadership? _____

Your assessment of on-brand behavior will help you determine whether the employer brand you now have is in fact creating real results you can substantiate—in the actions and behavior of employees. Or whether the commitment of your employees to on-brand behavior, as well as the availability of role models, is falling short.

5. ARE YOU SATISFIED WITH HOW YOUR EMPLOYEES UNDERSTAND AND BELIEVE IN YOUR EMPLOYER BRAND?

After assessing what is happening on the outside, when you look inside the business, what do you see? Do your employee "customers" have a consistent experience that in turn motivates them to deliver to your customers in the marketplace? How comfortable are you with your reputation as a place to work?

Do you make an effort to train your people to deliver your brand equal to the effort you make to develop your brand? The first step to help your employees understand the brand promise is to explain the brand

When we were articulating the employer brand at Yahoo! we came up with some less-than-formal ways we would know if the employer brand was working. We said we would know all was working when someone would stop an employee on the street, eye the Yahoo! T-shirt, and say, "You're lucky to work at Yahoo!" Or when someone would stop an employee and say, "Don't you work for Yahoo!?" Or when a cousin of an employee would, at a family gathering, begin the Yahoo! yodel. When the kids of employees would identify themselves, proudly, as Yahooligans. We would know it was working when an employee would want to stay at Yahoo! simply because there is no other place like Yahoo! Or when Yahoo! is there with the employee through every possible change in life. When the employee realizes the work we do touches millions of people around the world. And when employees simply feel proud of the work they do.

—Libby and Mark

promise. And not in marketing terms. In simple terms. Appealing to the customer in each of us.

Do you take the time to interview your customers on the precise experience they expect to feel when the brand is delivered? And do you share these reports with employees? The first step to help your employees believe in what they can do to deliver the brand is to hear the first-hand experiences from customers. It will make it real.

Do you identify the touch points between your employees, the brand, and the customer? Carefully consider how employees can positively impact each touch point. The first step to help your employees *do* what it takes to deliver the brand is to help them see all the opportunities they have to exceed customer expectations. Even if they are not customer-facing employees. Ask yourself these questions:

If you asked the question, "What's in it for me to work here?" what would most of your employees say? _____

If asked by friends, "What's it like to work there?" what would most of your employees say? _____

If asked to recommend your business as a place to work, what would most of your employees say? _____

If asked what the business promises to employees, what would most of your employees say? _____

If asked whether they have the tools, resources, and skills to "get things done" at work to deliver what customers expect, what would most say? _____

If asked, at the same time, if they have what they need to get things done for their own lives, what would most say? _____

If asked what your business stands for, believes in, and values, what would most of your employees say? _____

If asked to compare what the business believes in and their personal beliefs, what would most of your employees say? _____

If asked to assess whether they "live the brand," what would most of your employees say? _____

Your assessment of the emotional commitment to the business will help you determine if the employer brand offers enough emotional content about the business for employees to make the connection or if something is missing. All together, your level of satisfaction with how employees understand your employer brand can help you determine what work you need to do. But don't stop here. In your next step, you need to take a close look at how your employer brand supports your talent strategy.

6. Does your employer brand support your talent strategy?

You can't look at your employer brand without looking at what your business needs to do with talent. In a nutshell, your employer brand should be the framework for how you address your talent blueprint.

A retail company was struggling to gain market share. The brand promised an experience of quality, cleanliness, and responsiveness. The marketing created a customer expectation of experiencing something beyond the usual. But the company had done little on the inside to prepare its employees to deliver this experience.

We did a few site visits to identify the customer touch points for ourselves. And we found a store that didn't quite look ready for company. The windows were dirty. The sidewalk in front of the entrance was covered with cigarette butts. The welcome mat had lost half its letters. The outside of the building was so dirty, in fact, that a note of apology was taped on the front door. The inside wasn't much better. The entry floor was stained.

Clearly the brand was experiencing a bit of breakdown. And the company, although not intending to disappoint customers, was creating a disconnect by not doing its homework to prepare employees to deliver the promise of the brand. They didn't realize that contributing to the brand promise is everyone's job, not just the people on the front line with customers. To repair the situation, the company reached inside, first to solve the operational issues, then to use this success to reengage employees—learning again that unless you get to the core of the problem, from the inside, it will not go away.

—Mark

Once upon a time there was an endless supply of eager employees. And most of them were willing to engage—until the weight of change and the lack of trust in business caused them to think twice. That's why this is the moment for employer brand. This simple language of choice—with its clear call to action, grounded in commercial reality—can effectively combine the functional and emotional components of an employee's relationship with a business as it gives a business a compelling and personal way to tell its story. This balance of commercial and personal, functional and emotional, is what makes employer brand a secret sauce to address talent issues.

"Today's talent is more demanding of the organizations they work for," says Diageo's Yvonne Larkin. "Compared with previous generations, the talent we need to attract is more mobile and potentially less committed to developing their career within a single organization. Increasingly, they want the values they live their life by to be reflected in the organization where they work. They are less willing to make compromises."

Every business has challenges *finding* the right talent. Every business has challenges *keeping* the right talent. Every business has challenges *securing the trust* of people. Every business has challenges *engaging* its people in its business and its brand. What's different today, as employees tell us, is that a business must do more to prove it will deliver what it promises. Business must pass a test before employees are willing to engage.

This talent situation is a far cry from what we experienced in prior generations. And it's a juggling act. On one hand, it's a talent challenge to engage the people we have in our businesses, to

We learned at Southwest that a robust workforce plan is a practical way to start. We developed a robust workforce plan that would report exactly how many candidates we had to interview to produce the number of qualified employees we needed in any given period of time. The only way the business could effectively plan how to use our resources to hire and keep employees was if we had a good idea of how many people we actually needed. So we started with facts. And we built the workforce plan based on the facts.

—**Libby**

deliver the brand to customers, and to perpetuate the experience we create internally so we can successfully recruit new people to support that external experience. At the same time, it's a talent challenge to effectively market the employee experience without resorting to hype. To clearly articulate the authenticity of the organization in a truthful, appealing manner. Business *must* wage war: on the outside, to get the people, and on the inside, at the same time, to keep and engage and inspire the people. And any military strategist will confirm there's nothing as challenging as a two-pronged campaign. That's where employer brand can help.

Have you thought about new sources of talent as the overall market for talent shrinks? Sociologists, demographers, business magazines, and thought leaders have been predicting since before 1995 that business would face a talent crisis by the year 2005. Others, most notably Peter Cappelli of Wharton Business School, seek to debunk this idea. Cappelli cites the effect of the baby boomers working longer at the same time that boomers' children are entering the workforce, as well as an influx of immigrants, the effect of offshoring, and the fact that the labor force will grow through 2014.[1] Although the workforce will not shrink, it will get older and more diverse. Whether or not the predicted demographics prove true, most CHROs complain today about not being able to find the people they need. The people with the right skills. Or they are anxious about losing people they need to win over their competition, especially if it's partly because the business is not viewed as a good place to work.

Do you have a hard time finding people with experience and skills in their industries or in specialties? Even if the overall numbers make it look as though you have surplus applicants, is the fight to get the best talent at its most intense? No business is immune. Some types of jobs, such as those in information technology, simply do not yield enough candidates for all the positions that need to be filled. This places extra pressure on every business to do everything it takes to secure the right people. And places more pressure on the employer brand.

Do you have enough people for the future? Have you anticipated the impact, as baby boomers get ready to retire? Do you know where the next generation will come from to help the business do what you need the business to do? What skills and experience will be required? How many people will you need in key jobs? How many leaders will you need to develop from within? Where will you find them? What training will they need, to do the job and deliver the brand? How well does your talent strategy address your workforce needs—and how well does your employer brand support your talent strategy?

Do you know what your competitors are doing to land the same talent? Competitive intelligence has always been important in running a business. Now it is equally important for recruiting. How well do you know what your competition is doing in the hiring arena? Investment analysts have discovered that cataloging job postings can indicate where a business is planning to go. Do you know what your competition is looking to hire? Do you know the packages they are offering? Have you asked declining candidates why they accepted an offer from a competitor over yours? Or asked accepting candidates why they chose you over a competitor? Over time, the rules of engagement between competitors have become less friendly. Once upon a time businesses in the same space might honor handshake agreements to refrain from actively recruiting each other's employees. Today telephones are ringing like mad and email inboxes are filling with invites for career open houses. Lawsuits are filed to stop "poaching" of employees. That puts more pressure on the business currently employing the person in demand—pressure to make sure the employee commitment is as strong as possible. The best defense is always a strong offense.

Does your strategy vary by workforce segment? Any business has difficulty successfully implementing a single talent strategy across divisions, locations, and specialties. There is not, in fact, one talent challenge for the entire business. Your talent challenge will be distinct in distinct parts of the business, based on what each part of the business is looking for.

Do you segment by level of employee? Smart companies segment talent. First, they recognize that the highest level of talent, such as executives and "super–creatives," produce high-impact results. The very presence of thought leaders in their fields can change the game for the business in a big way. Second, they recognize that some employees are core to the business, with core competencies that produce results. Third, they manage the variations of peripheral talent. Some may be employees, some may be outsourced. Work may be done offshore or by vendors. Branding the experience for each talent pool can support attracting and retaining the talent needed in each segment.

Do you target markets for employees in different ways—with a separate (but related) employer brand for each? Each segment may need its own strategy. The top tier may sourced and recruited directly by the company or through third-party recruiting agencies. They will be most influenced by what they have heard from their peers about the business or what they read in business and professional journals. They react to a solid corporate reputation. They follow well-known talent that act as magnets for their peers. The core group of employees, on the other hand, can be targeted through recruitment branding, advertising, and sourcing. Although reaching this peripheral group is closer to product marketing, others may be acquired through third party agencies or business partnerships.

A merger brings talent issues of an organization to the surface partly because so many issues must be addressed in such an intense period of time. So when two organizations were trying to come together, we knew the success of the merger would come down to employees making the choice to join and to commit to the new organization. We treated the staffing issues of the merger as we would treat one big recruitment of new employees to a business. We clearly articulated a compelling value proposition of what the business would offer as well what the business would expect. We made it very easy for employees to answer the "What's in it for me?" questions, with a very detailed web site available on day one of the new organization. And we promoted this value proposition with a range of informal and formal media. The result was an offering that employees could easily evaluate to make the decision whether the business made sense for them. By focusing on the issues from a recruitment perspective from inside the company, the company covered the necessary bases to articulate what employees needed to hear. And it worked.

—Mark

Do you (if yours is a mature business) find it difficult to compete with start-ups for top talent? So much of what drives a prospective employee is a sense of feel. What one feels the business stands for. What it may feel like to work there. How it may feel easy or difficult to access opportunities. In smaller new companies, people feel they have more authority and influence and can make a bigger contribution. All of these categories of "feeling" are easier for a new company to promise—and, in many cases, to deliver—than they are for an existing company, simply because the existing company has to deal with all the people who are already there and the natural baggage they bring to the party.

Do you find the search for diverse candidates even more challenging? The same concerns apply. These candidates, although certainly looking for what a business stands for, also specifically look for the organizational commitment to diversity.

Do you recognize that not only are employers becoming branded as places to work, but new workers are becoming their own brand? Fact is, top talent no longer actively seek out new opportunities; businesses find them because they are known in their field. The best companies have strategic talent-sourcing functions that search for the talent they want. They spend months, even years, cultivating relationships with prospects, eventually creating a compelling opportunity for the candidate. These sourcing functions use business competitive intelligence to know who to cultivate and who may be available, open, or interested. "Branded" talent can be sourced through employee referrals, speakers at professional conferences, expert bloggers, authors of articles and white papers, academic faculty, and so on. To attract these candidates, companies often have to think outside of the box. Creative ways to acquire this talent include creating start-up type ventures within the organization for those with entrepreneurial interests; acquiring small start-ups for the talent; creating joint ventures with university researchers; buying a candidate as if he or she were a company, including rights to intellectual property; and very creative compensation packages and work arrangements.

Do you recognize that people look for more than money? Without question, money speaks. And it will always speak. But as we talk with employees we learn, over and over, that people are sincere when they say they want a job to be more than a paycheck. Certainly they aspire to a job that offers more than a paycheck. And they want the business to stand for something beyond the financial rewards. Ask yourself these questions:

How would you summarize your business's current talent needs?

_____

How would you assess the workforce plan you have in place?

_____

How would you evaluate your analysis of your workforce needs—what people, what skills, what places, what timing? _____

What are your competitors doing to secure the same talent?

_____

How does your employer brand contribute to addressing your talent needs? _____

Your employer brand will be only as strong as its ability to support your talent strategy. And only as strong, too, as the talent strategy that supports your business. That's why it's so important for you to consider your talent strategy as you look at your employer brand.

> Many times we are called in to work with a business that is struggling with talent issues of one type or another. And many times those issues boil down to what we label the employer brand—the clear understanding of expectation between the employee and the business. At a financial services company, the HR staff simply could not believe that prospective and current employees did not "get it" about the value of working at the company. We had to show them, by mapping the actual points of contact between the employees and the business, that just wanting to create a productive experience for employees does not mean employees have a productive experience. They needed to carefully consider what can get in the way.
>
> **—Mark**

7. Does your employer brand support your recruitment targets?

In the end, you can judge your employer brand's effectiveness by how successfully it helps you land the people you need in your business. Otherwise it's an exercise. Not a productive strategy.

Do you get the résumés you need from potential employees? Are you having trouble with the pipeline? Perhaps you need to attract more qualified candidates for the jobs you need to fill. Is your candidate flow what it needs to be? Can you keep filling the jobs you need with the right people? Or is your talent pool starting to become a dried-up creek bed? Especially for those jobs the business considers absolutely essential? If so, your employer brand may not be doing its job.

What are your hiring rates? How long is it taking to fill open positions? Are slots open for weeks and months? Is your metric dashboard gauge going the wrong way?

Do you have trouble "closing the deal" with the prospects you want? Do you need to convert more qualified applicants into new employees? Does your business get the applicants but, for whatever reason, have trouble closing the deal? Do the ones you want simply go elsewhere? Take a look at what you are saying to prospects throughout the process. Do the messages you send to attract employees parallel your identity and values as a business—and your brand promise to external customers? How do prospects react to who the business is? What the business is? Why the business exists? What's unique about the business? And, most important, about what the business needs and expects from employees to deliver the brand promise and what the business offers employees in return?

What are your recruits saying about you? Are you asking them why they accept competitors' offers? Are you hearing anything to indicate they believe the recruitment experience is not what they expected? Does it provide a prospect enough opportunity to distinguish this business from the others? Do the recruiting materials make working at the business sound too good to be true? Or make the

One day, in a focus group, I talked with a lady named Judy. She has stuck with her company, through thick and thin, good times and bad, for over twenty-five years. She says she strongly believes in what the company is all about, what difference it makes to its customers, why investors should believe in its future. She even thinks she knows what the brand stands for in the market and how employees are essential to its delivery. She should be, by all accounts, with such "line of sight," the quintessential engaged employee. But Judy is looking for a job. And she admits that while she is on the look, she is not fully engaged in her work. She has, she reveals, simply given up on the company as a place to work. She can't handle the emotional stress. She feels overworked, over-stressed, underled, overmanaged, and, above all, underappreciated. Pay raises have been minimal, despite the company's achieving strong earnings. Career development feels almost nonexistent. Leadership feels detached. Her immediate management feels disconnected. So, as soon as another comparable job comes along, which she believes will be soon, she will leave. With no regrets. "I am so tired," Judy says. "I simply don't know, any more, what's in it for me to stay here. Maybe I'll feel better somewhere else. At least it will take a while for me to feel this bad."

—Mark

recruits want to join? Listening carefully to your recruits, just as you listen to your customers, can let you know quickly how healthy an employer brand you may be working with. Have you surveyed candidates about their experience?

Are you losing employees you want to keep? If your turnover is high, especially in key talent areas, there may be some issues with your employer experience and brand.

Does your business approach retention as a process of constant recruiting and rerecruiting of key talent? Or is there a pattern of letting these efforts lapse, then struggling to regain lost ground? Does the business build the brand into the fundamental messages all employees receive, to reinforce the value of working at the business? Ask yourself these questions:

How would you assess your success in recruitment? _____

How effective is your employer brand in your recruitment efforts?
_____

What is the impact of your reputation as a place to work on your recruitment efforts? _____

What aspects of this reputation need to change? _____

How effective are your efforts to rerecruit key employees? _____

How do your employer brand, and reputation as a place to work, help or hurt? _____

This close look at the practical effectiveness of your employer brand will help you consider its impact on your recruitment and rerecruitment efforts.

8. ARE YOU SATISFIED WITH HOW ENGAGED YOUR EMPLOYEES ARE IN THE BUSINESS?

Just as you listen to customers and recruits, you need to carefully listen to your current employees. They are, after all, the ones the business needs to deliver the brand. And they also participate in, as well as nurture, the internal environment in which their colleagues want to contribute and thrive.

A financial services company was addressing some performance management issues. As part of the work, we were talking with employees about what they actually experience at work compared to what they believed they were promised. We learned that, in fact, there was a significant say/do gap between what employees felt they were told and what they actually saw ... especially in the area of career development. That they had been promised a world of opportunity but in fact they couldn't find the entry point. That for them the promise was empty. And it was likely time to start looking elsewhere.

—Mark

Is there a say/do gap between what an employee hears and what an employee sees and experiences? Between what an employee may consider reasonable for the business to deliver and what an employee may actually experience? In fact, nothing can undermine a brand faster than when the day-to-day employee experience does not mirror how the employee remembers the employer brand promise.

Does your business portray itself as one type of place to work, whereas employees actually experience something different? Any say/do gap can be a problem. Do the rewards live up to what employees thought they would receive? Is the actual work the same as or different than what they expected—or, worse, do they believe the employer brand promises one type of job but they find themselves doing another? Or doing what they think is something different?

How do actual touch points between the business and employees compare to what they may expect? From the employee's first encounter with your employer brand through the last, what is the experience? And how does the experience undermine or reinforce the promise you express? What happens, stage by stage?

One day, in another focus group, I talked with a man named Jim. He pays close attention to the ways his company advertises its products. He tunes in to how his company positions itself. He listens carefully to the promises his company makes to its customers. And he realizes what the company expects of employees. He just doesn't see what the company offers employees in return. "I think companies are used to a time when the exchange with employees was a bit more cut and dried. The company said 'you give me this and I'll give you this,' and employees went along. But something happened a few years ago, and I just get the sense people are looking for something more. Although many of my friends are still looking for a paycheck—I mean, we have to eat—we also want to be attached to a company that somehow represents more than a basic commercial enterprise. So that's what I am looking for."

—Mark

Does the business actively use the employer brand to create advocates for the brand and the business, to reinforce word-of-mouth recommendations that can effectively attract and retain employees? Does the employer brand articulate your values, mission, and purpose? Does the employer brand parallel the promises to customers? Does the employer brand frame all the messages your employees receive?

Do you get complaints from customers saying the operation isn't quite what it used to be? Or that your products and services aren't as reliable as customers remember and expect? If so, the promise of your brand to customers may not be consistently delivered. And as a result, customers may be starting to vote with their feet and choose someone else. This may mean your employer brand—the intentional one you develop or the unintentional one you inherit—may not be working. Simply because your customers say they aren't getting what they expect. And satisfied customers are the ultimate result of a healthy employer brand.

Has teamwork deteriorated? Do you know that your people are not working together to deliver results to customers? Regardless of what customers experience and observe, what do *you* see as you evaluate results from the inside? When your brand is delivered, is it consistent with what you say the brand promises to customers? Or can you see gaps in what may be delivered —perhaps before it becomes evident to customers? Ask yourself these questions:

How would you summarize your current level of employee engagement?

_____

What signs are you seeing that employees are as engaged (or not as engaged) as you need? _____

How would you summarize your customers' view of how engaged your employees are? _____

How would you summarize your leadership satisfaction or frustration with your employee engagement? _____

How does your employer brand contribute to or undermine your efforts to engage employees? _____

Employee engagement is at the heart of your employer brand. And even though the two experiences are not precisely the same, the effort to engage certainly is critical to the experience of employer brand alignment.

9. HOW SATISFIED ARE YOU WITH HOW YOU TELL THE STORY ABOUT YOUR BUSINESS AND YOUR EMPLOYER BRAND?

Your sense of how you are telling your story (and how others tell the story, too) can help you determine the communication health of your employer brand. And what symptoms that health may actually reveal about what's happening underneath.

What about the materials you produce for prospective and current employees? And other stakeholders? As you look at the consistency of your communications with a range of stakeholders, including employees, you may see signs of an *unintentional* employer brand that is *not* working for you. Communications that follow the employer brand are crisp, to the point, ultimately simple, and tied to a clear call to action—just like communications that follow a consumer brand. So how do your communications stack up?

Is your web site clear, to the point, and meaningful—or is it a collection of favorite expressions of corporate-ese? Do your communications with employees speak in simple, human words or do they impersonally summarize rules and steps? Do your descriptions of business strategy bring the business closer to employees or simply sound like watered-down presentations to the financial community? Prospective and current (as well as former) employees will use their x-ray

> Dr. John Sullivan suggests that there are four categories by which an employer brand can be measured. First is media exposure. These metrics include number of positive citations in media outlets versus those of your direct competitors. Second, Sullivan suggests, is getting listed on best places to work lists. Beyond that, he suggests finding out what your target talent population knows about your business's employment brand. Finally, he says, look at metrics such as increased flow of employment applications.[2]
>
> **—Libby**

vision as they go through your communications. They will be attracted to and impressed by efforts of a business to parallel the experience it creates for customers with the experience it offers to employees. They will respond to being, as an employee, a part of what they already may experience as a customer.

Do current advertisements support the employer brand? Many advertisements of many businesses portray employees serving customers. If that portrayal does not parallel what actually happens—if it is, in fact, less than authentic—efforts to promote the customer brand may actually undermine the efforts to support the employer brand.

Advertisements may portray employees in an unrealistic way. The actors portraying employees may not look like real employees. They may not sound like real employees. And they may not do their jobs in the ways real employees do theirs. Real employees, of course, can see through this in a minute. And it can immediately prompt a logical question: "What's wrong with the way we actually do things?" Advertisements may also portray customer touch points that don't really happen. The x-ray eyes will see right through artificial portrayals—advertisements painting a picture of interaction that simply doesn't happen.

Advertisements may make promises the business can't fulfill. Employees will see, in a flash, if the ads make claims or promises that they know, at first glance, may be difficult to fulfill. If it sounds too good to be true, it usually is.

Advertisements may portray values inconsistent with the actual values of the business. The ads will undermine if the employee cannot see himself or herself in the portrayal of the business. If the values of the business in the ads are not the same as the day-to-day reality. If the business in the advertisements is not the same as the business where employees work.

Do you advertise for potential employees? Do you advertise for job openings? What do your current ads say about your business as a place to work? Do you list jobs on your web site? A branded jobs site? Does what you advertise accurately reflect the experience of people who work there?

What is the media saying about you? Are media reports about your business consistent with the employer brand the business projects?

No business can control how it is portrayed by the media, even though effective public relations can help. No force can undermine an employer brand as quickly and permanently as the media. Despite criticism of the media, most people still put their faith in the media without question. As the saying goes, "If you read it in the paper, it must be true."

What news reports, editorials, and speeches provide key insight into what is important to the business? What indications do these messages provide of what the business stands for? And believes in? Ask yourself these questions:

How would you summarize the effectiveness of your marketing materials to prospective employees? _____

How would you assess the impact of your web sites? _____

How would you evaluate the impact of your customer advertising?

_____

How would you consider the view of the news media coverage of your business as a place to work? _____

How does your reputation as a place to work influence what others say about you? _____

Business or news reports can paint a picture of the business as a place to work that is inconsistent with what the business says it is—or actually is. If the business says it offers one employee experience and the news media reports another, the credibility of the employer brand can suffer. A portrayal of business activity that is contrary to the values of employees will quickly undermine the employer brand—if employees see, through these reports, a business at odds with the value system they hold.

10. Do you have an employer brand crisis?

Now look back at everything you have considered in this health check, to determine whether you have a healthy brand on your hands, or a bit of a nuisance, or a significant employer brand crisis.

Depending on what you found as you collected data and answered questions, you can determine whether or not your employer brand, intentional or unintentional, is in crisis, or if you have enough concern that you need to make it a crisis.

How can you get your team to see the need to reposition your employer brand? One way is to create your own crisis. That's right. When I joined Yahoo! in the middle of the dot-com bust, we certainly had many crises. We had to change our business model. We were recruiting a new leadership team. We needed to reduce our expenses and unload our unprofitable products and business units.

In the midst of this crisis it would have been silly to bring up how we would brand ourselves as an employer, but I was thinking about it. I believed in our future success. I knew we had to set ourselves apart from other employers in our space. I knew it was a good time to help our employees understand what we offered that they couldn't find anywhere else. I knew we needed to further engage our people. After walking around and talking with many Yahoos and listening to HR teammates, I felt our issues were clear. But those issues may not have been the most important, at that moment, to our senior leadership team. They were focused on turning around the business. We needed a focal point.

We decided to audit our cultural health. To learn more about what our employees thought and felt about the culture. We needed valid, meaningful data as a basis for articulating our mission, vision, and values. So we surveyed our people. We learned that Yahoos value trust and working relationships, really like their coworkers, have positive working relationships with their peers, trust their supervisors, and use words like *pride* and *commitment* and *caring* and *energized* to describe our environment. We also learned we needed to improve how we help employees understand our vision and values and expectations. The data showed that clearly we had a crisis. And it gave us permission and helped us create support to explore the employer brand.

—**Libby**

Someone who moves into an older home may not like everything that's there but may decide, for any number of reasons, that it's OK to stay there and make the best of the "bones" of the old home. But some renovations may be needed. It may be the same with your employer brand. Hallmark's Dean Rodenbough says:

Even though we had a lot of research and brand initiatives in place, we realized that we needed to more proactively manage our brand.

The marketplace was changing. Our consumers' lives had changed. How they interact with our products had changed. And greeting cards were no longer top of mind for some of them. We needed to do a better job of reminding consumers about the relevance of our brand and products and we needed to begin with our employees, making sure they were engaged in their work and active ambassadors of our products. We considered employees an untapped resource and we needed to make sure they were invested in the brand's future.

The employer brand you discover may not be the employer brand you want. But you may decide to live with it. Or you may not. Only you can determine whether this employer brand is anything close to what you would want for your business. And whether your employer brand is in a crisis.

If a business from the outside tried to take over the business, would employees fight or welcome the takeover? If employees would not fight the takeover, the business may not have the emotional connection with employees that it needs to withstand less severe challenges.

If a business from the outside moved next door, would customers avoid or welcome the competition? If the loyalty from customers is not strong enough to weather the competition, employees who ideally would have an emotional connection with the business may not be creating the emotional connection the business needs with customers.

If a business from the outside went into business with an almost identical model but a different identity, would employees avoid or welcome the new face? Would they be inclined to leave or stay? If the new business on the block successfully steals employees, the reputation of your business as a place to work may not completely resonate with employees.

If your business wants to grow, will the employees support it? A business must look to its growth. An employer brand is essential to any growth strategy. Growth requires continuing to hire the right people in the right jobs at the right time. And keeping the current employees. This constant effort to recruit and retain demands that the business enjoys a reputation for people in the marketplace that supports its ambitions for growth. The emotional connection with employees, as expressed in the employer brand, is key to a strategy for growth.

If your business needs to change or possibly shrink, will employees stay connected? The emotional connection with employees will be tested most as the business faces challenges of reducing size without cutting out its heart. The employer brand will give people something to hold on to as their willingness to emotionally connect to the business is tested with each change. The essence of effective change management is effective stability management—giving people things to protect as they adjust to things that change. The employer brand will give people that emotional anchor as they react—perhaps emotionally—to how the business expects them to change. Ask yourself these questions:

> Based on the answers to the "health check," how would you summarize the crisis mode of your business? _____
>
> To secure leadership attention to the health of your employer brand, what do you need to do? _____
>
> To make this effort stick, whom in your leadership do you need to engage? _____
>
> To make this effort real, whom in your business do you need to involve? _____
>
> Are you committed to lead this effort as the employer brand champion?
> _____

Is it time to gather a team to address employer brand? If you find, at the end of this chapter, that your employer brand may be in crisis— whether self-created or naturally caused—then it's time to put together the cross-functional team and walk through a step-by-step process. You'll use the insight you gained from answering the questions in this chapter to steer the team to tackle those fundamental issues, from the inside.

One of my colleagues at Yahoo! told us a story about her former employer, a pharmaceutical company. They spent time and money to rebrand the company for the customers and rolled it out with much fanfare. "Drugs That Matter From People Who Care." Unfortunately, they did nothing to connect the employees to the new brand. Within a few days the employees had changed the slogan internally, to "Drugs That Matter, From People Who Don't."

—Libby

Five Essential Steps

1. Complete your "health check" for your employer brand, based on what your customers and employees experience, as well as what your business needs.
2. Carefully review your talent strategy. Without a sound and relevant strategy, your employer brand will have a difficult time making a real contribution to your business.
3. Consider how your employer brand supports this talent strategy. What it does and does not contribute and what changes need to be made.
4. Consider how your efforts in employer brand connect with your efforts to engage employees. Although these two experiences are not the same, they certainly do have a lot in common.
5. Consider where you are in the development of an employer brand. Have you worked to build one? Or do you need to begin by looking at what already exists and start from there?

CHAPTER FOUR

ESSENTIAL #4: PREPARE

OK, you have now determined your readiness to work on your employer brand. You know if you have a problem that needs to be solved. You have identified whether your employees are engaged or skeptical. And if there is a brand crisis, you are ready to save the company. You want to fix it. Now!

Your task seems overwhelming. A mild panic sets in when you begin to wonder: "How do I get this done?" That is the wrong question. You, alone, cannot fix it. You must avoid the temptation to go it alone. The brand, the culture, the solution to any emotional disconnect belongs to the business as a whole, not to one person or department.

Before you get started, keep a few things in mind. This is challenging. You can't underestimate what it will take to get it done. You need to prepare yourself to do this the right way.

Here are the steps to get started.

EIGHT STEPS TO GET READY TO BRAND FROM THE INSIDE

1. DEVELOP THE BUSINESS CASE TO BUILD OR REBUILD YOUR EMPLOYER BRAND.

Chapter Three guided you through the steps to diagnose the health of your employer brand. Your first step to "get this work done" is to turn that insight and information into the business case for your efforts.

Basically, this business case for employer brand should be rooted in the ultimate result it will create for your business. Based on what you determined in Chapter Three, begin to craft that business case with this end state in mind.

Your business case should include four key sections:

The need: Why the business needs to address employer brand.

Show them the money!

What is the burning platform for addressing employer brand? Financial results due to customer observations and buying patterns? Turnover results due to employee perceptions and experiences? Recruitment results due to prospect reactions and expectations? Or all of the above?

As you prepare the business case, attach the financial and opportunity costs to the conditions you need to address. What are the costs from unhappy customers? What extra recruiting costs do you incur to find the right candidates? Do you have to overpay people to close deals with new employees? As a result, are you ramping your compensation costs higher than your competitors'? What does turnover cost? How much are you wasting if your internal communications don't connect and engage? What costs can you measure if your advertising messages aren't considered authentic? Or if your corporate reputation is losing ground?

Based on your work in Chapter Three, clearly articulate the problem your employer brand is going to solve. Make your explanation direct and to the point, but do not exaggerate. Most likely this is not the end of the world, but it can prevent a business from achieving results. Be sure to realistically link your efforts to build the employer brand to the strategies of the business. Credibly convey the business need for this work.

This business case for employer brand must position the efforts as a *business* issue—not an HR issue, not a communications issue, not a marketing issue. Employer brand is essential to the business. Your business case must tell the reasons why.

The result: What the employer brand will deliver to the business.

What end-state difference will a healthy employer brand make to your business? Will it be in recruitment? Engagement? Retention? Financial results? All of these?

In addition to describing the problem, your business case must clearly state what the result will be, to justify the investment in the work. Your explanation must distinguish this from other strategies of the business; it must carefully position this as an essential connector among many of those strategies. Truth is, as we have experienced over the years, for every issue a businesses faces there is a talent component. And employer brand is at the heart of what happens in a business with talent.

As tempted as you may be, however, to claim what employer brand can do, be careful *not* to overstate the ultimate results. Promising *too much* may only lead to unrealistic expectations and possible disappointment. Instead, emphasize the incremental milestones that a focus on employer brand can achieve—and how those milestones ultimately connect to create substantive results for the business.

The barriers: What you must overcome to successfully build and implement the employer brand.

The business case you develop must not just focus on the positive side of this effort. You can't simply talk about the good things employer brand can bring. You must also tell the truth to the leaders of your

A consumer products company was building its business case for employer brand. But the team got so excited about what they *could* achieve that, in the business case, they overstated what they likely *would* achieve. And, no surprise, when they got into their approval session with leadership, the leaders of the business questioned their assumptions and their predictions. The team had not done its homework to get to the core of the difference an employer brand could make. Nor did it document the financial impact. What emerged was employer brand as a "nice to do" instead of a "have to do" simply because they were not realistic about the end state. They painted a picture of aspiration, not a detailed look at projected accomplishment. Senior leaders told them to go back and do more homework. Which they did.

—Mark

business about what can get in the way of your successfully building and implementing your employer brand.

Consider three potential barriers to your efforts to brand from the inside.

Culture. Is it challenging to your business to take a close look at what's inside? Is there hesitation to closely examine the inside? Is it more comfortable in your culture to simply continue with a comfortable point of view? To maintain the status quo? Could people invited to participate in such an effort react with something like, "Well, that may be good for some others, but it just isn't us"? To successfully brand from the inside, you must clearly see what's inside your business so you can create an authentic outcome. Otherwise it will be too easy to do a synthetic fix. If your culture resists such candid assessment, you should address this as a barrier in your business case.

Leadership. Is it challenging to your business to engage senior leadership in discussions about talent and culture? Or is it more comfortable for leaders in your business to talk about money and assume the talent will follow? At the same time, is it habit for leaders you may want to include in this process to delegate involvement to someone else—perhaps someone with less clout? Successfully branding from the inside requires the direct engagement, commitment, and sponsorship of senior leadership. Otherwise it may be too easy for this to be labeled an "HR thing" or a "Communication thing" or a "Marketing thing." If your leadership resists such involvement, you should address this as a barrier in your business case.

Silos. Is it challenging inside your business to get people to work across the traditional boundaries of department and function to focus on issues in an integrated way? Is it more comfortable for people to work within their comfort zones—with people who share their views of the business? And, as a result, do different groups of people often work to solve the same problems at the same time, without connecting? To successfully brand from the inside, you need the holistic view of the business from many sources. Otherwise the solutions will never be real and will not work. If silos are a challenge, just say so, and address them as a barrier.

The investment: What resources you will need to brand from the inside.

This business case, like any business case, must clearly specify the investment necessary to generate the return. You will have a better idea of the scope of this investment after you finish reading this book. Overall, to brand from the inside, your investment (in hard or soft dollars, depending on your internal resources) will likely include the following:

- *Employee and leadership research*—if you decide you need current data on how your employees and leaders view your talent, brand, and business issues.
- *Advertising agency support*—if your approach to brand from the inside will involve work with your advertising agency to connect to your customer brand work.
- *HR consultant support*—if your approach to brand from inside involves a significant amount of work on your people strategy, issues, programs, and systems.
- *Change/engagement/communication support*—if your implementation of your employer brand represents a significant shift in your employee point of view.

An energy company working on employer brand issues wisely decided, from the start, to engage senior leadership of each of its businesses. The internal champion of the effort personally contacted the heads of each business, explained the purpose and approach, and secured the involvement of senior leaders. This high-profile advisory team provided necessary guidance and grounding to the process as well as served as a "conscience" of the exercise. Their involvement in the actual building of the programs, policies, and messages that employees would experience grounded the development in the business, making it a business issue, not an HR or communications issue. And when it came time to implement, they served as willing speakers to the authenticity of the process and the outcome.

—**Mark**

2. PUT TOGETHER YOUR TEAM (AND BREAK DOWN THE SILOS).

Now, before you can put the team together, you need to name a team captain. You need to choose an employer brand champion. Every employer brand effort needs one.

According to the 2005 Hodes research, 72 percent of human resources professionals say that HR people lead employer brand efforts at their organizations. Someone in the business must wake up every morning thinking about the employer brand. Picturing what the employer brand can accomplish. Speaking in the language it creates. Someone who is passionate. Realistic. A strong facilitator. A strong believer. And that champion needs a team.

It's true that in business, people like to work issues in their own ways from their own comfort zones. That can be fine if the potential impact of the problem stays in that confined space. But if the problem can reach across the business, the efforts to work the issues and the team must reach across as well. And that takes a leader of the effort.

Busting the silos.

If you are as convinced as we are about the potential of employer brand—and understand what it can do for your business—you need to carefully put together the group of people who will take a look at your employer brand. Realize that others in your business may be working the same issue. And they may be quite a ways down the road. They may fear that by working with a team they will lose ownership and recognition. They may worry that you will encroach on territories. They may feel threatened by your efforts to bring them together. But you *must* bring them together if you want any chance to create a coherent employer brand. "The real key is a strong partnership among Communications, Marketing, and Human Resources," says Linda Clark-Santos at Washington Mutual. "We needed to capture the essence of the brand on the inside. So we sat with one from HR, one from Communications, one from Marketing. We said, you know, we need to figure out how to do this and make this happen. What came from our discussions was our employer brand campaign. We kept asking ourselves, 'How do we get this inside people's heads?' What resulted from our collaboration was a year of planned activities."

Building an employer brand is not a one-person effort. It's not a two- or three-person effort. It's not a one-department effort. To get it done right you must include many people. And extend your work group beyond the people you immediately work with.

The problem is that most businesses today thrive in silos that permit like-minded functions, product groups, business units, or geographical regions to operate together. On one hand, these organizational structures can work well when individuals need to work within their groups. But silos can create artificial boundaries that make it hard to integrate across the entire business. When individuals from various functions have to work together, silos can get in the way.

You won't develop an employer brand that sticks if you let the silos get in your way. No *one effort* to build the employer brand from *any* critical player can successfully do the job in isolation. That would be like an orchestra trying to play a symphony without all the instruments. The holes are immediately apparent.

You need to reach for representatives of three key groups—HR, Corporate Communications, and Marketing. You may also need to reach for others, such as Operations, depending on what business you are in. That's the only way to ensure you'll build an employer brand that authentically reaches each dimension of the employee's working life. Without such a cross-section, what you achieve will be limited by the narrow scope of the represented points of view. No one person or department can completely define the essence of the business. Silos get in the way.

Businesses resist real collaboration. They talk collaboration. They profess a commitment to collaboration. But they resist. They resist for good reason. Collaboration can slow things down. Collaboration can create internal conflict. Collaboration is harder work. So as they resist, they retreat to their comfort zones armed with lengthy PowerPoint documents unsuccessfully pointing to the reasons for whatever problem they are trying to solve. But collaboration is essential to employer brand.

Building the team.

So your first challenge, as a champion of an employer brand process, is to put the team together. You have to get the right people at the table, working together on the problem. You may need to call in some chips.

One of the challenges of having a powerful brand is the fact it has more than one owner. As we began to work on employer brand at Yahoo! we initially thought we were stepping on each other's toes. HR felt we were in charge of the lion's share of employer brand. Corporate Communications was the crafter of messaging our corporate identify and in charge of internal communications. Marketing owned the consumer brand. As a technology company, we had a tech team working on creating tech branding. We were all working on our parts of the puzzle. But it was a puzzle.

—Libby

Hallmark's Dean Rodenbough remembers, "We created a brand management structure with three teams—governance, strategy, and tactics—rather than a full-time, staffed department within the organization. Each team is comprised of members from Marketing, Creative, Human Resources, Communications, Legal, and the product areas. Before we decided who to invite to be a part of the brand teams, we thought about everyone in our business who may be helping to develop and nurture a version of the employee brand right now—even if they didn't know it!" At a minimum, your employer brand team should include the following groups:

Human Resources: The experts who define and sustain the employer brand through the people they hire, the leaders who are developed, and the programs, practices, and processes for those people. They develop the details of "the deal" with employees. How employees view that deal will strongly influence their willingness to deliver the brand externally. For your folks from HR, employer brand can frame how the function executes the development and implementation of processes that define day-to-day work at the business. Beyond that, employer brand can define how HR can become an agent of transformation, focused on the development of intellectual capital and knowledge management. Diageo's Yvonne Larkin observes, "Releasing the potential of our employees is key to Diageo achieving its performance aspirations. By using the insights gained from our employer brand work, we can better align our people strategy with our business strategy."

Marketing: The experts who tell a brand story on the outside. You need them and you want them. They know the customer brand promise and what employees must deliver to make the promise come true for customers. For Marketing, the employer brand can complete the internal steps to ensure a successful delivery of the customer brand. And can make sure the people inside are prepared to make a difference to customers. Eric Jackson, of FedEx, comments, "Because of our business model, our people are our product. So what happens inside FedEx is critically important to every go-to market strategy we devise. We know if we don't get it right with our workforce, we won't get it right for our customers."

Corporate Communications: The experts who tell the brand story internally and externally. On the inside you want to partner with them to embed brand messages into every dimension of employee communications. Just as important, on the outside you want to make sure the messages sent to the press, investment community, and other stakeholders are consistent with the employer brand promise. For Corporate Communications, employer brand can frame how to communicate key messages about the business to employees, using tools and language that are relevant to employees. It can ensure a consistency between internal and external messages. And it helps the business differentiate how it tells its story by focusing on the explicit communications and implicit messages employees receive.

Operations: The experts who deliver the brand to customers. They get the job done. And how they do that job will strongly influence what customers experience. They may not immediately appreciate the subtle nature of employer brand and the small things employees can do to make the brand come alive for customers.

These groups are the must-haves. Do whatever it takes to get them to the table.

Within each general area you may want to include specialists, such as the learning and development or recruitment people within HR, or the quality assurance people within Operations, or the advertising specialists within Marketing. Be careful *not* to throw the team off balance with too many from one specific area. This is a work group. Not a caucus.

Depending on the type of business, you may also want to include additional representatives. You may want to include Customer Service if you rely on customer-facing employees, the call center if you deliver the brand to customers over the telephone, the behind-the-scenes operations center if you deliver the brand online, Sales if the business's success depends on a connected sales force, and Technology if it is important to be known for the innovative technology you create. You may want to include external resources, too, such as representatives from partners in advertising or consulting.

Before you invite others to join your brand team, give yourself a quick silo check to identify who else you may need to include:

- Which parts of your business tend to do things on their own without consistently connecting with others?
- Which have the most potential influence on the customer brand?
- Which have the most potential influence on the employee experience?
- Which players are most likely to believe they should be included in a discussion of brand?
- Which are most likely to "do it on their own" if you do not invite them?
- Which silos do you need to bridge to build the employer brand?
- Which departments or businesses or sectors in the business thrive on their own and so become internally focused?
- Which silos must you invite to participate in the process?

At Southwest our first few meetings on employer branding were focused on understanding the concept of branding in general. We didn't even have the right language to understand how marketing principles and tools could be applied to the employee value proposition.

—Libby

> We once had a disastrous kickoff meeting with a client group. It was deadly. The leader was so excited about the topic that she could not stop inviting people. We walked into what we expected to be a group of ten and it was a roomful of forty. Our small focused party turned out to be a rock concert, with everyone competing for air time.
>
> **—Mark**

3. PLAN HOW TO INCLUDE EACH POINT OF VIEW FROM YOUR TEAM.

It's not just a matter of inviting a mix of people to be on your team. You need to involve them. And as the leader you need to coordinate (and plan for) that involvement. You need to work the team to secure a mix of views.

If a communicator alone develops the employer brand, the employer brand may be all about the message. Communicators like to create words and pictures. But the application of the employer brand in words and pictures, without the thinking behind the employer brand, is rather like a plateful of marvelous icing with no cake underneath.

If HR alone develops the employer brand, it will likely be all about programs and process. HR people like to develop and implement detailed programming, whether it be how people are paid, how they receive benefits, or how their performance is managed. But HR may get so caught up in the implementation of the process that they miss the big picture.

If Marketing alone develops the employer brand, it may be nothing more than an internal marketing campaign that sounds a lot like the customer brand but may not be grounded in the reality of the employee experience. Marketing people, thank goodness, focus on selling. Where would we be without them? But the skills that create sales on the outside can create hesitation on the inside simply because employees may not want to feel they are being "sold" a point of view.

Your brand isn't simply built by one group or nurtured by one department. It's the result of the efforts of many groups of people. Select your team to reflect the actual contributions your people already make.

4. CONSIDER HOW TO AVOID THE TEMPTATION TO REINVENT THE WHEEL.

Put any number of smart business people in a room and they will be tempted to reinvent wheels. It doesn't matter what topic. It's genetic. And you don't have time for that.

There are proven steps to follow to develop your employer brand. Fact is, a lot of the thinking you need to develop the employer brand has already been done. So much of the employer brand is how the business thinks through its soul as it prepares to define its offering.

So as you begin to work with the team, start with the work your business has already done. This will help you prevent unnecessary "wheel reinvention" and give each silo a chance to showcase their work. Be sure to cover these areas:

- *Corporate mission.* Does your business have a clearly articulated mission, vision, and values? (Most mature businesses do.) If so, bring these to your first meeting. All of these documents, and the thinking behind them, can provide helpful clues as you develop the employer brand. On the other hand, if you are a startup, you have a clean slate.

- *Marketing insights.* Has your marketing department initiated a recent external brand effort? What reports do they have? What evaluation of your external brand characteristics have they conducted? Marketers, as a part of their consumer branding initiatives, will have studies and research reports that give insights into how your brand compares with your competitors'. Consumer insights may define the characteristics and personality of your brand. Letters from customers may offer valuable clues about their experiences connecting with your brand. Customer satisfaction data may indicate how customers perceive your business. What pleases them about the experience. What frustrates. And how these observations support (or potentially undermine) your brand promise.

- *Sales.* What collateral material does your sales force use to promote the brand externally? What brochures do they use? How does your web site present what the business offers and stands for? (For examples, visit the sites we reference in this book.)

- *Advertisements.* How does your organization position itself in the marketplace? Do you brand the organization with a specific name or experience? Is your organization the parent for many consumer brands? Is your organization thriving behind the scenes, without a strong public face?

• *Engagement.* How does your organization connect with employees? Are your folks on board with what your organization commits to customers? Do they clearly see the role they play to create brand success on the outside? And are they motivated to deliver their best? Your business may have employee survey data that reports on the state of engagement. You may have done work to determine if your employees are on board with what your business commits to customers. If they see the role they play to create brand success on the outside. If they are motivated to deliver their best.

• *Customers.* What data do you have about how customers perceive your organization? What pleases them about the experience? What frustrates? How do these observations support (or potentially undermine) the brand promise you deliver outside?

• *Internal communications.* What data do you have about how employees perceive what they hear from the organization? Do they believe what you tell them? Do they trust the organization's message? Do they consider leaders credible? How do these observations support (or undermine) how you need employees to deliver the brand outside? Your internal communication people may have collected data about how employees perceive what they hear from the business. If they believe what you tell them. If they trust the message and the messenger. If they consider leaders credible. And how these observations support (or undermine) what you need from employees to deliver the brand.

• *Other information.* What else can you get your hands on to help you and your guests get smart before dinner? What employee materials? HR communications? Competitor information? Industry observations?

5. DEVELOP A CLEAR PICTURE OF WHAT YOU WANT TO ACCOMPLISH.

It's easy for any team, no matter the issue, to try to boil the ocean. To try to solve a problem too large for any one group of people or any one period of time. You and your brand team will work best if you try to work on one or two priorities you have carefully considered. And narrowed down.

Brands evolve over time. It is best to break up branding work into parts. Plow through, one part at a time. For example, once Yahoo! completed its rebranding efforts and a new brand, the business repackaged internal programs and communicated and marketed these to employees. Then Yahoo! tackled the external positioning of the employer brand.

One way to determine what you can accomplish is to consider the natural way in which employees will look at your employer brand. People must take small steps before they take large ones. Any employee will need to be familiar with an employer brand before becoming comfortable with it—and well before becoming intimate with it. This *intimacy* with the employer brand is a fundamental part of the emotional connection the employer brand seeks to create.

At the same time, it's important to have a picture of the on-brand behavior needed in your business. What on-brand behavior consists of at one business may be totally different than at another, simply because the role of the employee to deliver the brand will be different.

Finally, your picture must include the standards your employer brand must reach. Any external brand has standards—visually, in how the brand is displayed, and emotionally, in how the employee delivers. An employer brand needs standards, too. Part of your job, for every process you create that employees may touch, will be to consider what standards you must follow to create an on-brand experience.

Throughout this process, be true to your (business) self. This is not marketing. This is not hype. This is real life. You need to leverage your organization's DNA. Now, we are not scientists, and we do not portray them on television. But we know business. The DNA or essence of the business is essential to the employer brand because it defines what the business can be. Every business has DNA. It is who the business is, why it exists, and why it was started.

So, do you want employees to develop employer brand *identity?* And employer brand *commitment?* And to become employer brand *advocates?*

Yahoo! identified our target customer as internet-intensive users who are confident, curious, driven, optimistic. We observed that these were the kind of intellectually curious people who ask "What if?" The folks who milk life for all it is worth. These people have something special about them that we refer to as "the Y! gene." When looking for talent, we want to find and keep Yahoos with the Y! gene so they will create the Yahoo! branded experience for customers. So to begin extending our employer brand externally, we first had to set standards to assess whether or not a prospect had the Y! gene.

—Libby

Some people are simply *employer brand clueless*—without a clue as to what the employer brand is. In fact, there is no way you will get to begin your employer brand journey with a population that is already activating the employer brand. Until now, employer brand has been too elusive a concept to be openly embraced by the broad employee population. Even businesses that have set the world ablaze and filled many conference platforms describing employer brand efforts *still* have employees who are clueless.

Some employees, who experience employer brand *identity,* understand what the employer brand is and have a good idea of the roles they play to deliver the brand externally and experience the brand internally.

Some, who experience employer brand *commitment,* strongly believe in the brand, what it stands for, and what it means *to them* and demonstrate a willingness to *do something extra* to *make the brand live* internally and externally. There is no chance your employees will successfully deliver your external brand unless what it takes to deliver that brand is at the top of every mind—and at the core of every heart—no matter what job they may do.

Some become employer brand *advocates:* employees who consistently deliver the brand externally as well as fully experience and share the brand internally.

No matter how passionate you may be for employer brand, no one person can do this alone. It's a team effort. And the rest of this book will help.

6. PREPARE FOR THE TEAM'S WORK.

As the employer brand champion, you need to lead the process. You need to clarify what the team must accomplish. And do what it takes to make it happen.

Chapter Five outlines the specific steps to branding from the inside. In the meantime, here are a few tips to help you get ready.

Set a clear agenda with reasonable expectations.

No matter where you start, you want to manage expectations. To make sure you get everyone to attend, you should send out an agenda and homework assignment in advance of the session. The agenda for your first meeting should simply cover three or four key points you will be sure to cover, such as these:

- Define objectives
- Clarify what your customer brand promises to customers and how that compares to what customers actually experience
- Confirm who your customers are, including shareholders, employees, business partners, the media, and the community
- Identify how you can make the brand promise come to life within the organization to motivate employees to deliver the customer brand

That's it. That's enough. In subsequent sessions you can work through more of the details of the programs and processes that support the employer brand. And, if the discussion ever starts to slow down, keep in mind these three questions, simply to get people talking:

- What do you want customers to "tell their friends" about how *your* product or service compares to your competitors?
- Why will your customers continue to choose you the next time a competitor tempts them to make a change in brand?
- What role do your employees play in delivering the experience described above?

It's impossible to have an authentic employer brand unless it starts from the inside. That's the only way it can become second nature—if it reflects how people in the organization work and live. Otherwise, people will see through any effort to promise one thing and deliver another.

Working on your employer brand with your team is not about people singing around the campfire. Or wearing matching outfits while smiling at customers. The employer brand you create will have a clear focus on what must functionally occur for employees to engage, as well as what they must emotionally experience.

Functionally, employees will need to feel they can access the tools and resources they need to get things done. Emotionally, they will need to feel comfortable with how they are treated.

Developing the employer brand is half the battle. How you market and nurture the brand requires a persistent effort that you simply cannot underestimate. In fact, many believe it can be more effective to follow the strategy to *unbrand*—to avoid the natural inclination for the splash or the launch. And to simply let the employer brand be and become.

Have your own clear point of view.
So much of the work to develop and nurture an employer brand is a matter of creating influence. After all, no one can control how anyone may react.

Because this is a matter of influence, be prepared to address resistance to collaborating.

Perhaps the most powerful element of the Yahoo! employer brand is the clarification of the functional and emotional elements—as if giving permission to employees to, on one hand, expect the company to provide certain tools and resources to help them get things done and, on the other hand, hope for a stronger connection. What's interesting is that this balance came directly from employees in how they answered questions in our survey. And it was when we looked at the results and saw the trends in their responses that we realized they were describing a functional-emotional balance. It was only then that we realized the parallel to our customer brand—the life engine—the functional representing the engine and the emotional representing the life.

—Libby and Mark

For example, you may find that the people who can make a difference to your employer brand simply can't reach beyond the silos. You could let them continue to do their own thing. Or you could lead a process to build a team and real consensus to focus on the employer brand.

You may find that the people who can make a difference can't admit that their specific area of the business may need to change The mere fact that you called them to the meeting may make them feel threatened. You could let them continue in their silos. Or you could help them discover, through this process, that each part of the business is only as strong as its connection to another. And everyone could stand a little improvement.

You may find that the people who can make a difference tend to blame each other for what may not be working. Again, you can let this continue or you can help them discover, through the process, that blame is time-consuming and useless and ultimately will undermine the employer brand experience.

7. Engage leadership.

Although you're the strength of your team, you need the business's leadership in your court.

As Yahoo! Hot Jobs' 2005 poll results show, more than 95 percent of people on line looking for jobs consider it very important or important to be able to trust a company's leadership.

An employer brand that does not connect with the leadership of a business is doomed to disappoint.

Employees look to leaders to be the ultimate expression and representation of what they consider the brand to stand for. They look less at the marketing dimensions of the brand and more at the heart and soul of the business the brand represents. They will study whether the leaders appear to live the values of the business—as expressed in the brand—or instead fall into the say/do gap that plagues so many.

In his best-selling business book *Good to Great*, author Jim Collins describes five levels of leadership, with the ultimate level being an individual who is able to blend extreme personal humility with intense professional will.[1] According to Collins, this type of leader is most often found at the helm of companies that are able to go from good to great. We believe these leaders can most

effectively support the employer brand. They lead by example.
Because their behavior is on brand, others follow suit. Because
they communicate a shared vision and mindset, others do their
best work. They never forget that work is a personal experience. Best
employer brands know that leaders aligned with the cause will be
the keepers of the brand and the culture. And to make this happen they provide regular development opportunities so all leaders
share the same messages with their teams. Southwest, for example,
prepares talking points for leaders and schedules regular leadership luncheons and meetings, so everywhere across the system our
leaders (supervisors to directors) hear the same messages and
share the same with their teams.

To credibly address the role of leadership in your employer
brand, you must consider the importance of trust.

This may be the elephant in the middle of the room.

And it could be the most important element your employer
brand team tackles. Because without trust it's impossible for an
employer brand to thrive. Or to be at all authentic.

No matter what employer brand you implement or how you
implement it, you will have messages to share with employees. And

---

An energy company completed all the steps to develop an
employer brand in record time. It had a clear vision. It had a well
articulated set of values. And it pulled out all the stops to implement worldwide. But it left out one thing—the behavior (and, frankly,
the credibility) of its leaders. It simply did not do what it needed to
do to clarify the attributes and behavior demanded of leaders to
successfully support the employer brand. So employees heard one
thing, saw another, and believed yet another. Ultimately, the actions
of leaders betrayed the commitment of the employer brand
because the leaders did not live the brand. And, no surprise, the
employer brand failed. Simply because employees could not trust
the promises the employer brand made. Much like customers who
lose faith in a product after a series of disappointing experiences,
the employees lost faith. And ultimately moved on.

—Mark

those messages will be received, and internalized, only if employees fundamentally trust what the business has to say. "This is not about putting up posters and letters," says GE's Linda Boff. "It's about making certain managers and leaders understand the brand." Libby Hutchison of WaMu agrees. "We believe the best thing we can give people is a good boss. And we're free to say to someone, 'You are not acting in accordance with our values.'"

New workers are savvy. Many are merely looking for an employment relationship they can depend on, with a business that has meaningful values and that is consistently and reliably faithful to those values, that tells them the truth as early as possible, that would never give them cause to be ashamed or embarrassed.

A loyal employee will no longer naïvely commit. The new loyal employee is informed, rededicates again and again, and rationally chooses to stay engaged with the business—through good times and bad—only for good reason. And the new loyal employees have every right to expect that their business will be loyal to them. When you break that understanding, you may say good-bye to your people. Trust fuels productivity much more effectively than any other motivational technique. We break that trust, for example, by not adhering to our stated values, by announcing layoffs without warning, by poorly executing and integrating acquisitions, or by implementing the latest fad in management science without careful thought.[2]

According to Robert Levering and Milton Moskowitz, in the best workplaces there exists an atmosphere of mutual trust between management and employees.[3] Trust, according to these experts, is defined by a partnership between employees and management as well as the recognition that employees add value to the organization. In fact, one of the Fortune 100 "best places" companies made the list simply because of the trustworthy way in which it handled layoffs.

So as you prepare to lead the effort to develop your employer brand, you need to have a clear idea in mind of where people are in the business in trusting the leadership. That way, as you begin to plan, you can influence how the messages are developed and delivered. Yvonne Larkin of Diageo comments, "Commitment from the senior leadership team is critical to sustaining the focus on nurturing the employer brand. They have to truly believe in why it is important and be prepared to change their behaviors and actions if they are in conflict with the brand essence."

It is a fact in business life that nothing hurts as much as watching a company that has done so much, so right, absolutely toss it all away for reasons its employees find nearly impossible to understand. This company began as a merger of competitors. We helped them think through their first vision statement and their initial values, all of which contributed to their first employer brand. And they did all the right things. Used the employer brand to frame the employees' day-to-day experience. Used the employer brand to frame the employee communications. Used employees, in fact, to tell others—inside and outside the company—the stories about what the employer brand meant, what it meant to work there, why the business must exist and succeed, and why they, the employees, must stay. And then it all went away. The business faced severe external challenges, after which leadership tossed out the fundamentals at the core of the employer brand—the fundamental values and principles, for example—in place of whatever the business style of the moment was. Looking back, it seems like overnight, the mission ended and the employer brand died. Simply because the business decided the values it stated were no longer relevant to the challenges it faced. It was as simple as leadership abandoning the values, even as HR and Corporate Communications tried to keep doing the right things. So it all went away.

—Mark

In recent years, following a wave of high-profile corporate scandals, there's been a shift around the issue of trust. More and more jobseekers are emphasizing corporate ethics when determining whether to join and stay with a business. In a study by the Work Foundation, 20 percent of employees found employers who were socially responsible. Companies with strong commitment to local, national, or global causes are able to build a sense of community internally and externally.

HR plays a major role in establishing and nurturing an employer brand. And according to Tom Gibbon, president and CEO of J .Walter Thompson, if you are an HR executive you'd better begin to take on a leading role, or you'll run the risk of being marginalized in employer branding efforts.[4]

8. FIND OUT HOW OTHERS ARE DOING IT, BUT RESIST THE URGE TO COPY.

People like to take shortcuts. In business, this is driven by a need for speed, or to improve productivity and process, or the quarter-by-quarter mentality that pervades business today. People are driven to produce instant results and measurable value.

Sharing best practices and learning from the work done well by other businesses *is* good business, but carbon copies work only for paper. One cannot simply lift what one sees working at another business and assume, automatically, that what works in one organization will automatically work at another. It's great to get ideas from a conference presentation and handout or a book, but don't assume, incorrectly, that best practices work everywhere they are applied. And don't think, incorrectly, that you can skip some of the fundamental steps to work an issue and still get a good outcome.

There are no shortcuts to developing an employer brand that works. You have to do all the work we outline in this book to build an employer brand.

"It takes time to build great brands," says Diageo's Yvonne Larkin. "Patience and persistence are key!"

To make the most of how you embrace the power of brand and what you discover about the potential of employer brand, you must

Mark and I were giving a speech about employer brand at a conference for communicators, and a person from a major technology company asked a question about our internal branding campaign at Southwest. My jaw dropped when she said, "I heard you speak about this when you were with Southwest. You know, we bucketed our offerings in the same eight categories as you did. We didn't call them 'Freedoms,' but somehow they just didn't work." I was kind of taken aback, you know—the thought of someone simply lifting an idea born in a specific culture and thinking it would work somewhere else. She later admitted that may not have been the best approach, and they were planning to start over and do it the right way.

—Libby

work through all the steps in this process. Otherwise you will not have the employer brand you aspire to create. The business *must* commit to doing what it takes to build the employer brand the right way. As Ruth Mortimer comments, "There was a time when the brand was a logo on packaging or the message in an advert. But this is no longer enough. Companies are turning to internal branding strategies and asking their employees to 'live the brand.'"[5]

Imagine a fast-food company that thinks everything can be cooked in a minute! This was a business looking for instant solutions to employer brand issues. Few, if any, of their customers believed in the experience the external brand promised. Few, if any, employees believed in the employer brand, and even fewer saw how the two connected. Employees could not see how their jobs contributed to the delivery of the external brand. Customers walking into the restaurant expecting a fine dining experience found a less-than-clean, less-than-appetizing, certainly less-than-brand display of product and service. The company knew it had a problem and understood it needed to focus on the operation of the business: getting employees to do simple things like clean the facility and make the food more attractive. Fundamental brand "blocking and tackling" for a place that encourages people to eat. But the consensus ended. Staff simply could not initiate a collaboration that reached beyond their silos. Each was entrenched in a part of the business, disconnected from others. Each key department (HR, Communications, Marketing, Operations) viewed the challenge from their own limited points of view. And blamed each other for what was going wrong. According to Operations, the problem was all in the quality of candidates HR delivered and the lack of good training that HR should deliver. According to the marketing lead, the problem was the consistency and discipline of the operations and the quality of the managers of each facility. According to HR, the problem was all Operations (uh-oh, two votes, could get you voted off the island), because they could not keep the restaurants clean. And according to Corporate Communications, the problem was all Marketing, because they did not coordinate their brand messaging with what was communicated externally and internally. They needed to start over from the beginning.

—Mark

Add It Up

On the inside, engagement in the employer brand means the employee embraces the experience of working at the business, pursues the opportunities the business offers, and values the rewards.

On the outside, the employer brand is all about the behavior and skills needed to successfully deliver the brand to customers. An engaged employee will internalize the promise the business makes to customers, develop the skills necessary to deliver that promise, and display the behavior necessary to deliver that promise.

According to Jon R. Katzenbach, pride is a primary source of energy and emotional commitment in organizations that outperform their competition. He describes "institution building pride" or "intrinsic pride" fed on character that builds a collective sense of emotional commitment. He points out that a monetary scorecard is less relevant in these organizations than basic performance factors, such as customer satisfaction and quality factors.[6]

At Southwest it took a cross-functional team to come up with the freedoms. Working with a room full of people from Advertising, Public Relations, Marketing, Operations, and HR, we went to work cataloging the products, services, and experiences offered by the company that employees wouldn't get if they worked somewhere else. We defined the employee experience that we branded as the Freedom to pursue good health, create financial security, learn and grow, make a positive difference, travel, work hard and have fun, create and innovate, and stay connected. Our employer brand message was "At Southwest, Freedom begins with me." To make the emotional connection with employees, we then translated our freedoms into outcomes, always linking those outcomes back to the freedoms in all our messages. Working in partnership with our ad agencies, benefits consultants, employment partners, and so on, we created great employee-related products and services and tied them together under the Freedom theme with creative on-brand packaging.

—Libby

Your employer brand team will have its work to do. When you find yourselves experiencing a bit of your own brand fatigue, just consider the importance of this work. And what a difference it can make to the business and the people.

So what silos do you need to bridge? And how can you get started?

The steps to follow are in the next chapter.

Five Essential Steps

1. Find out who in your business may be working on employer brand now. Or has worked on employer brand. Try to see their work. Identify the likely groups and individuals to invite to work on the employer brand.
2. Find the work your marketing group has done to advance your external brand. Consider how that work could connect to your work developing the employer brand.
3. Find the work your HR group has done to advance your employee experience. Consider how that could connect.
4. Find the work your corporate communications group has done to create a line of sight for employees to the way the business operates. Consider how that connects as well.
5. Get ready to get employer brand team together, following the steps outlined in Chapter Five.

PART THREE

GET IT DONE!

ESSENTIAL #5: CREATE

Our mothers taught us that cake mixes, no matter the brand, list the directions on each package for a purpose. Regardless of how many times someone has baked a cake, it never hurts to be reminded to add the butter.

It's no different with employer brand.

You and your interdisciplinary team may be tempted to get right to the point and start crafting that employer brand.

But as the champion of the employer brand, you need to view your role as that of an internal consultant. You can ensure that the result of your work will be more lasting and effective if you carefully follow the proven steps to create an employer brand. Approach the development of the employer brand as a consulting project. Organize your work as a consulting project. You are the consultant. We'll look over your shoulder.

This chapter details steps that have been used successfully with many organizations. Use them yourself. They can even help you put together your agendas and exercises for your team meetings to plan your employer brand.

You and your team will work through four steps. First, you will set your ground rules. Second, you will do some homework. Third, you will set aspirations for your employer brand, so that in the fourth step you can add it all up to articulate your employer brand. The business case you developed in Chapter Four will be very helpful. And if you ever start to wonder if it's as important a cause as you think it is, just imagine the impact of one negative customer experience.

You may, in fact, want to share the following story with your team.

It's our favorite "employer brand nightmare" tale. You may have others.

Picture the scene. A late night. Two worn-out business travelers, Tom and Shane. They check into a popular nationwide hotel in a major city. They believe they have reservations guaranteed for late arrival with a valid major credit card.

But there's no room at the inn, despite the brand promise and the credit-card guarantee. The night clerk quickly reports that the only rooms left are off-limits because their plumbing and air-conditioning are out of order. So much for brand functionality. And he shares that he gave away the last functional rooms three hours ago.

Now, much to the dismay of Tom and Shane, this trusty clerk has not done a thing to find them alternate accommodations. So much for on-brand behavior. Even though their reservations are, according to the brand promise, guaranteed. Worst of all, the clerk is deeply unapologetic. In fact, he goes on to say, "Most of our guests don't arrive at two o'clock in the morning."

This last comment is, no surprise, the crowning blow for our weary travelers. According to a PowerPoint account of the story widely circulated in email inboxes across the world—and shared by author and well-known speaker Tim Sanders in his speeches to tens of thousands—the travelers go on to discuss the inner meaning of the term "guarantee" with the night clerk, even calling on a dictionary for a proper definition.

Part of that definition is "a promise or an assurance, especially one given in writing that attests to the quality or durability of a product or service." But the night clerk just doesn't care; it's as though he bet they wouldn't show up. When our duo suggests the least he should have done was line up other rooms in advance, the clerk bristles and says, "I have nothing to apologize for."

So, with the clock soon approaching three, the clerk slowly starts to dial for beds around town. They finally find rooms in a "dump" several miles away from downtown, which will make a big difference in morning rush-hour traffic. And to add insult to injury, only smoking rooms (for these confirmed nonsmokers) are available.

After they survived the ordeal, Tom and Shane shared their story in the PowerPoint presentation "Yours is a Very Bad Hotel." When they send the presentation to hotel officials, they add that they'll be sending it to the parent company as well as to friends, whom they hope will share it with their friends.

Remember that brand adhesive? That's how we got this story to put in this book. What an example of a brand failure caused by one employee who chose, for whatever reason, not to live the brand promise![1]

THE FOUR STEPS TO BRANDING FROM THE INSIDE

STEP ONE: CLARIFY YOUR GROUND RULES.

Before your first meeting you will want to set the stage for what you will accomplish. For your team, you will reconfirm why you are building an employer brand and what it can contribute to your business and your employees. This can be as simple as an email to the team with prework assignments you send before the meeting. And to get their attention, look around for a customer horror story like the one above—but from your own business. Chances are you will find one.

When the team gets together, as a team-building exercise ask them (as we did in Chapter One) what brands they remember being dependent on as children, what brands they can't live without now, and what their brand habits tell them about brand. We all learn from our brand dependency.

1. Share the need with your team.

One of Libby's favorite Yahoo! executives has a habit, in meetings that get off track, of asking "What problem are we trying to solve?" It sounds so logical, and it's absolutely critical, yet how often do we determine this at the outset? And as it is for any business issue you try to resolve, starting with "Why are we doing this?" is critical to your employer brand team. Without a commonsense reason, focusing on a potential result may be challenging. Share the need with your team by addressing the following five basic questions as part of the initial discussion. You know your perspectives; theirs may be enlightening as well.

What's happening in your business that may make employer brand an issue to address? Are there issues with your customers? Are you concerned with their satisfaction? Are there issues with sales? With your operation? Is everything clicking along in a way that satisfies what you promise to customers? Have you gone through a merger or acquisition, business downturn or growth?

What's happening to your talent? Are you having any challenges finding and keeping the talent you need? Are you at all concerned about your reputation as a place to work? Are you differentiated in the employment market in the right way? How you are doing in the "war for talent"? Do your employees know why the business exists? Its purpose? Do they share a sense of mission and direction? Do they feel they get a return on their emotional investment in the business?

What's happening with your employee engagement? Are there issues with employees? Concerns over recent survey scores about employee engagement? Are you getting signals that employees may be emotionally disconnecting from their work or the business? Do you observe distrust? Skepticism? Or worse, cynicism? Are employees delivering your brand promise to customers? When your employees speak to your customers, do they speak the voice of the brand? Do they communicate confidence in your brand? Do they know your brand promise? Are they committed to delivering the brand? Can they articulate what the business stands for and what it is like to work there?

What's happening with your customer brand? Are you relaunching your brand? Redefining its promise or characteristics? Applying it to new products? Is there a new advertising campaign about to be launched? With new promises to customers?

What's happening in your markets? Are you facing more intense competition? New competitors? Is it more difficult to differentiate your brand and products? Is price pressure making it more difficult to command higher yields? Do your employees think with creativity and innovation as they develop products and services for the business to take to market?

2. Record your ideas.

Here are some ideas for how to use flip charts or a whiteboard to transcribe what you hear in the meeting (see Table 5.1). Record your answers for when, later in this chapter, you'll build your employer brand.

After doing this work for so long, I think there are some patients who don't want to be cured. Take a well-known Fortune 500 company in a highly branded industry. A company people talk about all the time. And wonder about quite a bit. They asked us to lead them through a day of employer brand planning because the business was about to rebrand the brand promise to customers. And they thought it would be a good idea to get the employees on board in advance. Good idea. Well, we should have known we were headed on a one-way trip when the agenda was revised twelve times. And when we got there, it was clear there was no champion and minimal commitment (people kept leaving during the meeting or answering their PDAs). And every page we turned to, every exercise or question we asked, was met with objection. Oh, we can't do this. Oh, we tried that. At the end of the day little had been accomplished. But lunch was very good

—**Mark**

TABLE 5.1. ISSUES AND IMPLICATIONS FOR EMPLOYER BRAND.

Issue	Implication for Employer Brand
Business	
Engagement	
Brand	
Market	
Talent	

3. Clarify your objectives.

It's common sense in business that without a clear picture of the end state you want to reach, based on the need, it is difficult to get there.

This is especially important with employer brand, simply because there are so many directions in which you can go. It can be easy, as we said in the previous chapter, to try to "boil the ocean" and tackle too much.

Talking about the business as a place to work without a grounding in customer reality doesn't complete this work. That's why you need to pinpoint what you want to accomplish—and set priorities, based on your business need. Start with your output from Step One as you consider what your employer brand can do. Here are a few questions to prompt your thinking.

- *Business:* What difference can it make for the business to develop an employer brand?
- *Engagement:* What can the employer brand mean to employees on the inside of the business? How can the employer brand impact the emotional connection employees have with the business? Can it help them understand their role? What is expected? What they can expect in return?
- *Brand:* What do you want employees to understand and believe about the business as a place to buy?
- *Market:* How can the employer brand help employees understand what's happening in the market?
- *Talent:* What do you need prospective, current, and former employees to understand and believe about the business as a place to work?

Table 5.2 presents another idea for how you can chart your work.

4. Specify your goals.
Now consider the specific things you need your employer brand to accomplish. And what the priority must be. What your employer brand must accomplish to make a positive difference to your business and to your employees.

TABLE 5.2. ISSUES, NEEDS, AND EMPLOYER BRAND OBJECTIVES.

Issue	Need	Employer Brand Objective
Business		
Engagement		
Brand		
Market		
Talent		

Consider, for example, what behavior you need from employees to support the external brand promise. What foundation the employer brand can provide for the experience you create for employees. The guidelines your employer brand can provide to the rewards you offer. How you can rely on your employer brand as a basis for the policies and programs HR develops. And how the employer brand can help you plan the content, style and tone of your employee communications.

Using Table 5.3 as a model, record your output to use later.

TABLE 5.3. TOPICS AND STANDARDS FOR EMPLOYER BRAND.

Topic	Standard for Employer Brand
Behavior to support external brand	
Foundation for employee experience	
Guidelines for employee rewards	
Basis for HR policies and programs	
Content for employee communications	

At Yahoo! we went through a thorough process to clarify just what the brand means. So we could answer every question about what the brand means, what customers we serve, what connections we create. When we looked inside, we said, OK, how can we make the employee experience at Yahoo! relevant to the customer experience we create? Simple. By authentically reflecting, for employees, what we deliver to customers. And that's what we did. The parallel in our employer brand is the connection to employees. On the outside it's the connection with customers. We identified, on the inside, the functional and emotional connections we created. The functional connection is all about getting things done; the emotional is all about being fulfilled to making a difference. It's a combination of efficiency and accomplishment. And it's what our employer brand is all about.

—Libby and Mark

STEP TWO: DO SOME HOMEWORK.

Before the next meeting, you will want to ask your team to do some homework—before you start building that employer brand.

In fact, you need to collect a lot of input from a lot of sources. There are many places to look for clues to what the employer brand can and should be.

"We started with research," remembers Hallmark's Dean Rodenbough. "Our corporate strategy and marketing areas gained current insight about the brand and what it stood for as well as our vulnerabilities in the marketplace. Based on those insights we articulated a brand essence—what the brand stands for—in today's terms to become a lens for decisions and choices. That work also led us to a simplified mission statement of "enriching lives."

Your customer brand.

An excellent source for "clues" is the brand your business takes to customers. Your customer brand will offer many clues that can help you define your employer brand. To help you take your customer brand to the inside. Look at your customer brand for clues to use as you build your employer brand.

What is the brand promise your business makes to your customers? Is there an overall promise, from your business, as well as specific promises for specific products or services? And how does this promise come through in your brand?

One way to consider how you are positioned—and how to position your brand in comparison to others—is to look online for the actual words from the top brands.

Consider, for example, how Hewlett-Packard says on its internet site that "everything we do, we do to make technology more practical, usable and valuable to our customers."[2] Harley-Davidson claims "we fulfill dreams."[3] Heinz, the company that make catsup, says its business is all about "doing a common thing uncommonly well."[4] Pepsi Bottling Group says, simply, "we sell soda."[5] Your customer service team may have already done some of this work. If so, ask them to present what they have discove;ed and how they ensure the promise is delivered at the next meeting.

What is the brand personality your business conveys? Is there, in fact, a distinct personality your brand portrays? Are you publicly "fun" in the spirit of Southwest, "cool" in the manner of Gap, or "friendly" in the pattern of Hallmark?

Again, an online search reveals clues. For those who trade online, eBay promises "to provide a global trading platform where practically anyone can trade practically anything."[6] And for those who enjoy a six-pack, Anheuser-Busch promises that, through its products, "we will add to life's enjoyment."[7]

Your marketing team or advertising agency may have already completed this work, too. If so, ask them to present their insights at the next meeting.

What "big idea" can connect your brand with customers? Beyond the specifics of your products and services, what is the "big idea" your brand stands for? Today's employee wants to know, and feel comfortable with, the larger idea a business represents. The employer brand can crystallize this purpose in a few words and images. It can convey the essence of the business and make it relevant and appealing. Like a fine recipe, this identity must contain just the right ingredients that simmer at just the right temperature—with a pinch of values, mission, and purpose.

Amazon, for example, describes itself as "a place where people can find and discover anything they might want to buy online."[8] Dell promises to "make computing accessible to customers around the globe";[9] Motorola says it can help you find "the people, things and information you need in your home, auto, workplace and all spaces in between."[10]

General Mills says it makes "some of the most trusted and respected food brands";[11] Kraft envisions "all the ways we can eat and live better, such as the enjoyment of a dessert, the convenience of a microwave meal, the safety and value of our products and the services and solutions."[12] Coach proclaims that every product embodies the "perfect balance between aesthetics and functionality";[13] Ritz-Carlton says its hotels "are renowned for indulgent luxury."[14]

What would your brand say? Could you speak with the clarity of BP, which says "our business is about finding, producing and marketing the natural energy resources on which the modern world depends"?[15] Or the candor of Williams-Sonoma, admitting "we are here to please our customers—without them nothing else matters"?[16] The essence of the employer brand is what the business values. What the business stands for. How you brand the soul of the business.

Your marketers may have done this work as well. If so, ask them if they will share. As Diageo's Yvonne Larkin observes, "We know that our reputation can be and is used as endorsement of the quality of our products. This is a key commercial lever."

Add it up. Your answers to the three questions in Table 5.4 will help you solidify what you need your employer brand to accomplish. Take your answers and describe how they will ultimately influence your employer brand; review these at your next gathering.

Your identity.
An employer brand must help an employee answer the question, "Why does this business exist?"

How would your employer brand do this?

Once upon a time, business was so stable people just knew what a business was about. Ford was about cars. Maxwell House was about coffee. Today business is more complex. And the employer brand must explain the identity of the business. The simple declaration of "This is who we are, what we do, and why we're here." The ultimate purpose. The essential reason.

So why do you exist? What is your mission? Your purpose? Why do you stay in business? What would happen if you no longer existed? Why do your people come to work? Your corporate

TABLE 5.4. EXTERNAL BRAND INFLUENCES ON EMPLOYER BRAND.

External Brand	Influence on Employer Brand
Brand promise	
Brand personality	
"Big idea" behind the brand	

communications group may have already led this work. Ask them to share what they have.

Your employer brand must, at the same time, reach beyond a statement of identity to clarify the ambition of the business—a clear description of "This is what we can mean to our business, our customers, our people." So when an employee wonders, "Just how far can we take this business?" he or she can secure an answer from the employer brand.

GE's Linda Boff observes, "GE promises to be a brand that is first and foremost about integrity—what people take pride in. Putting our imagination to work. We say the same thing inside and outside. We solve our customers' toughest problems and, we believe, some of the *world's* toughest problems. To be a good and a great company for our employees, customers, investors and for society at large, it has to start inside." Over at FedEx, Eric Jackson comments, "Most great companies recognize that they have a higher calling. For FedEx that higher purpose is that we change what's possible for our customers. The employer brand is all about creating that higher purpose inside the company and bringing it to life, internally and externally. Any great organization must have a higher calling to provide the incentive for their workforce to consistently go above and beyond."

What is your ambition? And how does it compare to others? Are you similar to Pfizer, which states on its web site its ambition to "improve the quality of life of people around the world and help them enjoy longer, healthier and more productive lives"? The site goes on to state, "we dedicate ourselves to humanity's quest for longer, healthier, happier lives through innovation in pharmaceutical, consumer and animal health products."[17] This clarifies to employees the "bigger idea" the business stands for.

Intel wants to "change the way people live and work,"[18] Coca-Cola wants to "benefit and refresh everyone,"[19] and Nokia wants to connect "people with each other."[20] How would you, in one sentence, describe your business—its purpose, identity, and reason for operating? How do you want to be remembered? What about our business would be the most difficult to copy? What is the ultimate result you create, the difference you make, for customers? The community? Employees? What impressions do you want to create?

Take your answers to these questions and select the five that are most important to your business and your employees. Record these as five key elements your employer brand needs to address as it captures the essence of your brand identity.

The Five Key Elements of Your Brand Identity

1. _____
2. _____
3. _____
4. _____
5. _____

Before our marketing team was ready to work on rebranding, HR and Corporate Communications worked together to help the company define our mission and values. This process began with an employee survey, a series of meetings with founders, employees, and executives. We wanted to answer for employees the question "What does Yahoo! want to be when we grow up?" Corporate values seemed too traditional for such an irreverent young company. One of our founders asked us "Why do we have to have a list of values? Why can't we just have a list of 'what sucks'"? And that is exactly how we marketed the values, paired with a "What sucks and aren't you glad you won't find these at Yahoo!" list. The values became the foundation for our new brand. As we launched our rebranding, our marketers conducted an inside-out and outside-in review of the company, with HR as part of the internal review team. Internal workshops were held to explore brand characteristics, competencies, values, territories. A brand audit was conducted with internal stakeholders through one-on-one interviews. Extensive marketing research tools were used to learn what our customers thought about the company and our brand. This led to the identification of our core competencies and core experiences for customers. We defined our target customer as an intensive internet user (with that special Y! gene) seeking efficiency, engagement, and expansion, and we defined Yahoo! as the "Life Engine" with everything a customer needs or wants to do.

—**Libby**

Your values.

How do you want your employer brand to clarify the values of your business?

Years ago, most businesses seemed to stand for much of the same things. And for the most part any business could be trusted. Employees didn't have to pay as close attention to what a business believed because they could pretty much believe in everyone.

Today employees look closer. Many want to look beneath the surface to see what the business *believes in* and will ultimately *stand for.* And how those *values* line up with their own. They want to know *why* this business makes a difference. Who it touches. What contributions it makes. What conviction it brings. What boundaries it will operate within. When it will not budge.

At Washington Mutual, according to Libby Hutchison, the values are simple and clear. "Our values are the core of our employer brand: to be fair, caring, human, dynamic and driven."

So what do you stand for? What are you willing to fight for? What actions do your leaders take beyond words—the say/do? What would your business "go to the mat" to support or prevent? What would they simply not permit? How do your values connect with your brand promise?

On the outside, Hallmark articulates a brand that stands for enriching lives. "We are here to enhance relationships, to enrich lives." On the inside, it articulates an employer brand that stands for enriching careers and experiences. "Hallmark is here to help people define and express the very best in themselves." And the company brings this to life through the small things it does for employees. "For much of Hallmark's history we translated the consumer brand attributes on the outside to the inside with distinct practices that survive today. We send, for example, gifts from the company when employees get married or have a baby, and acknowledge deaths with flowers or charitable contributions."[21]

People want to work for companies they feel they can believe in, that stand for issues and commitments that parallel their own values. Many have little tolerance for companies they believe don't hold strong values or don't put their words into actions. Employees look for actions *beyond* words.

At FedEx, the Purple Promise is strengthened by the company's statement of values. As it says in its materials for employees,

"The Purple Promise is simple and profound: I will make every FedEx experience outstanding. The Purple Promise is part of a broader platform of ideas we must all embrace—a shared way of thinking, acting, and believing. This platform of our corporate mission statement, our strategy, our shared values dictates how we will respond to our customers and to each other, no matter where in the world and what we do in our work. These are the things that make us FedEx." The company clearly reinforces its fundamental values of people, service, innovation, integrity, responsibility, and loyalty. "The Purple Promise is more than what we say—it's what we do. It unites us."

So what do the words about your business say about your employer brand? And what should your employer brand say? Are you like Porsche, for example, which says on its internet site, "we take the values of the past and those of the present into the new millennium"? The site further states a commitment to "trust in our staff, maximum independence, highest possible level of competence and transfer of responsibility, originality in the implementation of projects, greatest possible integration of staff into company processes" and the "emotional unity of the staff and their work, being part of the Porsche team."[22]

According to Diageo's Yvonne Larkin,

> When the organization was formed, we defined four key values: freedom to succeed, being the best, being proud of what we do, and being passionate about consumers. After considerable thought and deliberation, we recently added a fifth value. Recognizing that we need to release the potential of every employee and indeed every other stakeholder relationship as a company, then understanding and valuing their needs and contributions, is critical; hence we concluded that our fifth value should be valuing each other.

Johnson & Johnson, on the other hand, says it "strives to attract people with strong, positive values, and we develop, reinforce and reward those values";[23] Boeing says it is "committed to a set of core values that not only define who we are but serve as guideposts to help us become the company we'd like to be."[24] BP sets its boundaries by saying "in all our activities we seek to display some unchanging, fundamental qualities";[25] Shell says "our core values of honesty, integrity, and respect for people define who we are and how we work"[26] and General Mills says its values are "the source of our strength and the heart of who we are."[27]

What are your values? How would you, in one sentence, describe what your business stands for? Believes in? Would fight for?

Any business should ask how willing employees would be to fight for the business. If threatened, what would it take for them to carry a rallying sign? Employees who are not willing to take action to support the business when times are tough may be less likely to deliver the brand when times are less threatening.

Whole Foods Market, which says its core values "are the soul of our company," positions its values as a fundamental part of its brand promise to customers and employees. This includes "selling the highest quality natural and organic products available" and a "passion for food." The business says "by maintaining these core values, regardless of how large a company Whole Foods becomes, we can preserve what has always been special about our company." It continues "these are not values that change from time to time, situation to situation, or person to person, but rather they are the underpinning of our company culture."[28]

IKEA says its values "create a sense of belonging" for employees;[29] Heineken says its core values—"quality, respect and enjoyment"—shape its employment policies.[30] And Starbucks attributes its growth to its "uncompromising principles."[31] What are your values? What about your business?

Take your answers to these questions and select the five most important to your business and your employees. Record these as five key elements your employer brand needs to address as it captures the essence of your brand values.

The Five Key Elements of Your Brand Values

1. _____
2. _____
3. _____
4. _____
5. _____

Customer experience.

At the core of any employer brand is how you clarify the behavior you need from employees to deliver the brand you promise to your customers. Every brand experience carries a defining moment that will determine how a customer reacts. What a customer will say. What a customer will do. Your customer service people may have done some of this work.

As you build your employer brand, identify the touch points between your customers and your brand, to consider how to influence every possible interaction.

Your assignment is to create an actual map of the experience your customers have with your business and your brand, to identify each opportunity for a connection with one or more of your employees.

On a white board or flip chart, draw a circle in the middle and write the word *customer* inside. Draw a line from the circle to represent each possible touch point or influence a customer may experience. Be as specific, detailed, and thorough as possible. Think of every possible influence on the customer from every possible source. Here are a few suggestions.

Messages.

What advertisements and promotions do your customers see? What promises do they make? What experience do they promise? What type of service? What behaviors do they anticipate? What expectations do they raise?

What other messages about the business do your customers see? What news reports? Editorials? Reviews?

What do your customers likely hear from other customers?

Touch points.

What are the touch points between the business and customers? List all the formal and informal encounters. Walk through, step by step, what a customer experiences with your business and your brand.

What do customers observe about the business and the brand from a distance? What impressions could they form? What could they learn by watching others use the products or services? What could they learn visiting your location or facilities?

What is the buying process customers experience, from the customer's first encounter with the brand, product, or service, through the last? What happens, step by step, in a location where the product or service is offered?

What does the brand promise at (and for) each interaction with a customer? What expectation is built into the advertisements or communication?

Employee interaction. For each touch point you identify, indicate how the employee can make a difference to the customer. Specify the behavior the employee can bring to the interaction. As you consider the potential of employee interaction, answer these questions.

How can employees influence what customers observe about your brand from a distance? What behavior? Attitudes?

How can employees influence the customer buying process? Positively? Negatively?

How can employees undermine the external brand? Skills? Attitudes? Behavior?

What impression can employees create about what your brand stands for? How can they reinforce or accidentally undermine the brand messages?

What can be the difference between an employee "doing a job" and an employee "delivering the brand"? What does it take to make the difference?

What is on-brand behavior? Behind the scenes as well as with customers?

From your answers to these questions, select the five most important characteristics of on-brand behavior.

The Five Key Characteristics of On-Brand Behavior

1. _____
2. _____
3. _____
4. _____
5. _____

Our eight freedoms at Southwest are the best practice in how to frame and articulate the employee experience to find, keep, and engage employees, while successfully and consistently delivering the customer experience. But for many years before we articulated the freedoms, we planted the seeds for the freedoms. Like when we introduced BenefitsPlus. Focusing on the business and the customer gave us a freedom, if you will, to step out of the world of HR to explain an HR program in a manner immediately relevant to the employee, as immediately relevant as any product they may choose on a grocer's shelf. Our retail approach to the communication made information immediately relevant to the employee in the context of a consumer. We learned from that experience what business can achieve when we place the details of an HR communication in the context of the business, the external brand, and the customer. The seeds of employer brand showed us how to communicate what HR delivers in a natural way.

—Libby

In addition to specifying what on-brand behavior is, your employer brand should clarify how your employer and customer promises connect.

Customer expectations from the marketplace define how employees must deliver the products and services the business offers. The customer brand may articulate "what the business is all about"; the employer brand translates this brand message for the internal audience.

So how clearly does your employer brand articulate the employee role in your customer brand? Kellogg's says "we want people to know us for our commitment to their well being as well as for high quality, wholesome foods."[32] Gap says "we create emotional connections with customers" with brands designed "to make it easy for people to express their personal style."[33] IKEA says "our business idea is based on a partnership with the customer."[34]

The employer brand can help articulate (and reinforce) the customer brand to employees, providing an overall context for why the business does what it does. Within this context, the employer brand can help the business specifically describe the behaviors and

To introduce our new brand internally at Yahoo! we gave every employee a chance to advertise what makes Yahoo! their life engine by giving out license-plate frames that are customized: "My [fill in the blank]—Engine." We also held an essay contest for employees and customers to describe how Yahoo! is their life engine, with a Harley-Davidson as the prize. The Life Engine brand worked just as well internally as externally, so we began our efforts to make it come to life for Yahoos—our employees. This would involve finding the unique attributes that attract the right people, creating the right experience for Yahoos, so that we bring out the best in our people and they can bring their best to their work. We began with an online survey to determine which Yahoo! benefits, amenities, affinities, and experiences our employees valued most. We used the results to define our employer brand and to position it internally by applying brand to every dimension of the employee experience. We want the employee experience to fuel the life engine and career of Yahoos. We can do this by making it easy for Yahoos to get things done and engage by offering tools for life, guides to make it easier to navigate through the company, and special amenities that create the "Wow" experience for Yahoos. We repackaged our benefits under the label My Life: My Benefits. This program will describe our offerings by life stages to make them real. Total compensation became My Life: My Rewards. Career development was packaged as My Life: My Career. We gathered all of our amenities and perks under one site, My Life: My Perks. And we anticipate adding to the My Life: My _____ series. Our typical HR policies became MyGuides. We added MyGuide: Working at Yahoo!, MyGuide: Paying at Yahoo!, MyGuide: Recognition and Rewards at Yahoo!, MyGuide: Interviewing at Yahoo!, MyGuide: Retention at Yahoo!—and we have only just begun.

—Libby

expectations that go with the customer brand. Ultimately, a clear description of the employer brand can help the business create loyalty and trust with employees, which can create competitive advantage.

That may be why a company like the Container Store says that "when customers walk into any of our stores they immediately sense the 'air of excitement' that exemplifies the entire company. This excitement is fostered by the spirit of our store employees."[35]

And why Whole Foods says its customers "are our most important stakeholders" and "the lifeblood of our business."[36]

External messages reinforce internal priorities. Nordstrom, for example, simply says "we remain committed to the simple idea our company was founded on, earning the trust of our customers, one at a time."[37] And American Express says it is "committed to making a positive contributions to our customers' lives."[38]

Now, with your answers in mind, complete a flip chart modeled on Table 5.5. For each touch point you list on the left, indicate the skills, behaviors, and attitudes your employees need to bring. This will help guide you to what needs to be included as you develop your employer brand.

Basic sensing.

Before you move on, you need to do some basic homework about what your employees are thinking about the brand. You need an effective measure of your starting point so you can plot the "arc of change" to create brand engagement, as we describe in Chapter Six.

Now, to get this insight from employees, you will likely not need to do a full-blown survey. You may be able to get what you need from employees willing to answer a few questions on line, on paper, or in focus groups.

TABLE 5.5. TOUCH POINTS AND EMPLOYEE SKILLS, BEHAVIORS, AND ATTITUDES.

Touch Points	What skills does an employee need to bring?	What behaviors does an employee need to bring?	What attitudes does an employee need to bring?

Some type of research is essential to a successful brand effort. It's impossible for even the best of internal teams to imagine every reaction real people might have. Just impossible. We learned that when working with a consumer products company. In previous years we had visited a number of locations to check out the health of messages with employees. This time around, with the focus on employer brand talent, they were hesitant at first; the internal team really resisted going to the field to do any research. "Oh, our people are over surveyed," and "Oh, if we ask them questions they will expect something." Finally they agreed—and the results were quite surprising. We conducted a series of highly structured focus groups, following a script of open-ended questions. Employees could see right through any efforts of the company to "spin" the work experience. And they could immediately spot the holes in the experience (in this case, the offerings for career development). We never would have learned that if we hadn't asked. And if we hadn't asked, and had not addressed the career development issue, we might have flopped when we took the employer brand messages public.

—**Mark**

Here's what you need to find out.

How aware are employees about the brand? In general, how well do they understand what the brand is all about and believe in what they think the brand stands for? What do they know about the brand promise to customers? What would they say that your *customers* would say you stand for? What would your customers miss the most if you were not in business? And what do they believe customers trust most and least about your brand?

Do they experience the cocktail-party effect? How important is it to your employees to tell other people they work for your business? To what degree does your brand and reputation influence recruitment and retention—that experience when, at a social gathering of some type, employees like to tell others where they work? How important is it to them to tell other people where they work? How did this influence the decision to join? To stay? How would they react if the business did something publicly embarrassing? How could a negative reputation influence their decision to stay? Or leave?

What is the residual customer effect? Before they joined the business, to what degree did your employees' past experiences as customers influence their perception of what life might be like as an employee? What did they experience as customers that led them to expect certain things as an employee? What did their experience as customers tell them about what the business believes in? How did their customer experience motivate them to join as employees? Or not?

What is the residual employee effect? Before they joined, to what degree did your employees' impressions of current or past employees shade their expectations of the business as a place to work? What did they hear from past or current employees that led to certain expectations? What did they hear from other employees about what the business stands for, believes in? What did they hear from other employees about how the business treats employees? What did you hear about the business as a place to work?

How do the dots connect? How do employees see the connection between what happens inside the business and outside the business? How can they impact a customer's experience? How can they impact a coworker's experience? How do their jobs affect the ability of coworkers to do their jobs? How does what they do make it easier to deliver the brand?

Before you move on, fill in Table 5.6, listing in the left column those key elements you recorded earlier from your discussions. Then record what you have learned in terms of what you need employees to *understand* about the brand, *believe* about the brand, and *do* to make the brand come alive.

Check the files.

What are you already saying about your employer brand—even if you don't realize it?

What articles in your employee publications talk about your business as a place to work? And what messages, in presentations from your leadership?

What observations from customers, in letters they write, give you clues to how they react to your brand and your employees? What research is available from your marketing group? What collateral material is prepared for your sales force?

Find what you can and bring samples to your next meeting. Spread them out on the conference room table. Do they have a common look and feel? What do they say about the company? Follow Table 5.7 to record the responses.

TABLE 5.6. WHAT EMPLOYEES NEED TO UNDERSTAND, BELIEVE, AND DO.

Key Elements of the Employer Brand	What do employees need to understand about the brand?	What do employees need to believe about the brand?	What do employees need to do about the brand?

TABLE 5.7. ANALYZING THE BUSINESS'S COMMUNICATIONS.

Topic	What have you communicated?	Your external brand promise	Employee skills and behavior to deliver the external brand	Your employer brand promise	The experience you create for employees as a place to work	"What's in it for me?" to work at the business

STEP THREE: STATE YOUR ASPIRATIONS.

Next, as you consider what the employer brand should include, take a close look at what you want to say about the business as a place to work.

Every business is a work in progress.

And every business has places it hopes to travel to.

Your employer brand should specify what you aspire to for your business and, specifically, for the experience you create for employees.

Address "What's in it for me?" so the employee can answer the question "Why would I want to work here?"

In the end, few employees will support what a business needs to achieve without a satisfactory answer to the question, "What's in it for me?" if they were to make that contribution.

There's absolutely no more important question for the employer brand to answer than the prospective employee's "What's in it for me?" if they work there. It's kind of the foundation for everything the employer brand can and should accomplish.

A global technology company realized, after talking with employees, that the fundamental question that needed to be answered was, yes, "What's in it for me?" (WIIFM). The company developed a clear, concise employer brand promise, but refrained from "announcing" the message. Instead, it launched a multimedia communication effort to "plant the evidence" in the population of everything available to employees to enrich the work experience—all successfully directed to answer the WIIFM question. The "anchor" was a quarterly web site, with a link sent to all employees via email, each quarter highlighting a specific dimension of what the company offers to enhance employees' relationship to the company, build employees' careers, and help employees manage the various parts of their lives—all designed to help employees answer the WIIFM question. And because the company carefully avoided hype and followed the principles of its brand, employees reacted favorably to the "evidence" and the conclusion it produced.

—Mark

Unless employees believe in what a business offers, it will be challenging for them to see the benefit of a commitment. Does your employer brand clarify the role an employee can play, the contribution an employee can make? Ultimately, just as a brand articulates a value proposition to a customer, the employer brand must clearly express the potential of connection with the business. And how the company values its employees.

That's why so many top brands create clear messages about the importance of their people to what they want to accomplish.

On its internet site, Pizza Hut says "the only thing that tops our pizza is our people,"[39] eBay says "our people are the reason we've come this far,"[40] and Gillette says its commitment is to help "bring out the finest in every individual."[41] American Apparel "sees all its employees as long-term investments";[42] Heineken says "people are as essential to Heineken as hops and yeast."[43]

Tiffany says its people "are the talent behind our reputation."[44] Johnson & Johnson claims "a company's character is not derived from its buildings, its products or its business strategy. It is a reflection of its people."[45] To Williams-Sonoma, the potential "of our company has no limit and is driven by our associates and their imagination."[46] Porsche candidly says "it is in manual work, which is still, as ever, greatly valued, that the true ability and the real emotions can be found."[47]

Businesses also focus on the specifics of benefit programs for employees. Pfizer states their benefits offer "the variety and flexibility to help address their [employee] needs at different stages

We learned at Southwest that a robust workforce plan is a practical way to start. We developed a robust workforce plan that would report exactly how many candidates we had to interview to produce the number of qualified employees we needed at any given period of time. The only way the business could effectively plan how to use our resources to hire and keep employees was if we had a good idea of how many people we actually needed. So we started with facts. And we built the workforce plan based on the facts.

—Libby

in life."[48] Merck ties rewards to an employee's role with this statement: "While you're busy taking care of the world, Merck makes sure someone's taking care of you."[49] Restoration Hardware says its benefit package is "designed to help you live healthy and work well."[50]

"We were a pioneer in American business when we introduced profit sharing in the 1950s," says Hallmark's Dean Rodenbough, "making us one of the first companies to make employees part owners. We have always been family oriented—through our benefits, leaves, flex time, part time, telecommuting—and socially responsible, with a significant volunteer program and a matching gift program to charities when employees volunteer."

What would your business say?

How would you describe, in one sentence, the "What's in it for me?" for employees to work at your business? _____

_____

Articulate the experience an employee can expect.

Someone looking at a business as a place to work will likely look beyond the broad issues to get a realistic idea of what happens day to day in the workplace. Inquiring minds want to know how the programs and policies and resources the business develops actually influence an employee's daily experience.

So it's no surprise that top-branded businesses talk about what it's like to work for them. When Pfizer says, on its internet site, "your talent can touch the lives of people everywhere," it taps into what employees may aspire to contribute.[51] Merck states that employees "want an environment that expands their thinking, and values their ideas, perspective and individuality"[52] and IKEA says "we employ people who really care about customers and colleagues—people who are prepared to work hard and want to do their very best."[53] Such descriptions paint a picture for prospective employees of what life may be like.

Apple steps beyond general description to state, on its site, "we look for the finest minds in the industry. People who take pride in their work and inspire those around them to be the best." The site goes on to define a work environment "where you're encouraged to defy routine, to explore the far reaches of the possible, to travel uncharted paths."[54]

American Apparel, based in Los Angeles, details a strong commitment to the quality of work life, stating on its site that "we believe that the nature of the work environment has a direct impact on the caliber of work." The site goes on to detail the environment it offers as including "proper lighting above sewing machines" and "free English classes to our workers" and "five certified massage therapists."[55] It even describes how it introduced a bicycle-lending program during a transit strike.

For people who look for a sense of belonging, eBay may strike a chord when it says "we enjoy our work and we'll be the first to admit it" and that "we've created a place where people can come together, exchange ideas, share experiences." The company says "our people are the reason we've come this far. And the reason we'll succeed tomorrow. So as we grow (and we are) we'll try our darnedest to retain the fun, community feeling that makes eBay so unique."[56]

Employees at Amazon, according to its site, can expect to "work with and learn from an unusually high proportion of smart, focused people who are passionate about their work" who work "in a casual but accountable environment" and "have fun."[57] Starbucks says it provides "a great work environment" where people "treat each other with respect and dignity."[58] Williams-Sonoma says it is "committed to an environment that attracts, motivates and recognizes high performance"[59] and Whole Foods says "we strive to create a work environment where motivated team members can flourish and succeed to their highest potential."[60]

Painting a picture of opportunities, in addition to the work experience, is an important part of the employer brand message. SAP says on its site "we hire the most talented and creative employees";[61] Gap says "we offer exciting opportunities to learn, stretch and grow."[62] Tiffany is proud of its "extraordinary training and support" opportunities.[63] Gillette says "individuals in every job function find the challenges, training and resources that make for a rewarding career."[64] Nordstrom describes its commitment "to encourage and support the success of each employee."[65] Boeing says "we'll give you the resources and vision to go farther, faster." It challenges employees to "join us and take your dreams as far as you've imagined or change your mind in midstream if you like."[66]

Diageo says it offers "a stimulating work culture" where "people can grow, learn and have fun."[67] Intel says it creates "an inspired workplace where inspiring ideas are rewarded."[68] And when Kellogg's says "you can't beat being part of a company that's like a family" you can immediately sense a warmth.[69]

So, with all of these ideas from top-branded business, what could describe yours?

How would you, in one sentence, describe what your employees experience?

Clarify who the business is looking for.

An effective employer brand not only positions the business but should also clarify what an employee must bring. Nike, for example, is very clear: "We aren't looking for workers. We're looking for people who can contribute, grow, think, dream and create. We seek out achievers, leaders, visionaries. We love winners."[70] JetBlue is looking for "creative, dynamic people to work with us to help develop the airline that brings humanity back to air travel."[71]

Anheuser-Busch says "success is determined by your own vision, commitment and drive to achieve your potential."[72] Amazon says it wants "more smart, big picture thinkers to help us innovate, to take us into new markets and new product and service categories."[73] Starbucks says its "ability to accomplish what we set out to do is based primarily on the people we hire" and that it wants people "who are adaptable, self-motivated and passionate."[74]

The Container Store says "hiring people who are self-motivated and team-oriented with a passion for customer service is key."[75] Coach specifically remarks "we seek out individuals who are not only technically skilled and knowledgeable but who enjoy challenges, who seek to develop themselves."[76]

What do you want your employer brand to say about the people you are looking for?

How would you, in one sentence, describe who you are looking for to join your business? _____

Show how the business appreciates its heritage.

Some say great businesses are those that make smart decisions for the short term because they keep the long term in mind. And they realize that long-term success results from short-term decisions—made for the long term. How would your business look at your legacy?

Your employer brand may in fact be one of the few places where you can freely talk about the roots of the business.

That may be why Pfizer states on the internet that "throughout our history, a legacy of caring for others has been at the heart of everything we do."[77] Kellogg's conveys its appreciation for its "strong past and a bright future" as it reinforces the personal mission of its founder, W. K. Kellogg, "to help people help themselves."[78] Heinz refers to a favorite saying of its founder, Henry J. Heinz: "heart power is more important than horse power."[79] Pizza Hut tells the story of "two brothers, mom and $600" that "turned into the recipe for the world's largest pizza company."[80] And Boeing describes how "over the last century" the company "has grown from building planes in an old red boathouse to become the largest aerospace company in the world"—a company "with a history as renowned as the history of aviation itself."[81] Diageo says "we are today's caretakers of these brands which will continue to be cared for by our people for decades to come. We are as passionate about their future as we are about their legacy."[82]

Hallmark's Dean Rodenbough says,

> To begin to prepare for our centennial in 2010 and remind us of our brand heritage, we have started a program called "Stories of Hallmark." It is a speaker series in which we invite people to share their recollections about the evolution of the company and talk about critical decisions that helped shape the brand legacy and enduring history we enjoy today. The first speaker was our chairman, who is the son of our founder. Others have included the first woman to lead our creative department as well as the individual who helped establish the corporate and family foundations. We are currently convening two presentations a year and videotaping them so that they can be available on DVD for use in future employee sessions.

What about *your* business? What about your legacy should be included in your employer brand?

How would you, in one sentence, describe the legacy of your business?

For two companies merging, employer brand issues were at the core of the issues of the partnership. And this was as close to a merger of equals as you might find. Even so, there were quite a few people at one of the companies expressing hesitation about the change. We realized we would never get past the hurt if we didn't acknowledge the hurt and move on. So we put together a traveling "museum" of artifacts, products, clippings, and stuff from the heritage of the business, and we took the "museum" on a final road tour to all the company locations. It was quite moving and it did help people adjust.

—Mark

Clarify the commitment to diversity.

Back when we first looked for jobs, few companies talked about their commitments to social issues. Or to diversity of thought, opinion, and culture. Today, however, such issues are at the forefront of what employees are thinking about and what an employer brand must convey. And it's no surprise that our internet surfing reveals many commitments to diversity.

So how clearly does your employer brand articulate a point of view on diversity? Pfizer, for example, states, "the diversity of our workforce provides the competitive edge—our goal at Pfizer is to create a culture where all people are valued and where their ideas are encouraged and respected."[83] Nike says, "we thrive in a culture that embraces diversity and rewards imagination."[84] Merck links diversity to its business mission. "We've come to understand that it takes a rich mix of talents, viewpoints and experiences to deliver the kind of leading-edge therapeutic solutions Merck is known for. The best solutions come from people with a variety of backgrounds coming together and building upon each others' knowledge, skills and abilities."[85]

HSBC declares "diversity is central to our brand," and it connects this issue to its values, clarifying, "we believe the world is a rich and diverse place full of interesting cultures and people who should be treated with respect and from whom there is a great deal to learn."[86] Kellogg's says "we're dedicated to the things that set us apart and make us better . . . it's all about being yourself, being accepted and being successful."[87] Gap says "everyone's ideas are welcomed and treated with respect."[88]

Heinz defines diversity as "recognizing and understanding the difference in culture, beliefs and values" each person brings to the workplace.[89] JetBlue says its commitment to diversity enables them "to better anticipate, understand and meet the needs" of customers.[90] Anheuser-Busch says "appreciation for differences is at the core of who we are." This includes a commitment to the development of minority- and women-owned companies by purchasing good and services from those companies.[91]

Commitment is a common word when branded businesses talk diversity. Dell says its commitment is "to make technology more affordable and accessible to people and institutions around the world so that they can take advantage of the tremendous economic and social benefits of more pervasive technology."[92] Shell says *its* commitment to inclusiveness "means a workplace where differences are valued; where everyone has the opportunity to develop skills and talents consistent with our values and business objectives."[93] And the Container Store says *its* commitment to diversity is based on "focusing on talent rather than titles."[94]

Some directly apply the issue to the business. UPS says it considers "diversity a mindset of inclusiveness, respect and cooperation."[95] General Mills believes that diverse teams "create more and better solutions."[96] Johnson & Johnson believes "diversity fosters the exchange of ideas within the workplace,"[97] and GE recognizes "the power of the mix, the strength that results from inclusiveness."[98]

What about your business? What commitment to diversity should be included in your employer brand?

How would you, in one sentence, describe the commitment of your business to diversity? _____

_____

Clarify how the business views its social responsibilities.
How a business views its role in a larger world has become more important to people looking for jobs. What should your employer brand say about your business? What larger issue do you want to attach to your reputation.

Social contribution is central to the employer brand at Washington Mutual. "One of the things that 'seals the deal' is we give people four hours a month to do volunteer work. It is a key investment in the community," says Libby Hutchison.

"At UPS," says Tom Pizutti, "each year since 1968 the company has sent a group of managers away from their homes, families and jobs. For one month they spend time helping others in the Lower East Side of New York City, the rural hills of Tennessee, the border towns of Texas, and our newest location in San Francisco. They feed the homeless, visit the sick and elderly, build homes for the poor and work with prisoners. The goal of the program is to make the managers better understand people and what impacts UPS can have on a community." As well, at UPS, thousands of employees participate each year in a week of synchronized volunteer service around the world as part of the Global Volunteer Week.

Procter & Gamble also takes social responsibility very seriously. "We try to create a meaningful impact to help people live, learn and thrive," according to Diana Shaheen. "We focus on where and how P&G can uniquely make a difference. For example, our global Children's Safe Drinking Water program transforms contaminated water into safe drinking water. Crest Healthy Smiles promotes dental skills training around the world. We are also committed to funding and involving employees in new schools, like in China through Project Hope."

Live, Learn and Thrive is P&G's "corporate cause." It focuses on the development of children in need, globally, up to age thirteen. P&G resources help children *live* by helping to ensure a healthy start; provide places, tools, and programs to enhance the ability to learn; and offer access to programs on self-esteem to help them thrive. "We're proud of the impact we're making with P&G's corporate cause. Our programs have reduced cavities by 60 percent in Poland and Russia, built and remodeled more than four hundred schools from Mexico to China to Egypt to Pakistan to other countries, and taught personal health habits to 80 million children in China," says Sheehan.

Again, a canvass of internet sites reveals that top-branded companies like to talk about this issue.

Merck, for example, says it cannot "succeed as a business" unless it lives up to its commitment to global communities.[99] SAP says it "recognizes our responsibility to contribute to the communities in which we live and work," and that "the private sector plays a vital role in generating strong economies."[100]

Kellogg's expresses an understanding of what it means for a business to be socially responsible. "We believe that businesses can play an important role in helping many of the challenges and social problems facing people and communities today."[101]

Toyota "believes in helping people improve the quality of life in their communities."[102] Heinz says its social covenant includes "improving nutrition, the environment, health, food safety and education."[103] CitiBank commits "to making the communities in which it operates better."[104] American Express highlights its "long history of philanthropy around the world";[105] Gillette expresses its commitment to "improve the communities" where it operates.[106]

American Apparel goes a step further, saying its goal "is to make garments that people love to wear without having to rely on cheap labor" and "to establish new ways of doing business that are efficient and profitable without exploiting workers."[107]

For some businesses, social responsibility directly connects to its products. Heineken believes its responsibility extends to "being a part of society" in all the places where it sells its product.[108] Anheuser-Busch believes its social responsibility extends to "promoting the responsible use of our products by adults," believing that "doing good by the public and doing well as a company go hand-in-hand."[109]

Whole Foods believes "companies, like individuals, must assume their share of responsibility as tenants of Planet Earth." Specifically, they contribute to food banks and neighborhood events, compensate team members for community service work, and contribute "at least five percent of total net profits to not-for-profit organizations." They describe an obligation to educate their stakeholders "about natural and organic foods, health, nutrition and the environment."[110]

Half Price Books believes "everyone should have the opportunity to learn to read" and is dedicated to literacy efforts.[111] In explaining its focus on global communities, Coca-Cola says "it's a special thing to have billions of friends around the world and we never forget it."[112] We remember when all Coca-Cola wanted to do was to teach the world to sing. In perfect harmony.

What about your business? What is social responsibility to you and your employer brand?

How would you, in one sentence, describe the commitment of your business to social responsibilities? _____

_____

Articulate the employee's opportunity for work-life balance. There's more to life than work. And a key part of any employer brand is the commitment to support work/life issues. How would your employer brand fare?

Hewlett-Packard, for example, commits to support employees as they "navigate through their work and personal life challenges."[113] Amazon says it recognizes its people "have a life outside of work and need a break every once in a while" as it commits to "match the pace of your life."[114]

General Mills is committed "to an environment that supports the varying needs of our employees inside and outside of work."[115] Boeing states "we know there is a world outside of work and we endeavor to provide you with programs that help you make the most of it. No matter how your life changes, from getting married to having children to caring for an aging parent, Boeing offers resources that protect you and your family."[116]

One of the challenges of telling the brand story within a business is finding credible channels people will access and respond to. At one global organization, we created a quarterly intranet message titled simply "Look what's in it for you" to help employees, yes, answer the question "What's in it for me?" to work here. What makes the approach work is the use of actual employee stories of real things that happen in real places in the business (to real people). The release on career development opportunities featured, yes, testimonials from employees about the opportunities they experienced. And the release on social responsibility featured, again, testimonials from employees about the ways they give to special causes—and are supported by the business. Somehow hearing from real people makes it all feel, well, real.

—Mark

What do you believe your employer brand should say?

How would you, in one sentence, describe your business's commitment to work-life issues? _____

_____

Step Four: Define your employer brand.

Now it's time to take all the input and put together your employer brand.

You want to end up with one sentence that articulates what it means to work at your business—and how that supports your brand delivery to customers.

That sentence will frame what you offer and how you communicate to prospective, current, and former employees.

A hotel organization, for example, stated its employer brand was "we care for you so you will care for our guests." In that one statement the business clarified its promise to employees ("we care for you") and how that connects to customers ("so you will care for our guests"), which would later frame every aspect of HR policies and programs as well as employee communication. Southwest says, "At Southwest, freedom begins with me."

To get to your one sentence, however, you need to go back and pick up the key words from all of the steps and exercises you have completed in this chapter.

Key words.

Return to the various ideas you jotted down throughout this chapter and select five to ten key words to incorporate in your employer brand, entering them in Table 5.8.

Key phrases.

Next, turn those key words into five key phrases to summarize what you want the employer brand to say, entering them in Table 5.9.

Key commitments.

Next, turn these phrases into five key commitments for your employer brand, entering them in Table 5.10. These will in turn shape how you implement the brand—a process we discuss in detail in the next three chapters.

Table 5.8. Key Words for Your Employer Brand.

1.	6.
2.	7.
3.	8.
4.	9.
5.	10.

Table 5.9. Key Phrases for Your Employer Brand.

1.

2.

3.

4.

5.

Table 5.10. Key Commitments for Your Employer Brand.

Key Commitments	Employer Brand
Brand promise	
Brand personality	
"Big idea" behind the brand	
Brand values	
Emotional connection	

Your employer brand.

Finally, in one sentence, declare your employer brand. To help you write that sentence, begin by "filling in the blanks" in the following sentence.

At _____ *we promise to deliver to employees*

_____, _____, *and*

_____, *expecting in return that our employees*

will deliver _____, _____,

and _____ *to our customers.*

Next, take this sentence and modify it into your own simple, clear employer brand. Before you finish, check your employer brand against your external brand—just to be sure it fits.

And now celebrate! You have an employer brand!

In the chapters that follow you will "operationalize" the employer brand to address each stage of an employee's relationship with the business as well as plan how to use the employer brand as a foundation for your employee communication.

I spoke on a panel on employer branding last year. The speaker before my panel was the HR leader from a well-known consumer products company. They had created an employee experience that was second to none. Their employer brand clearly articulated that they were a different kind of company who intended to be an employer of choice. Employee offerings included extended parental leaves (for moms, dads, and adoptive parents) and a myriad of childcare programs, including learning centers, day camps for kids, overnight care, and sick care. Work/life balance, commuter programs, scholarships, learning and career opportunities, and diversity councils. Only one problem—the employer brand was disconnected from the consumer brand.

—Libby

Five Essential Steps

1. Set your ground rules. What your employer brand result must be.

   Find the need: Why you are doing this work in the first place.

   Clarify objectives: What you must accomplish.

   Specify your standards: What your employer brand must be—and must do—to make a positive difference.

2. Collect the input. What the employer brand is based on.

   Your external brand: What you promise customers.

   Your identity: Why you must exist.

   Your values: What you stand for.

   Customer experience: How employees, the brand, and customers interact.

3. State your aspirations. What you want the employer brand to be. Few will support what a business needs to achieve without a satisfactory answer to "What's in it for me?" to make the contribution.

   The experience an employee can expect: Get into the reality of what happens day to day in the workplace, including the programs, policies, and resources the business develops that influence an employee's actual contribution.

   Legacy: Long-term success results from short-term decisions—made for the long term.

   Social responsibilities: How a business views its role in a larger world has become more important to people looking for jobs.

4. Declare your employer brand.

5. Get ready to apply the brand—stage by stage—in the next chapter.

CHAPTER SIX

ESSENTIAL #6: APPLY

Any business idea, unless carefully developed, can disappoint.

Your employer brand *may* disappoint anyone it touches, unless your business carefully operationalizes your employer brand through each stage of an employee's relationship—from the first consideration of your business as a place to work through how they notice, consider, apply, join, work, leave, and remember. (And occasionally whine.)

If your brand disappoints on the outside, customers may be disappointed. Leaders of the business may be disappointed as well, along with, yes, employees and their families. On the inside, your employer brand may disappoint if what your employees actually experience differs significantly from what they believe they are promised. So, to make the employer brand real for your employees, emotionally *and* functionally, it must live during each part of each day of an employee's experience. In what employees can access. How they get things done. How they feel about the business and the brand. Otherwise it is just a management idea. That's why, over the years, we have found that a key to successfully making your employer brand live is to apply it stage by stage. Even though, according to the 2005 Hodes research, only 36 percent of human resources professionals around the world say an employer brand can set a standard and framework for all HR activity.

Those committed to employer brand use it as a foundation for the employee experience. Eric Jackson of FedEx observes, "The Purple Promise manifests itself a thousand different ways to create a more unified culture within the company. We bring the Purple Promise to life through every part of an employee's life at FedEx, including all training, compensation, rewards, and recognition."

The stage-by-stage approach to applying the employer brand came out of our looking at talent issues for a retail organization. Struggling with how to make the employer brand real. We knew what we wanted to say, but it felt too much like marketing hype. It didn't feel real. So we decided to look at the employee experience the same way the business looked at each customer experience—stage by stage—from the first moment a customer heard about the organization through the moment a customer told someone else about an experience. We found that by looking at the employee's experience in just the same way, we forced ourselves to ultimately be practical about what programs and policies were developed for each stage as well as what messages were communicated. And it kept the employer brand authentic and real.

—Mark

THE STAGES OF THE EMPLOYEE EXPERIENCE

Only by addressing each stage of an employee's experience can you truly make an employer brand come to life.

Think of your employee as the internal customer of your business.

What the employee, as the internal customer, needs when joining your business will fundamentally differ from what's essential later in the career. And what will motivate the employee to commit will differ, too. That's why we use the seven stages of the employee-employer relationship as a way to frame the employer brand. And following these seven stages is the key to *operationalizing* the employer brand. Once this happens, it comes to life and fuels itself almost naturally.

Most of the burden of making this happen will fall on Human Resources. They design the policies, programs, and processes that define the day-to-day work experience—from the dress code to pay, benefits, facility rules, and guidelines for employee events—and they influence the people who make the difference to employees every day, on the job: the managers and supervisors.

But the stages of the employee experience are not just about HR. They should frame the way everyone in the business collaborates to make the employer brand real. As if developing "products" to "market"—to *functionally* and *emotionally* satisfy the internal, employee customers. That enables the real potential of the employer brand to come through, without disappointing anyone.

It's time to apply your employer brand to the seven stages of an employee's experience with your business:

STAGE ONE: NOTICE	STAGE TWO: CONSIDER	STAGE THREE: APPLY	STAGE FOUR: JOIN	STAGE FIVE: WORK	STAGE SIX: LEAVE	STAGE SEVEN: REMEMBER

In the first stage, a prospective employee *notices* a business. In the second, a prospective employee *considers* your business as a place to work. In the third, a candidate will go through an *application and screening* process that, if successful, is followed by the fourth stage: the candidate's *joining* your business. In the fifth stage, the employee *works* for your business until deciding (or being asked) to *leave* your business—the sixth stage. And, finally, in the seventh stage, a former employee will *remember* (and, perhaps, relate) the experience of working at the business. And what it was like as a place to work.

Your employer brand will come to life only if you embed it in each of these stages. We'll show you how.

Just as your business creates an experience for the external customer, you must create an experience for your internal customer—through each of these stages—based on your employer brand. Once again, this will occur *if* HR and Communications collaborate, with others getting involved as needed. HR can effectively design elements of the experience; Communications can creatively package, market, and tell the story. Neither can make it happen alone. The collaboration—step by step—is essential to employer brand.

STAGE ONE: THE PROSPECTIVE EMPLOYEE NOTICES.

The relationship between an employee and your business begins with an impression.

A person may hear about your business from a friend. Or see something in the media—perhaps a news story, perhaps an advertisement. They may experience your business as a customer. Or

A retail store considered its primary pool for new employees to be its customers. The reasoning was simple. Customers had made the emotional commitment to the business by shopping at the store over and over. Especially the ones who spent a lot of money. Well, chances are they might be influenced by the chance to work a few hours each week and get an employee discount (always a motivator!). And their enthusiasm for the store was obvious and contagious. So we embarked on a campaign for employees to recruit customers to become employees—simply by talking about how much fun they were having "on the inside" of the store. And it worked. In fact, the company still uses the same strategy today.

—Mark

observe your business from a distance. Or talk with someone who works for you.

Collectively, these encounters create an initial reputation for your business as a place to *work*—which may or may not connect with your reputation as a place to *buy*. What prospective employees see and hear about your business, before they may decide to try to join, will surely affect how they ultimately perceive your business. First impressions can be hard to shake.

Dean Rodenbough addresses this:

For Hallmark, this opportunity to create a positive first impression begins with its visitors center at the headquarters complex. It conveys the history of the brand, the scope of the company's operations and tells the story of all the elements that have contributed to our overall brand awareness—with displays about our products, the Hallmark Hall of Fame, memorable commercials, and specialty stores. A guided tour of the center is also on the agenda as we orient new hires or try to sell prospective job candidates on the company.

Earlier this year, Crown Gallery, a new, permanent exhibit in a "high traffic zone" within our main headquarters building, was opened for employees to showcase the essence and legacy of the brand. One of the Crown Gallery exhibits features a giant video screen with employees reciting the Hallmark brand essence statement. Beside the screen, our beliefs and values are imprinted on the wall, and close by is a giant sign with a Hallmark logo imprinted on top of the names of more than thirty thousand Hallmark employee.

So the lesson for any business is, as you market to and serve customers, you are also making an impression on prospective employees. Depending on the customer experience, that can be good news or bad news. A prospective employee will arrive on the doorstep of any business with ideas about what the employee experience may be, formed by these initial observations. Some ideas may be right. Some may be wrong.

What will prospective employees look for?

In most cases, a few simple things.

If people seem to enjoy what they do. That sounds simple enough— people liking their jobs. And as simple as it sounds, this is about as important as anything a prospective employee might observe. After all, who would willingly join a business where people seem unhappy?

If people seem to get along with each other. Again, this one sounds simple, yet its importance can't be overstated. Would any of us want to be surrounded by people who don't appear to like each other? Carping can be amusing in a New York deli, but would you want to work there? At the same time, for any new employee, one of the most important initial questions is, "Will people like me"? And

A retail company considered every possible way to hire what it considered a more sophisticated type of worker, someone actually closer to the type of customers the company wanted to attract. So it did some research to find out what people observe when they shop at the store and how those observations actually affect hiring. Well, we learned that prospective employees were actually making a lot of decisions about the business as a place to work based on what they observed as customers. And this was actually working against the business, not for it. So before they could upgrade the staff they needed to focus on the customer experience.

—Mark

the answer usually comes from, "Do the people seem to like each other?"

If people seem to think it's a good business to work for. This one gets a bit more serious, and in fact it goes directly to an employee's response to the question, "What's in it for me?" And how the prospect, in general, views the reputation of the business as a business. Is the business ethical? How does the business appear to treat people? Any negative press a business receives can seriously damage this part of its reputation. After all, what we read in the papers we assume to be true.

If people seem to think the business is fair. Ultimately, prospective employees will evaluate a business on the perceptions of trust. Certainly, fitting in and working with likable people will be important, but it's difficult for any employer brand to recover from perceptions of unfairness. And these, if they exist, will likely come from current employees or friends of current employees or people who may remember talking with a current employee. Someone always seems to know someone who worked there. And who reached conclusions about the business as a place to work.

If people seem to be able to get things done. And if they seem to have everything they need to do the work. From a functional perspective, the prospect will view the efficiency of the business, to make sure it looks as if employees can get things done, access resources they need, and receive the support they may look for.

A retail company was trying to make the most of its launch of a new brand promise. The simple use of buttons that employees wore, with the simple message, "Talk to me about [our brand]," opened the doors for customers to observe (and comment) on what they saw from employees from the perspective of what they felt the brand promised. And the outcome brought a few surprises. Customers offered many constructive ideas about how the business could be more effective in making the brand come to life. Ideas the business hadn't thought of.

—**Mark**

So what does it mean to a business for prospective employees to notice?

Well, your business doesn't have to sit back and wait to hear what people think about it. Working from your employer brand, your business can proactively influence what prospective employees observe and hear.

Your business can tell its story. The better your business prepares your audience for what they may experience, the better you can manage how they respond. So it makes sense to take the employer brand story outside to proactively discuss what your business is all about, using the same news media outlets your business may use to make important business announcements. A prospective employee just starting to hear about your business will need to hear, in such stories, what your business believes in, why you exist, and what difference you can make to the people you touch, internally and externally.

Your business can focus on your customer experience. It's no accident that a customer visiting a Starbucks sees an employment ad. Or a customer at Target reads stories about how the business contributes to the community. Or a customer at The Container Store reads an invitation to join the staff.

Prospective employees pick up a lot about the employee experience simply by connecting with your business as customers. So, rather than simply letting this happen naturally, you can proactively manage what customers see about what employees experience. Like the way in which, when you're at Wendy's, while you're waiting to order lunch you can read all about what the company values. That may not make a difference to your appetite. But it could make a big difference to your career choice.

That's one reason why well-known businesses, with names synonymous with their brands, are consistently perceived as better places to work. A study by JWT Specialized Communications indicates that a short list of employers' web sites is second only to networking with friends as the best way to find a job. The implication is that companies *not* known as being choice employers may only hope to hire those who are *not* selected by top employers.[1]

Your business can carefully monitor what public message boards and blogs are saying—and quickly respond if needed. In the old days people had to gather in a coffee shop or at the water cooler to gossip about a business. You know, to share horror stories of bad food or lost bags. Now we just log in to the many public or job-related web sites and blogs to vent anything we want to about a business. And to hear what others are saying. So a business that wants to pay attention to what people observe can (and should) take the time to monitor what circulates on these sites—and quickly respond to any messages that get out of control and require quick attention. Your business can easily and quickly learn what's up with at least some (and in many cases the most extreme) parts of your customer populations. And message accordingly.

Stage two: The prospect considers (as the business recruits).

Every business, at some point, needs to look for employees.

And depending on what's happening in talent, this can be a cakewalk or a challenge.

Two companies were going through a rather challenging merger. For any business going through a merger or acquisition, the relationship between the employer brands can be a big factor in how the employees react. So it's important to monitor what people are saying. As we tried to create messages of credibility, we would test them on the public gossip sites—the ones where people can go to read what others say about businesses. There was actually a chat room for employees affected by this merger. So we would go in, anonymously of course, and "water drop" certain possible messages we were considering. Such as "What if the company said this?" or "Do you think the company should let us know this?" or "How would you react if you heard this?" We received fast, candid feedback. And we used it.

—**Mark**

To encourage the prospect to consider your business as a place to work, your business uses advertisements. Now, the first employment ads were undoubtedly "Help Wanted" signs hung in the windows by shopkeepers. When newspapers began to include business announcements, ads for jobs were interspersed among other business notices, called "tombstones" by those in the business. These ads simply announced a job opening and assumed a never-ending supply of workers. Many jobs were filled by walk-in candidates who went door to door looking for work.

Recruitment branding and advertising has come a long way in recent years. Now, we are old enough to remember when ads were boldly discriminatory, looking for young men, recent graduates, and gals Friday. Twenty-five years ago a progressive business would use an oversized ad in a Sunday newspaper, including a corporate logo, a well-written job description, and a pithy marketing message—as well as the "equal opportunity employer" announcement—to reach potential employees. Employment advertising agencies were hired to write and design the ads. Thick employment classified sections

At Southwest, due to our low-cost strategy, we couldn't attract people with money. So we reached beyond the pocketbook to inspire people to join because of the quality of the work experience. We painted a clear picture of how people could come to Southwest and fulfill their personal aspirations and dreams. We made the most of the fun of working for a place where you could "color outside the lines." We leveraged our reputation as a place to fly to interest people in Southwest as a place to work despite our pay scales, which were competitive for the airline industry. And that required the now-famous focus on the Southwest work experience. As we considered at the time, what they don't earn in pay they will experience in fun. But it wasn't all about fun; we were able to show that even though entry salaries were low compared to some industries, the potential for career growth was huge, and the company offered more security than most.

—Libby

in the weekend editions were the place where active candidates could find work.

And these ads usually delivered the right candidates. Baby boomers and our predecessors grew up in environments where jobs were scarce and job seekers did all the work. Once in a job, most employees planned to stay for the long haul. The best candidates found the best companies and, for the most part, they stayed—*unless* they were recruited away by a headhunter. The grass has always been greener in someone else's lawn.

The first recruitment advertising campaigns focused on branding the corporate culture to give candidates "reasons to buy"—by touting a narrow set of reasons why someone would want to join a business. The best campaigns featured real people telling real stories of why they joined, stayed, and recommended the business. According to recruitment guru Gerry Crispin, these initial recruitment advertising campaigns drew from the experience and lessons of product advertising.[2] The emotional pull would connect with the customer. Following the lessons of product campaigns, early recruitment efforts included traditional print advertisements as well as visibility in radio, television, job fairs, corporate events, movie ads, and billboards—with specific messages targeted to specific candidate groups.

In the last decade, as talent began to get scarce, advertising ventured to the radio, national print ads in journals and magazines,

> At Southwest we were looking for folks who didn't take themselves too seriously. Even before we established our employer brand, we knew that recruitment advertising needed to appeal to the right personality types. So our ads said "Work Where Pants Are Optional" (these highlighted our uniforms, which included shorts), or my favorite: "Work Where Elvis Has Been Spotted" (with a picture of chairman Herb Kelleher dressed as Elvis); the fine print says "If you see him dressed as Ethel Merman, ignore him; we are trying to cure him of that."
>
> **—Libby**

outdoor, and television. When large numbers of employees were needed to open a new plant or office, employers ran targeted campaigns to attract candidates in mass. Many employers began to realize it was prudent to advertise beyond the current openings—to use the media to create recruiting campaigns in the talent marketplace to differentiate the business and communicate why someone should join.

The game changed once again with the emerging internet and job boards. The early years basically brought recruitment advertising online, making it more accessible and relevant. Businesses who understood the importance of messaging employer brands to prospects discovered that, as we saw in the previous chapter, a corporate web site could be an effective way to reach out to job seekers.

Yvonne Larkin of Diageo comments, "Our employer brand is key to our recruitment strategy. When we launched our career web site three years ago we tried to convey that the strength of our values was in our DNA. This was deemed critical in order to attract and ultimately retain people who would flourish in our environment."

When we had hiring challenges at Southwest, we realized we could not deliver an unconventional message to potential employees (who might be on their way to the nearest fast-food restaurant to accept a job) in a conventional way. So instead of traditional interviews, we held events to educate potential candidates about the career experience. That sounds dry, but we made them really fun, just like the experience of working at Southwest. We helped candidates see that, while initial pay might seem low, there were many steps on the career ladder (including three pay increases the first year of employment) and clear progression throughout a career. And that we were committed to promote from within, with a management track accessible to anyone who might be interested. They came, they listened, and a whole lot of them joined.

—Libby

Gerry Crispin, who evaluates such corporate websites, believes the sites *should* address the fundamental employer brand questions, including why people should join and stay at the business. "To become world class you must do it in a way that is memorable. That means you have to describe the challenge, and make it compelling. The messaging has to be congruent with the experience. A candidate should have a pretty good picture of a day in the life at that company, and in that job." According to Crispin, effective sites target the desired candidate, engage with messaging and answer the "why" questions, inform with relevant content, and respect candidates with acknowledgment and feedback.

A convenience store had a genuine interest in elevating the quality of employees in their stores—to, they hoped, raise the quality of experience for customers. A great, connected ambition. And they thought improving the benefits might be just the ticket to attract better people. But we weren't sold on that idea. So we said, how about if we do some research before you spend your money? We surveyed current and prospective employees about what would interest them in working at this company and what would deter them. Interestingly enough, their answers were in total parallel: they picked the same strengths and weaknesses. And we learned the reason the company had trouble finding and keeping the right people had nothing to do with benefits. It had everything to do with the overall negative impression of the customer service. They told us about the cleanliness in the stores, the friendliness of the staff, and the jokes by late-night comics. So rather than spend money on richer benefits, the company focused on upgrading the customer experience, which in turn would make a difference to hiring and retention. And it worked. The company confronted the core of the problem, acknowledged the connection between the customer and employer brands, and made a difference.

—Mark

So what can your business do?

Here are a few ways to use your employer brand to help with your recruitment efforts.

Use your employer brand to strengthen the sense of choice. Just as strong consumer brands make it easier for customers to make buying decisions, your employer brand can improve the quality of candidates applying for jobs and simplify the selection process. Your well-identified, well-executed, and persistent employer brand can help your business attract and retain candidates who fit needed profiles. And your clear articulation of the brand (and, specifically, the required on-brand behavior) can encourage candidates to self-select—and to decide to pursue you as a prospective employer only if you match their values, culture, and passion. You can use your employer brand to frame, in a clear and compelling way, how your business tells prospects what you are, what you stand for, how people get things done, and how your business is unique. Good candidates always have options. And as they select a business, they are in the driver's seat.

Use your employer brand to create "buzz." Great people are attracted by great people because they want to work with only the best. Your employer brand can articulate the qualities and attributes common to your best employees as a guideline for who to hire. Cultural fit, in most businesses, is imperative. So if your business hires someone who doesn't fit into the culture, no matter how strong a worker, that person will not succeed there. Articulating your

> You know, about the same time we redid the recruitment experience, we created a new recruitment communication piece to market the "What's in it for me?" value of working at Southwest. And the piece talked a lot of about the type of people who would succeed at Southwest and what the value of their work experience could be. Talk about a glimpse into the ultimate employer brand. And we coined that great line, "We're looking for people who color outside the lines."
>
> **—Libby and Mark**

employer brand—with those specifics we discuss in the previous chapter—can help your business avoid costly mistakes. And as your employer brand becomes well known, people can choose whether they want to work for your business before they even bother to send a résumé. That saves everyone's time and reinforces the fact that the stronger that message, the fewer bad fits may accidentally slip through.

Use your employer brand to make recruitment advertising real. Recruitment advertising, when done well, is more than slapping a logo on some communications; it extends your employer brand externally so prospects know what your business will promise to employees in return for what they bring to your business. This is more than an ad campaign. Although recruitment advertising should include well planned and coordinated media efforts that are consistent with the consumer brand, employer brand, and corporate identity, your employer brand can go a step further. It can actually attach meaning, value, and personality to what your business offers to employees, resulting in a compelling promise to prospects that clearly communicates what they will experience if they join.

Use your employer brand to make recruitment advertising relevant. Search engines have changed the recruitment game. Candidates now search for jobs in their desired fields and location using just a search window. Search engines can "scrape" jobs listings to give candidates access to openings in their fields locally and globally. Employers can use the same technology to build databases of candidates that match current and future roles. The dot-jobs domain is becoming a reality, which means that job seekers will know where to go to find jobs at desired employers.

Yahoo! Hot Jobs, for example, reports they are beginning to see client interest in employer branding rather than just listing jobs. The emergence of rich media on the Internet creates better ways to communicate what an employer offers. One client using rich media branding with job listings experienced a 70 percent increase in applicant interest, with a 300 percent increase in applicant quality as measured by how far the candidates made it through the application process. Rich media can bring new life to recruitment videos, making it easy for any candidate to experience more than just photos and descriptions of what it is like to work at a business.[3]

One of the legends of Southwest is how we created the job candidate experience. When we instituted the now-famous "group interview," we thought we were being careful to support the external brand, even if we didn't say it in just those terms. But we were looking at it from a cultural vantage point. In this interview candidates are required to simply get up in front of other candidates and talk about themselves. At the time, we reasoned that people who could not succeed at this task would likely have a difficult time thriving in the culture, because the environment demands that employees be outgoing. As time progressed, we realized this simple exercise defined an experience that, even for those not selected to join, motivated them to support the customer mission. What we accomplished was an ideal integration of the employer brand into the candidate experience. The group interview, with its relative zaniness and personality, perfectly represented the fundamental fabric of Southwest—an organization where, to achieve business success, we acknowledge the freedom of people to be individuals. We wanted them to feel good about applying and to take a close look at themselves and decide if they really wanted to go to work for Southwest—and we wanted to make them want to fly Southwest even if they were not selected!

—Libby

Use your employer brand to open recruitment advertising to new ideas. Social networking and social media are also emerging as effective ways for job seekers to network online. Although there are too many companies in this space, and a lot of hype, this will eventually become a valuable tool for job seekers. Employers will be able to use it effectively to mine candidates, too. If tied to applicant tracking systems with talent relationship management tools, businesses will soon have more powerful tools to build relationships with future employees.

Ultimately, employers will be able to use behavioral targeting techniques to find the right candidates. Employers may finally begin to find those elusive passive candidates where they live on the Internet by targeting them—based on interests and online behavior—and serving up customized rich media recruitment messages that are much more likely to be relevant to them. This is ideal for new entrants to the labor market who have been heavily influenced by brands. From early TV to MTV, they have been bombarded with brand messaging. And Gen Y is the first generation of employee to grow up online. Now we know how to reach them.

STAGE THREE: THE PROSPECT BECOMES A CANDIDATE (AND APPLIES FOR A JOB).

For most prospective employees, the experience of seeking and interviewing for a job is intimidating at best and downright frightening at worst.

It's an emotional experience to send a résumé for a job and wait to see if a response comes. Unfortunately, more often than not these days, someone who takes the time to submit a résumé online doesn't ever hear back, at least not from a human.

However, waiting to hear back from an interview is a hundred times worse. Let's face it: we hate rejection. We're human. We want a job for any number of reasons. And we don't want to get turned down. After all, a job says so much about us: who we are, what we do, where we work. Identity and ego are touchy things.

The hiring processes at the best employer brands become legendary through word of mouth and media. How your business handles the candidate experience and the process that supports it demands a strong understanding of your employer brand. And the commitment to bring it to life at this stage.

No matter whether a candidate submits a résumé for an open position, is referred by a friend, is solicited by your business, or is

One lesson from Southwest is that surprise can be a gold mine. And we realized we had to reach people at times when they might least expect a message about a job and a place to work. So at the height of our talent battle we advertised on television during NFL games and on billboards where we would usually advertise flights. Our planes were full, but we needed "butts in seats" at *work*. And we learned that our value proposition to employees was in direct parallel to our value proposition to customers—a positive place to work, an easy place to emotionally commit to, a fun place to join.

—**Libby**

internal and applying for a new role or promotion, the candidate needs to be treated well and, if rejected, deserves to know the reasons why and what he or she could do better the next time. Every interaction a prospect has with your business will reinforce or undermine your employer brand.

Your business *must* focus on the experience you create during the process and how that experience can positively impact a candidate's impressions of your business, *regardless* of whether the prospect is hired or not. If the prospect is hired, this experience sets the stage for a positive acclimation to your business. And if the prospect is not hired, your business will *still* want that person to carry a positive impression of how she or he was treated during the experience. For *others to hear.*

HR designs the experience and supporting processes your business follows to collect the information from people who want to be selected for jobs. This may include the use of your own jobs site, with an online tool candidates can use to submit résumés and assess whether or not the job is right, or perhaps use of a job board for this service. HR also designs how the business selects which candidates to pursue, conducts interviews, makes selections, communicates offers, and expresses regret to those not selected. But although these processes must be highly efficient, the trick is to make them invisible from the candidates, invisible from hiring managers. Only HR should see what happens behind the curtain.

What will candidates look for throughout their experience?

In most cases, a few simple things.

> One of the strongest declarations we made of what it meant to work at Southwest was when we merged with Morris Air. As with all mergers and acquisitions, there was concern over how the cultures would mesh. And we had the job of helping the Morris people get comfortable with the very different Southwest culture. So we explained how Southwest's serious approach to business is what gives the business the permission to have fun. And we summarized it all with the tag line, "We are serious about having fun." People loved it. It opened the door.
>
> **—Mark and Libby**

If people act interested in the candidate as a person. None of us likes to be overlooked. And we all want to make the best impression we can. So at every point of interaction the candidate will test whether your business (and the people handling the process) is expressing genuine interest—or is simply going through the motions.

If the experience is efficient and organized. Nothing will throw a candidate faster and cast a more negative shadow on the brand than a candidate experience that appears to be disorganized and haphazard. It will not say much about the ultimate reliability of the brand if, for example, your web site doesn't work. Or if your business is not efficient at getting back to the candidate when promised. Such faux pas will not motivate the candidate to have much confidence in your process or your business.

If your business acts like a good place to work. In many ways, the interview experience is like dating. And if your business fails the first date, it's unlikely the prospect will want to say "yes" a second time. A savvy prospect will look for clues, throughout the interviewing process, to how your business operates and, most important, how your business treats people. It's just like those touch points between a customer and the business. How will each interaction contribute to a reputation? And a feeling of what this place may be like as a place to work? How many times have you heard a candidate remark, "If you all are like this during the interview, what must you be like during the employment?"

If your materials follow the standards set by external communications and marketing. Prospective employees will expect a certain look and feel from the external marketing materials they have seen from your business. And though few businesses allocate the same dollars for internal or recruitment communications as they do for external materials, the look and feel should be consistent and have at least a standard level of clarity. And they must be in line with the employer brand.

If everything seems to work. Prospective employees will react to the fundamentals of the experience. If they're submitting a résumé online, does the site work? Does the site promise that the résumé will be reviewed by a real person who is trained to do this for the particular role and function—and does this indeed happen? Best employer brands use consistent systems to select the best candidates, put them through consistent interview procedures, and deliver the same basic kinds of onboarding and training in all businesses, departments, and locations globally. Hiring must be a most efficient business process to consistently deliver the right kinds of people throughout all the businesses and locations. And to maintain the employer brand.

If the interview—if there is one—is challenging. You don't want a gauntlet that creates an unprofessional experience, but the best candidates expect to jump a few hurdles to prove themselves worthy of a job. Interviews must be thorough and challenging, and interviewers should be well prepared and well informed. However, no candidate should ever be treated rudely. A noteworthy candidate experience will have a most positive effect on your employer brand. But a bad one will—well, you remember brand adhesive.

So what does that mean to you? Design your candidate experience with top talent in mind, so you do not unintentionally turn off your top prospects along the way. Create an interview that is engaging and packed full of thought-provoking questions. Coach the interviewer to show sincere interest in the candidate as a candidate and as a person. And remember, each step of each process is a touch point with a prospective customer.

If the candidate feels the interview—if there is one—is thorough. Every candidate wants the chance to "give it my best shot." We want to feel we have a chance to create a good impression. So be sure to consider the process flow the prospect will experience. Who will the prospect talk with? Does each interview build on the next? Will the business present what the candidate needs to know about the role, the coworkers, the business, the boss? And are the interviewers prepared to help the candidate feel as at ease as possible? The most important reaction for any candidate, upon walking out of the interview, is to feel the interviewer was interested and to feel the selection process offered the opportunity to shine. The prospect must feel he or she has had every chance to "give it my best shot" in front of people who will carefully consider the relative merits of the candidate. This might be the first signal a candidate has about whether or not a business is ethical. And they will remember whether this experience is consistent with what they believe your employer brand promises.

If the expectations are clearly understood. While a candidate is actively pursuing your business, you have a captive audience. This can be an excellent opportunity to begin to convey what skills and behaviors your business expects of employees to deliver your brand to customers. This can in fact serve as an opportunity for prospective employees to self-select if they feel your business and your job are right for them. But only if you make the expectations clear.

If the values feel aligned. As well, the candidate experience offers you the opportunity to clarify what your business stands for and believes in—and if the candidate is prepared to support what your business stands for. More and more, with each new generation entering the workforce, what a business values has more influence on the hiring decisions. And that's one reason it's so important to brand from the inside.

Everyone has a bad interview story, but not every one is published in a national business magazine. A recent *Fast Company* magazine article, "Why We Hate HR," recounts a story about a talented MBA who accepted a job offer with a large media company out of business school.[4] She was interested in several open positions in different business units, but HR steered her to one opportunity, saying that it was the sole offer that she would receive. She later discovered that she would have had several options. And she felt railroaded into the job, under the supervision of a manager who was not well respected. Obviously she felt damaged enough by this experience to share it with a reporter, and it has now been shared with the world.

—Libby

If the prospect feels your decision process is fair. At the conclusion of the screening experience—whether it ends with an acknowledgment that a résumé was received and reviewed, whether an in-person interview was conducted or not, whether a candidate was hired or not—your business must do what it takes to make sure each candidate leaves with a sense of fairness. The way you treat candidates will be talked about.

If rejection is handled with respect. Even if you quickly determine the person isn't right to do the job, keep in mind that that person is a customer who may influence other customers and potential employees. Candidates who have negative experiences remember them and publicly share the details for years.

The functional dimension of the employer brand is very important at this stage (to make sure everything works), but the emotional dimension is what really counts. Your business can say more during the application process about yourself and how you value people—in the way you *turn people down* and treat them with fundamental respect—than at any other stage. And your business can convert any and every candidate from someone interested in the job to someone connected to what the business is doing.

According to *Fortune* magazine, during the mid-1990s Microsoft's hiring machine took on mythic proportions. The behemoth put candidates through rigorous interviews, asking brain-teasing questions and asking programmers to code on demand. According to the former PR man running recruiting, Microsoft discovered three secrets to recruiting. First, involve employees at all levels in hiring. Second, create a process that works. And third, use innovative interviewing techniques, which included solving riddles or problems. But to snag the best candidates they had to sell the company and the role. Methods included asking Bill Gates to call the best candidates to close the deal. The challenge was to convince candidates that they were still innovative.[5]

—Libby

STAGE FOUR: THE NEW EMPLOYEE JOINS.

If seeking a new job is one of the most emotional of experiences, the actual moment an employee joins your business is the one time he or she is the most open to making an emotional connection.

The purpose of onboarding is to begin to make emotional and functional connections with new hires so they begin to feel a profound sense of commitment to your business. And it should last more than a day. At P&G, for example, onboarding covers an employee's first year with the company, with milestone events held at or after the six- and twelve-month anniversary dates.

One of our biggest challenges at Southwest was new-hire orientation and onboarding. We had transformed the recruitment process. But how could we make our culture come to life, while making sure employees understood important details of their benefits in the first few weeks of work?

One day, by accident, we started talking about things—loose brainstorming. We came up with a fill-in-the-blank idea, kind of "I love Southwest so much I would [blank]." And we said, well, we would shout, we would scream and laugh and finally sing. And that was it. Let the Southwest employees sing to new employees about what it means to work here. So we rewrote the lyrics to about a hundred songs (to offer our messages to new employees) and we took our cue cards, our background recorded music, and our video camera to all these Southwest locations to create instant karaoke. It worked.

These were not necessarily the most professional of performances. In fact, they had not been rehearsed. That's what made it great. To capture the essence of Southwest, musically, we simply recruited employees to perform at work, from airport concourses to office hallways to the maintenance hangar and Reservations. In true karaoke style, we gave them a songbook, asked them to choose a song, and turned on the camera. (Rehearsal can destroy spontaneity.) Herb Kelleher said, simply, "It's the best representation of the Southwest culture ever created."

—Libby and Mark

For any business, the ultimate opportunity to imprint the employer brand is when a new employee joins. In this brief window of time, the employee is an absolute sponge for every belief the business wants to instill. Open, willing to believe, and not yet influenced by others. At this moment they have yet to go native.

Because the right candidates won't walk into your business ready to deliver the brand promise to customers, employers focused on a strong brand make sure a robust onboarding process is in place. Onboarding starts when the job offer is extended and lasts until the person can perform well and begins to be considered a fully functioning team member.

As people who represent the employer brand and want to create an emotional connection, you and your staff can maximize the opportunity that this moment provides. In fact, there is no better time, no time when people are more willing to absorb, than the first few days on the job.

People start new jobs with hope. Wanting *this* to be the place where it all works, where they find opportunity and recognition, where they feel they fit and connect, and, in most cases, where they believe they can make a satisfying contribution. And get a paycheck to make ends meet or perhaps to improve their lifestyle.

Onboarding, in whatever form it is delivered, is your business's best opportunity to solidify the brand impressions people carry over from the first two stages, when they *hear* and *apply*. In fact, the onboarding experience should maximize how people absorb your employer brand. And it should last beyond the first day—through several months, in fact—with "buddy" programs and other offerings to help new hires understand your business and what is expected.

Certainly, when people join the functional requirements are significant. The details have to get processed. And technology can certainly make this more efficient. This experience should include the following elements:

Functional acclimation. How your business connects the new employee to the various resources you offer that can be helpful for getting things done.

Location orientation. How the employee learns the fundamentals of where to park, go to the bathroom, sit and eat lunch.

A global energy company was trying to apply the employer brand to the onboarding process, so we asked employees who had recently joined the company what they wanted to learn and when. They told us that on the first day, all they really cared about was where the bathroom was and where to park the car. A lot of the rest of the messages were lost on them. They just needed to get a handle on how to get around. Within a few weeks, however, they would be ready to hear all the details. So we took new-hire orientation and cut it in half. The first part was all about the logistics. The second part, thirty days later, was all about the employer brand. This new arrangement acknowledged the emotional state of the new employee who wanted to know, first of all, where to park, how to log on, where to find the bathroom. It embraced the new employee's insecurities, from "Will I fit in?" to "How will I connect with my boss?" to "How will I know I made the right decision to come here?" And it recognized that it can't all be done on the first day. That's why the heavy stuff comes thirty days later.

—**Mark**

Fundamental facts. How thorough your business makes the experience to educate the new employee about the fundamentals of your business, including how it works and how to contribute.

Through all of this, the employer brand should be at the core of how new employees onboard to your business. The secret to the employer brand at orientation is to capture its essence as quickly and powerfully as possible—recognizing this as a key opportunity to imprint new employees with the employer brand. Think about the power of the employer brand for someone who walks in the door, fresh, with all the hope and belief a new employee brings. It will keep the brand fresh. The emotional opportunities are incredible. This is a time to lock in the emotional connection that employees want to feel. And all it takes is for you, at the same time you are being efficient, to also step back and acknowledge the reactions new people bring to this new chapter in their lives.

What will new employees look for?

During the onboarding experience, they will be noticing all these factors:

If the paperwork is handled in an efficient way. In fact, the less paperwork the better. Most can be done online, but in some cases signatures and paper documents are required. New employees will "test" the reliability of the business, and the consistency of the brand experience, as they complete the necessary forms and steps to "register" as a new employee. If it feels bureaucratic or inefficient, this may sound alarm bells that the brand isn't quite as it has been portrayed.

If essential questions are effectively handled. The personal touch, so important to the impressions left with potential employees, is just as important as a new employee comes on board. Making certain that informed sources are easily available to the new employee can effectively address questions before they become issues.

If a new employee has a chance to culturally assimilate. Every new employee at every business wants to know they can fit into the new place of work. They search for clues to what it takes to be accepted, connected, included. This is an excellent opportunity to discuss the cultural dimensions of the employer brand—the details of what it means to be an employee at this business. They also want to know what it takes to succeed, and to move ahead in a career. Generation Y employees entering a new job are as likely to be thinking of what their *next* job will be as about their current role.

If the experience is consistent with the brand of the business. New employees may enter a business with expectations based on interacting with the business as a customer. Capturing the tone and feel of the brand in the onboarding experience can, in subtle ways, help connect new employees to what the business is all about. And what role they can play.

If the experience promotes the brand of your business. Ultimately, the hope for any new employee (and for the business) is that the employee will become a contributing member of the staff, helping to deliver to customers what the business promises. Promoting the brand, and what it means, throughout the onboarding process can help secure understanding of and belief in what the brand stands for. And what it requires.

A well-branded entertainment company wanted to make onboarding more entertaining. As well as more efficient. Top priority was function—to make sure the paperwork (most of which was moved online, via an extranet that employees accessed before the first day of work) was efficiently handled so employees could get to work when they came to work. But the emotional dimension was very important too, especially to lock in the employees' positive views of the brand as it related to customers as well as to new employees. So the business made orientation fun. Lots of activities, entertainment, videos. And all very consistent with the brand. Realizing they had this one opportunity to solidify the commitment.

—Mark

STAGE FIVE: THE EMPLOYEE WORKS.

So now the real experience begins.

It's no surprise the emotional dimensions of the employer brand are most tested during the ups and downs of an employee's experience with the business.

Every day brings a new set of emotional challenges, from how an employee feels treated by a supervisor or colleague, to how an employee reacts to a message from leadership, to how an employee feels telling someone where he or she works.

Simply put, every functional dimension of your employer brand, from payroll to performance management, carries an emotional dimension as well. Not only must the process and tools work, but the ways employees are treated at every step along the way must adhere to brand standards.

And when new employees join a company, they expect a lot. The 2005 Yahoo! Hot Jobs poll reveals more than 95 percent of people looking online for jobs say they must be able to access tools and resources they need to do their job. And more than 94 percent say they must be able to develop skills to advance their career.

"We have had a rigorous HR process for decades," says GE's Linda Boff. "We evaluate leaders and employees on business results and values. To succeed you need both. You must perform very well, do great work, and you must live great values. We make it very clear to people in evaluations, and everyone who comes into GE signs a letter. We take it seriously and it is a 'no strikes you are out' approach. Our values, our integrity are palpable in everything we do in promotability, career planning, leadership."

As we have said, every employee of every business asks (at one time or another and at times very frequently) "What's in it for me to work here?" To answer this question, an employee must have the chance to internalize the identity, mission, strategy, and values of the business; the tasks, skills, development, rewards, and environment related to the job; and the tools and resources to help manage day-to-day life.

The employer brand can crystallize what it means to work for a business—no matter what an employee may expect, or fear, or aspire to accomplish, and no matter how the business may be changing. The employer brand can be a *constant* in the ever-changing experience of working for any business. And something to hold onto during the ups and downs of any job.

Behind the scenes.
The employer brand can provide a framework for HR and other corporate services to operationalize many of its attributes.

This will include such routine experiences as a paycheck getting deposited on time, health benefits that get accurately processed, expense reports that are reimbursed on time, and coffee machines that actually produce fresh hot coffee.

And it will reach more substantive issues, such as the alignment of competencies to support brand behavior, how the business shares knowledge, and how it supports employees as they plan their careers.

Monitor and manage performance. One key opportunity for your employer brand is the focus on building capability and performance in the business. Libby Hutchison of WaMu observes, "Our employer brand is at the heart of our goal setting process." Yvonne Larkin of Diageo agrees: "Our employer brand is at the core of our people and organization strategy. It touches every part of the employee's experience, from recruitment to orientation to performance management to pay and benefits. For example, our

Every topic that is communicated with employees, no matter how seemingly mundane, offers an opportunity to advance the brand. Few people realize the first official introduction of the "freedom" theme at Southwest was actually to help people get comfortable with telephone enrollment for benefits! We had just introduced our new branding, "A Symbol of Freedom," and introduced the freedom branding outside the company. We needed a way to promote the phone, and we thought, well, the phone frees people from the large enrollment form it replaced; the phone frees people from having to be in one specific place when they enroll; the phone frees people from having to enroll at one specific time of day when everything may be in front of them. So it was all about the freedom to enroll. So we called it one of the "great moments in freedom."

—Libby and Mark

global performance managment process, which operates in all our businesses worldwide, has been designed to reflect the importance of valuing each other, creating mutually fulfilling relationships, diversity, and growth."

Potential can be unlimited when a business fosters a healthy, high-performance culture. When the spirit of passion, innovation, and dedication are in place, and the principles and values of the business become self-governing. When this occurs, the employer brand will self-replicate, enabling business leaders to focus on market and growth objectives.

According to Jon R. Katzenbach, "The most evident characteristic of any peak-performance workforce is the energy level it exudes. Walking into the workplace, you feel its energy, which is noticeably different from that of any average performing workplace. Activity levels are more intense, attitudes are more positive, interactions are less constrained, and formal positions are less evident. People work hard, but they have fun at work and take full advantage of a widespread sense of humor."[6]

How HR supports a high-performance culture will be unique to any business, and will most likely include these processes:

- Performance management systems
- Pay for performance
- Segmentation of employees by high performers and high potential, with appropriate rewards
- Weeding out of lower performers
- Emphasis on learning and development
- Two-way communications and feedback loops
- Dashboards and metrics that promote results and accountability
- Cultivation of leaders
- Building of a leadership bench and succession planning
- Open communication
- Distributed decision-making
- Rewards for innovation and risk-taking

By looking at these processes as "products" to market to employees, such offerings will be made equal, consistent, and employee-oriented throughout all locations. And they will be invisible, not awkward—employees won't feel processed. The most effective employer brands differentiate themselves from the pack by being able to demonstrate that each individual employee is highly and equally valued; their employees are very much involved in making decisions about their work, products, and priorities. These businesses fight hierarchy, distinctions, elitism, and bureaucracy like the plague. Their employees can access opportunities to develop, grow, and learn, and work-life issues are important.

Each time we work with a business to rethink and reposition performance management, we go back to the essentials of that brand promise to employees. Because nothing gets to the heart of the integrity of that promise like the way a business treats this most important and sensitive process. As we worked with one organization, we concluded that performance management was all about bringing out the best in people inside the business so they in turn would bring out the best from the business to the market. That summarized the essence of performance management—and the employer brand, too.

—Mark

A major hotel chain was going through a lot of change. Over the course of a few years it merged with one company, acquired another, was acquired by another and yet another. It was, for employees, a whirlwind. But they never took their eyes off working, because the employer brand remained the constant. To help employees see the benefit of a larger organization, the company emphasized the concept of world: "anywhere in the world of this company they could find a home," people to support them, the opportunity to move ahead. And so, for employees, the employer brand gave them something to hold onto during all the change.

—Mark

Make rewards make sense.

How employees are recognized and rewarded is critical, too. There is an overwhelming tendency to look first at compensation programs, to align employees' and business interests. When there are retention issues, compensation is the first suspect as a root cause. Compensation is important, but not only for obvious reasons.

Let's face it: pay is very personal. It is material, one's livelihood, and symbolic. For most, each step up in pay symbolizes another rung on the corporate ladder. Compensation is a powerful way to drive performance and to align employees with the goals of the business. How you pay employees says a great deal about what you value as a business. If you pay far below the market, employees won't join and won't stay. However, there are legendary employer brands that are proud of the fact that many take cuts in pay to join.

Best employers create rewards and recognition that promote the culture, behaviors, and values your business stands for. Rewards programs are designed to attract and retain employees who will be linked psychically with the mission of the business. Rewards are focused on strategic business and financial objectives and on creating shareholder value.

Best employers often make over rewards programs and create new incentives that position the business in the public's mind as not only a great place to work but also a terrific business to support through their buying decisions.

Rewards can be a creative and dynamic opportunity to demonstrate, in real and meaningful ways, exactly what your business's values and beliefs are, what its mission is, and what steps you're taking to make that future happen.

Your total rewards programming must leverage compensation philosophies—to brand it—in such a way that employees see a clear connection between what they do and how it's valued, all the way up to the C-suite and by customers and shareholders. It is that psychic satisfaction that has much greater staying power than the thrill of a bonus check, a pay increase, or "in the money" options.

Make benefits make sense, too.

Today, as the administration of benefits becomes more efficient (and more electronic), too many businesses think the communication of benefits can be handled with a flick of a switch, too. But it doesn't work that way. Benefits continue to be an ultimately personal expression of the commitment of a business to the security of the employee. And how a business communicates this message can make a difference in how people react.

We have seen, over the years, what can happen when the communication of benefits is handled as creatively and carefully as the communication of any business issue. The seeds of the employer brand at Southwest were planted in our early communication of

When we rebranded the Employee Assistance Program at Southwest, we hadn't yet discovered the power of employer branding, but we knew we had to brand the program in a retail context, tied to the business, relevant to employees. Also, the plan had become known by the vendor's name, and we didn't want it to be the vendor's plan; we wanted it to be our plan. That way, if we changed vendors, the name of the plan didn't change. So we followed a brand process just as we would for any product. We clarified the brand promise—to help you avoid the turbulence of day-to-day life—which directly led to the brand name, Clear Skies.

—Libby and Mark

benefits. Today, the effective communication of benefits is all about making the story personal, giving the employee the facts in an easy-to-understand way, and providing access to experts so employees can easily get the answers they need. Much like the support any customer expects when using a product or service the business offers.

STAGE SIX: THE EMPLOYEE LEAVES.

At some point, it will make sense for the employee to leave the business.

Some may leave when they want to leave. Some may leave before they want to. Some may even leave after. Regardless of the timing, the focus on employer brand demands that you create a positive experience for departing employees—realizing that as soon as they leave, they will talk and others may *hear*. That's why, according to Diana Shaheen, P&G focuses so much effort on keeping retirees and alumni (those who leave to go to other organizations) connected. "We place a priority on maintaining the P&G community," she says, "so we can continue to nurture loyalty and pride."

The employer brand carries different meaning for people departing under different circumstances.

Today every business talks about rising health care costs and how to figure out ways to help employees recognize the impact of the cost. We did that in the early 1990s in our "plane facts" campaign for Southwest. Each month employees would see a new "plane fact" linking the cost of health care to something the airline bought or sold. So people could easily see the threat of rising costs to the employee and the company. One "plane fact" was how many people would have to fly on one day to pay for a day of health care coverage. And another was how many bags of peanuts Southwest could buy for what it paid for one day of health care coverage. And so on. And it worked. People engaged. Costs leveled. And we planted another seed for the employer brand.

Retirement

The business should ensure that the process to prepare an employee for retirement is as sensitive to emotional issues as the process to work with customers in somewhat trying situations. Employees preparing for retirement may carry a range of emotions about the impending change; as a result, they may bring more emotion to the proceedings than the employees they work with.

Resignation

The process should facilitate an employee's departure as efficiently as possible, realizing that the departing employee may carry some negative views about the business. This means it's critical for the process to be foolproof, from the processing of paperwork to the handling of benefit claims. Again realizing that tomorrow these people will be on the street answering questions from others about the business.

Termination

The business should ensure this process is as fair and sensitive as possible, realizing this is not an easy situation; at best, you can make sure nothing goes wrong to create lasting bad memories of the business. Sometimes the way the termination is handled can create a secondary assault to the employee. Not only were they fired, they were treated inhumanely. "No surprises" is the best rule for the process, because surprise may have been a part of the initial announcement.

Southwest was a young new company for so many years, but as we approached our thirty-year anniversary some of our long-term employees were beginning to retire (many as millionaires). I was having farewell drinks with one of our retiring flight attendants when she told me that it took three visits to Dallas and meetings with four departments to retire. So our first branded piece was a brochure with a picture of an airplane seat with rockers on the bottom. It said "You've Earned the Freedom to Retire Southwest Style" and the content covered, step by step, what to do and think about as an employee prepared to retire.

—Libby

Functionally, the employee will be watching the exit process. Is there a specific set of steps to follow for the employee to exit? Are exit interviews available? What is the process to inform the employee about benefit issues after termination? And what is the process, if necessary, to handle ongoing paperwork?

Just as carefully as in the onboarding experience, the process of terminating employees (regardless of who decides it's time for someone to leave, the business or the employee) should focus on respect for the employee and adherence to the brand.

Employees should feel, as they leave the business, the best possible reaction to the business as a place to work, regardless of the circumstances. Care should be given to make sure administrative details are handled with efficiency and fairness.

Finally, for many businesses, the process of engaging alumni in the employer brand enables the relationship with the employee to continue beyond employment. Again, the focus should be on respect for the former employee and adherence to the employer brand.

So what will a departing employee look for? Many of the same things they have been looking for all along. Emotionally, just as the onboarding process must be personal, so must the exit process, carefully managing how the departing employee views the last stages of employment. Unfortunately, a disorganized departure can solidify any negative impressions of the work experience that the departing employee may carry. This is easily remedied by making the process as efficient as possible.

An airline, renowned around the world for its customer service, carefully helps departing employees "bridge" to what they describe as "a new chapter in the relationship with the company." They strongly believe that treating departing employees with respect is a key symbol to prospective and current employees of how the business values people. And they embed this sense of value in the steps they put people through as people depart the company. Because they still want departing employees to want to step on board one of their airplanes!

—Mark

Stage seven: The employee remembers.

At some point, every employee leaves.

And when they leave, they carry all the memories of the experience and will likely tell others what it was all about. That ultimate adhesive of the employer brand experience becomes a megaphone.

The final dimension of the employer brand, as a result, is how alumni carry the brand back into the marketplace once they leave the business.

Consider, for a moment, all the people they may touch: the prospect, who may be hearing about the business for the first time or perhaps in the midst of recruitment or orientation. The current employee, who may be going through a period of change with the business. And certainly the competitor, who may be trying to figure out what's going on inside.

The potential impact of the alum on the brand demands a strong employer brand that embraces the alum. In the same way a college strives to keep connected with alumni, for many reasons, a business that focuses on managing the perceptions of departed employees can experience an added potential of the employer brand.

The reach of the employer brand never ends. In fact, the effort to reach alumni, in its circular motion, directly influences what people may hear about the business and its employer brand.

Ultimately, every employee who encounters your business will tell someone else a story about the business.

Some may listen. Some may not. But a business's efforts to manage how people *remember* the experience can make a difference as such stories are shared.

For some companies, this is *the* reason for handling the departure experience with as much sensitivity as possible—to leave a lasting impression of care and concern. For others, it's a matter of carefully maintaining networks of alumni to continue the opportunity to influence the former employee's impressions.

Adding it up.

As the employer brand must reflect the stages of an employee's work and life, it must also frame the programs the business offers to address each stage. Each program and approach must address

> One of the great experiences in anyone's career is to visit a retiree club of a company that has effectively maintained the engagement with departed employees. A major energy company does this beautifully, with a web site for retirees, company-sponsored functions for retirees, special health programs for retirees, and, most important, a commitment to engaging senior people from the company to maintain the connection with retirees. Plus they offer retirees the opportunity to volunteer back at the company. They strongly believe it's a key part of their value proposition to employees.
>
> **—Mark**

two dimensions of an employee's experience—the *emotional* and the *functional.*

The programs must be efficient—to achieve a *functional* level of success—but they must also satisfy the *emotional* needs an employee brings to each stage. This blended approach must be a part of each stage of the employee's experience, from the first opportunity to hear about the business through the opportunities to remember what it was like to work at the business.

In fact, the *emotionality* of the employer brand touches every experience of employees, from the day they join through the day they depart, and all the days before and after.

Employees don't arrive at companies completely engaged in the brand—although they can be quite a ways along the path.

Brand engagement must be experienced at every stage of the relationship between an employee and the business—from the first consideration of it as a place to work through the final stage. And each stage of this relationship demands something new from the employee and places new pressure on the brand.

That's why the employer brand map must address each stage of the relationship, from when the employee first hears about the business through the day the employee leaves. And all of the days in between.

In addressing each stage, the employer brand provides the framework for HR to develop the programs and Communications to develops the message—and the two converge to create the experience.

Five Essential Steps

1. Consider what prospective employees may notice about your business as a place to work—from what they may see at your locations (if you have public locations) to what they may observe or read about you. And consider if you need to revise how you position yourself as a place to work.
2. Take a close look at your process for recruiting potential employees—and what it says about your business as a place to work. Specifically, look at how you use your employer brand in your recruitment advertising and efforts.
3. Take a close look at the experience you create for prospects and candidates—and what that says about your business as a place to work. Specifically, how you handle the interview process—if people feel they get a fair shake—and the rejection process—if people feel good about the experience.
4. Look at your onboarding (or orientation) as an ultimate opportunity for you to share the value of your employer brand. This is the moment the brand should shine. And people should celebrate their decision to join the business. Focus on your employer brand as you design and communicate all the many details of the day-to-day experience in the business, from pay to benefits to performance.
5. Carefully manage how you handle an employee's departure from the business—and your efforts to stay connected with departed employees—realizing they will talk about you to those people just starting to consider the business as a place to work. And, yes, the stages begin again.

CHAPTER SEVEN

ESSENTIAL #7: MARKET

The young professional sits at his computer. He is looking for a job.

Once upon a time, not long ago, he would have checked the classifieds in a printed newspaper for specifics and listened to trusted observers for the inside scoop. But not any more. Today the Web is his gateway to the world of working in business. That makes it an essential place for a business to live its brand. The prospective employee looking at potential places to work relies on a brand just like a prospective driver checking out cars or a shopper walking the grocery aisles. The brand represents the experience. It *is* the language of choice. And now it's online.

Like many in his generation, for the young professional what he sees on the screen is his first glimpse of the soul of a business where he may want to work.

He quickly scans the home page, much like a private investigator hunting for clues. What does the business do? What does it believe in? What does it value? Who are its customers? What would it be like to work there? Will I fit in? Will I advance? What does the business stand for? Why does the business exist?

So when this young professional finds Porsche's claim, on its internet site, that "the journey into the future is by no means a journey into the unknown," he wonders, is this a possible place for me to work?[1] Or when he reads Diageo's claim—"the customer is at the heart of everything we do"—he ponders, would I fit in here?[2] Or when he considers a statement by Johnson & Johnson that "we believe our first responsibility is to the doctors, nurses and patients, to mothers and fathers and all others who use our products and services," he thinks, well, maybe I can make a difference here.[3]

All those years ago, when we were first brand-dependent, there was a show on television with a man named Art Linkletter, with a segment called "Kids Say the Darndest Things." (The series was *House Party.*) We remembered that show when a telecommunications company wanted to demonstrate the simplicity of the company's values. An "everything I learned about values I learned in kindergarten" kind of thing. So what did we do? We got six kids from kindergarten to portray the senior leadership in a video spoof. The kids played it completely straight. The video was shot in a totally serious manner. And the result was right on target. Values even a six-year-old could understand.

—Mark

The Internet—and, inside a business, its intranet—have fundamentally changed how people find answers and insight about where and how to work. No longer is perspective limited to what is immediately within reach. Today anyone can find out what anyone thinks at the stroke of a fingertip on a keyboard. No prospective or current employee must pound the pavement to learn what a business is all about. Online opportunities, from job boards to blogs, are gateways for people within and outside of organizations to exchange information and ideas. Employer brand is right in the middle—or let's say it *should* be. A business that wants to reach its current, past, and potential talent must rethink how it communicates—in the same way, as we discussed in Chapter Five, that it must rethink the experience it designs. Your employer brand offers your business the chance to rethink how you use formal and informal communication to connect with employees. And to market the employer brand—message by message.

It's easy to recognize the importance of employer brand messaging. After all, it's at the heart of the whole issue. In fact, the 2005 Hodes research reveals that some 91 percent of human resources professionals say their organizations use the company web site to deliver employer brand messaging; 61 percent use print, 49 percent stage events, and 36 percent use email. At the same time, however, only 48 percent say they have an integrated brand communication effort.

FOCUS ON THE EXPERIENCE

Once upon a time—that is, before the Internet—any business had limited ways to tell its story. It could print brochures. Or it could plant stories in newspapers. Or it could make videotapes. And the media, because of the limitations, demanded a great deal of creativity. A business had to creatively articulate its message to catch the attention of its audience simply because everyone used the same few vehicles for outreach.

The differentiator, for many a business, was *not* the *media* selected to deliver its message but the *experience* created to support its message. So when it came to recruiting new employees, the promotional brochure certainly helped reinforce the sale, but the key selling opportunity was the in-person interview, career fair, or recruitment event. And when it came to engaging current employees and developing their support for the brand, the written materials may have reconfirmed the key messages, but the key opportunity for persuasion occurred during the face-to-face exchanges between an employee and a colleague or an employee and a supervisor or manager.

Now, the Internet, simply because it makes transmitting information so easy, makes it very easy for a business to *think* it is communicating. After all, just about anyone can set up a web site and populate it with content and—with broadband becoming pervasive—with streaming video and multimedia. But building that site in a way that attracts the user? Well, that's a different type of challenge.

The lesson of employer brand, in the internet age, is a reinvention of the ways business traditionally tells the corporate story. We must move from an emphasis on business saying what it wants to say, to an emphasis on articulating what employees (and prospective employees) need to hear—the "What's in it for me?" found in employer brand. And we must move from a reliance on media to *transmit* information, on and off line, to creating an *experience* that helps people solidify the key messages authentically *before* they are reinforced—again, on and off line.

For UPS, in 2003, the launch of a new logo "represented more than a cosmetic change," according to Tom Pizutti. "It was a signal to our customers, our shareowners, and our people that we're well-positioned within the global economy to synchronize their commerce around the world. The updated logo reflects the values, culture, and legacy of our past, yet marks the expanded vision of the company. To support the change and engage UPSers, on the day of the launch every UPSer received a small box that contained a lapel pin along with a message from our CEO, Mike Eskew. The brand mark was unveiled on our buildings, trucks, and airplanes and represented us as more than a package delivery company."

Basically, the successful communication of an employer brand must follow a specific sequence—to lead any internal and external audience from initially *experiencing* the message to *understanding* the message, *believing* in the message, and finally *doing* what the message is designed to motivate. What's unique about this approach is the emphasis on the experience—the opportunity to envelop the audience with the key messages before actually trying to help the audience understand or motivating the audience to believe.

Here's the messaging sequence for communicating employer brand.

EXPERIENCE	UNDERSTAND	BELIEVE	DO

And here's how it works.

First, the business should create the opportunity for the audience to *experience* the business and the brand. Before the business spends a great deal of effort to *tell* its story, it should create in-person, live, face-to-face opportunities to *live* the messages. The objective here is to create an experience so compelling and memorable it will motivate the audience to absorb the messages the business wants to convey. And these are not simply the traditional employee meetings, with a speaker and too many slides. The idea here is to entertain, stimulate, and motivate the audience with an experience that articulates the brand in a multisensory way. And though a face-to-face experience is always preferred, creating a sense of online experience for those who surf their way to employer brand can also be very effective.

For Hallmark, the annual Brand Week celebrations offer employees an opportunity to connect with and celebrate the power of the brand. As Dean Rodenbough remarks, "Three years ago, we held our first brand week celebration. It was an opportunity for employees to stop and think about the brand in new ways, with an emphasis on the opportunity for employees to become brand ambassadors. We encouraged them to talk about our products with their friends and acquaintances, encourage others to shop in our stores and use the products themselves. The annual Brand Week celebrations offer employees an opportunity to connect with and celebrate the power of the brand."

At the 2005 event, themed "Enriching Lives Begins With Me," a series of celebrations and events reinforced the brand connection and the role employees play as brand champions. To bring the theme to life, the meeting content and print and electronic media featured profiles of employees explaining how their job supports the company's mission of enriching lives. For example, employees were encouraged to wear branded or plum clothing as well as special lapel pins given out that year.

Among the week's events was a seminar on "Meaningful Moments," featuring a group of greeting-card writers and artists talking about their interactions with consumers on a recent publicity tour. Their comments underscored how important consumers made them feel about their work and how greeting cards had genuinely touched their lives. One of this year's employee forums featured presentations from two employee panels talking about their work. "One panel comprised greeting card writers who shared stories from consumers and how they were impacted by the cards they had created," says Rodenbough. "Another panel featured employees from a manufacturing facility and their comments about ensuring the quality of our products that consumers depend on."

Employer brand demands a new approach to employee communication, based on what an employee experiences. "When I come to work every day, it is 'How can I do the most credible job of telling the WaMu story?'" says Libby Hutchison of WaMu. "Our employer brand is infused in all communications throughout the company." In traditional employee communication, the emphasis is on the content people receive; in contrast, employer brand demands that an employee first experience the brand that the content will support.

For two companies in an acquisition, the reaction of the acquired employees was not going well. They viewed the acquiring company as a key competitor (and a tough one) that for many years had made life difficult for their business. So it was difficult for the employees to consider this company an ultimate partner. We determined that we could never get the support of the acquired employees if we relied on a traditional way to explain the business. Instead, to introduce the company, employees experienced an event focusing on all of the charitable activities the business was involved in—with representatives of each of those charities telling the story of how this business had made a difference. Employees experienced what this business could be by seeing the results of its actions rather than by picking up messages from a few printed or online words. After all, actions do speak louder than words.

—Mark

This *experience* of the employer brand will motivate the audience to take the time to *understand* what the business and the brand are all about. The *experience* can prompt a curiosity about the business that, when exercised, can help people *understand* the business, its purpose, and its values. And though most businesses rely on web sites to convey this understanding, the web sites of smart businesses (many of which are referenced in this book) are the ones that view the art of building understanding as a positive result of the experience of living the brand—even if just for a short time, even if just online.

Now, the *experience* of the employer brand, beyond motivating people to *understand,* will also persuade people to *believe.* In fact, the messages to motivate belief will be most effective if they directly connect to the *experience* the business creates—again, even if just online.

Finally, the effort to build the *experience* to motivate people to *understand* and *believe* must close the deal by persuading people to *do*; to take the necessary action or adopt the needed behavior to support the brand and the business. Again, this is much more effective and successful when directly connected to the *experience* the business develops.

Now, this sequence—from *experience* to *understand* to *believe* to *do*—should be carefully implemented in a mix of senses for the audience, so they never tire of any one approach and so they can't avoid the message. Here's how the sequence can apply to different ways to reach the audience. We have put together an overall framework for your communications of your employer brand (see Table 7.1). To put this into action, simply develop an action plan for each of the twelve squares in the grid. Your audience (primarily prospective and current employees, and, as appropriate, others as well) *will* notice. And you will see results.

When it introduced its new brand, Washington Mutual held brand rallies at some thirty locations across the country. According to Libby Hutchison, "The message was simple: 'You are WaMu.' We had a brand jingle for brand attributes. We made it fun, We made sure to show people rather than tell people. We named the people who use the brand *WaMulians*. We focused on what the brand means and what each person plays." To reinforce the experience, WaMu selected brand ambassadors to be role models for the brand, to "make the brand come alive inside," according to Hutchison.

"The campaign was anchored by 75 brand ambassadors representing all lines of business and functions," says WaMu's Linda Clark-Santos.

> The ambassadors were chosen by our executive committee because they were good living examples of our brand attributes. These brand ambassadors were passionate about the brand and support our efforts to bring the brand to life inside with our employees, so it could do the same outside with our customers. Each brand ambassador was responsible for taking the brand to a specific constituency. When we launched our brand in 2002, our brand rallies were the landmark events. Nearly 95 percent of our employees participated in the rallies. In some locations we had local talent contests, where people were invited to figure out a skit or a song that represented the brand to them, and the best of the best performed at the rallies. It was a grand home run and, two years later, nearly 85 percent of the employees could rattle off the brand attributes.

TABLE 7.1. ACTION PLAN FOR COMMUNICATING EMPLOYER BRAND.

Medium	Experience	Understand	Believe	Do
In person	Create experiences to envelop the audience in the brand and to brand imprint messages	Position and train leaders, managers, and supervisors to credibly convey key messages	Position and train leaders, managers, and supervisors to "walk the talk" to demonstrate on-brand behavior	Position and train leaders, managers, and supervisors to recognize and reward brand delivery and results
Online	Adapt the in-person experience to the online environment, focusing on how to make the business's web sites online destinations	Use the web sites to convey key messages and build fundamental awareness of the brand and the business, in a user-friendly way consistent with the experience	Use the web sites to help the audience question and confirm key beliefs forming about the brand and the business, using the interactive nature of the Web	Use the web sites to celebrate the brand delivery and results that people create from the inside, using the speed and immediacy of the Web
Offline	Adapt the in-person experience to any offline materials, such as traditional print and video	Use traditional print and video to support the effort to build fundamental awareness of the brand and the business	Use traditional print and video to confirm key beliefs forming about the brand and the business	Use traditional print and video to celebrate brand delivery and results

At its heart, employer brand is a new language for your business to tell your story—to employees, certainly, as well as other stakeholders. And if your employer brand raises the stakes on how your business creates an experience for employees, it brings your employee communication into a brand new world. For this is no longer the transmission of facts. This is the marketing of the idea on which your business is built.

Here are the eight basic standards to follow for your communication of your employer brand.

EIGHT COMMUNICATION BASICS

1. OFFER A GLIMPSE INTO THE EMOTIONAL RELATIONSHIP THAT CAN BE ESTABLISHED WITH YOUR BUSINESS.

To clearly communicate the employer brand, your business must reveal its core and define its relationship with your employees. Just sticking to the facts won't cut it. Prospective and current employees must see the parallels between your employee and customer experiences.

Consider the impact when Whole Foods Market says "we look for people who are passionate about food" on its internet site[4] or

A hotel chain's focus on employer brand reached to external audiences, including investors and prospective employees. So rather than have some leader from the company talk about the employer brand, we asked employees all over the country to make their own "home videos" about what it meant to work there. The home video version of "What's in it for me?" to work there. An entertaining, enlightening, and ultimately human articulation of the employer brand. So we put out a notice, asking people to send in tapes, and we received hundreds. People sang songs, performed dances, did raps, put on skits, and just talked about the value of the work experience. And it was magic.

—Mark

when Boeing pleas to prospective employees, "you'll be making tomorrow better"[5] or when Motorola says it makes a difference "by making things smarter and life better for people around the world"[6] or when Porsche says, "our staff can proudly state there is a piece of them in every Porsche."[7]

It's no longer enough for a business to transmit facts and expect employees to respond. Your business *must* create the multisensory experience for your employees in which the brand is present all around, in everything they see and touch, every day they work for you. In fact, marketing the employer brand reaches beyond the message. The employer brand *becomes* the fabric of the business. It *is* the DNA.

2. RETHINK YOUR APPROACH TO EMPLOYEE COMMUNICATION.

To achieve this degree of emotional connection, your business can't communicate the same old way. Employees won't believe it.

The communication infrastructure behind the employer brand is often as critical to lasting impact as what employees experience. Businesses often rethink and reinvent how the employee communication works, inside, to deliver what employees need (and the business needs) outside the function.

Two pharma companies, after they merged, articulated a new value proposition for employees. They realized that unless they addressed how they get things done as an employee communication function, all the clarity in the world directed to employees would eventually get lost, because they would go back to working the same way they always had. They had to change inside so they could change on the outside. So we got the two groups together and, based on practical employee research we had conducted about the media patterns of the two audiences, we reinvented the employee communication function to better provide what employees might actually absorb. We made certain to match the structure and process of the function to what employees needed. An interesting parallel to employer brand.

—**Mark**

Today they look for more. They are hungry for more. Information must be personal and relevant; vehicles must be accessible and flexible; leaders must be visible and consistent.

Well, this is not our father's or our mother's business, nor is it how that business communicated with our fathers and mothers. People who do employee communication, though they may have the skills of journalists, aren't really working as journalists to report the facts of a business. At the same time, however, they are not really advertisers selling a product, because their audience won't be sold. So they often find themselves caught between conflicting needs: to tell the truth or to push a message—to hype or spin.

When we started our careers, in fact, few serious communications were created expressly *for* employees. Company newsletters and magazines focused on bowling tournaments and new babies instead of the issues of the business. And when serious business messages were needed, the employees usually received a warmed-over version of what had first gone to external audiences. Tailored analysis and insight for the internal audience were rarely attempted.

We learned when we were kids that actions speak louder than words. And we learned as adults that people tell the best stories themselves. For a manufacturer of large industrial products, the message of the employer brand at the time was all about the pride people take in their work space, to make the company safer and to make the products more reliable. The idea of an employee who cares for his work space and what comes from his work space is essential to the delivery of the brand promise to customers. Well, rather than some spokesman from the company telling this story, we went to the source—to an employee who had just made all these changes to his work space. In this large plant he had changed the lighting so he could see better, changed the way he stored his tools—all these small things that added up to a sense of ownership, a strong feeling of pride, and an improved contribution to the brand. And we let him his tell his story to the entire company through a company-wide videotape.

—**Mark**

Interestingly enough, one of the first opportunities to communicate a serious issue directly to employees came in the early 1970s, with a law called the Employee Retirement Income Security Act (ERISA). This benefits legislation introduced a required communication vehicle called the SPD (short for Summary Plan Description) to provide details of benefit plans to employees. All of a sudden a business had to communicate real facts about a real issue. And in real time. Or else there were penalties.

At about the same time, things started to significantly change in business, and business slowly started to realize it needed to keep employees informed to keep them engaged. New health care premiums. New benefit programs. New ways to pay people. All these HR issues opened the door to discussion of more serious and personal issues in employee communications. This ultimately led, within a few years, to more focus in business on communicating the various dimensions of the day-to-day life at a business. Smart businesses, in fact, used the credibility of HR communication as a foundation for all employee communication.

Over time, business began to realize the power of messaging directly to employees—and the potential impact on business performance and employee engagement. If business still fell short of a clear answer to "What's in it for me?" it did at least progress, through the '80s and '90s, to greater clarity in corporate messaging, a stronger leadership presence, and a greater sensitivity to employee reaction. At the same time, legal changes spurred by business controversy have led to a stronger requirement for internal and external transparency.

You can't ever underestimate, for the evolution of the employer brand at Southwest, the importance of all the benefit communications over the years. Certainly the materials were fun and creative and supported our brand. But they also had a lot of really good functional information that helped employees get smart about their benefits and do smart things with their benefits. That was, as we talk about with brand, the big idea. We helped people get smart about benefits. And they remembered, when we asked them to get smart about other things.

—Libby

And then came the intranet. Here it was, folks, the ultimate communication tool. Or, we should say, an ultimate tool to permit a business to *think* it communicates. On one hand, business relished the speed and flexibility of the new tool; on the other hand, we realized how quickly employees could compare notes about who was telling the truth. And how quickly a business could overtax the tool, with information shoveled onto one intranet site after another with virtually no chance of ever being absorbed. Here was a tool that could throw so much information to people—more than employees could ever absorb—that a business could easily live with the illusion that it was communicating. Never mind that employees were drowning in electronic messages. The intranet sites looked good. And they offered speedy, paperless transactions. Sometimes we call this the instant-gratification approach to employee communication. That is, posting the information online, and presuming people will receive it, creates instant gratification for the sender. But that's not who we should be worrying about. This communication is not about the sender. It's about the receiver, the user.

3. AVOID THE TEMPTATION TO SPIN.

For many years we had a favorite saying: "Start with the truth and then edit."

And if it was true then, when we started, it's especially true today.

We learned, for example, in a Towers Perrin study conducted in late 2003, that American workers were hungry for the truth but simply did not feel they were being fed.[8]

This study of one thousand randomly selected employees from American companies revealed that American workers were increasingly cynical and suspicious of information they receive from their own employers—no matter the topic. In fact, just over half (51 percent) of the respondents believed their company generally told employees the truth, whereas almost a fifth (19 percent) disagreed. At the same time, 51 percent believed their companies tried too hard to spin the truth. Employees believed their companies communicated more honestly with shareholders (60 percent) and customers (58 percent) than with workers.

Employees viewed information from senior leadership as the least reliable, with almost half (48 percent) agreeing that they

Not every employee cares about every message a business delivers. Or has the time to absorb it. For example, an energy company concluded it could only reach employees with brand-related messages if we could identify the "sphere of interest" they had about the company. So we conducted extensive research with employees to learn, basically, what interested them, in what sequence, and to what degree. The results confirmed that, in fact, employees had three spheres of interest. Which they described as, "First, I care about me. Second, I care about the immediate team I work with. Third, I might care about the company, but don't push it." The only way we would successfully reach employees would be to craft the messages according to the spheres of interest, starting with "me," then "my team," and, ultimately, "the company." For a health care organization, for example, we learned through a series of research questions that employees only had eight minutes a week to absorb all the messages the company would send. And that they would only be able to absorb 90 to 120 seconds' worth at a time. With this information about the realities of the employee experience in hand, we were able to completely shift the nature of the communications to fit the shortened time frames. And to make sure, if employees only had eight minutes to absorb, we weren't trying to send them much more information.

—Mark

received more credible information from their direct supervisor than from their company's CEO.

These results, in light of employer brand, revealed a worrisome employer-employee dynamic. Survey respondents believed their employer was least open when communicating the fundamental "deal" between the company and employees—specifically, what the company needed from employees and what employees could expect to receive in return. Only half believed employers were candid about what the organization needed from employees, and well under half (39 percent) believed the company was completely open and honest in communicating what the organization offers. More than 90 percent of employees, however, claimed they were ready to hear the truth about their companies and their jobs.

The lessons of this and other research are clear. Business must keep the message simple, clear, and transparent. There's no room, when communicating with employees, for corporate-sounding sentences with lots of big words. And lots of punctuation is not a hallmark of corporate-sounding sentences. Employees today want facts. Just the facts. The young professional looking at businesses online does not want to be slowed by hype. If hype is what he finds, he'll move on. Likewise, people at other stages in their careers become immune to corporate words that all sound just the same no matter the business. But they do respond to words that speak directly to what's important to them. A business must search its soul before it begins to package. Communication about brand is not about facts. It's all about ideas and feelings. And it should be a *sound bite* for everything the business is known for. So a business must avoid the temptation to explain. Instead, it should tell. Share. Show. Let other employees see when employees deliver the brand.

To authentically deliver the employer brand message, it makes a real difference to get to know the environment in which the message will be received. Talking with employees in focus groups about how they use communications can help. And it really can make a difference if you experience their workplace. If you, as the saying goes, walk a mile in their shoes.

A snack food manufacturer was set to communicate many issues to truck drivers who deliver products to grocery stores. These issues had everything to do with how truck drivers would answer the WIIFM question—specifically, around how they were paid for their work and how routes were assigned. Not necessarily crowd-pleasing messages. Before we could imagine how to approach them, we needed to absorb the environment. So we spent a couple of days riding the trucks with the drivers to deliver products to the stores. We did the work side by side with the drivers. This enabled us to absorb what they consider important, how they view the company, and how they would view these potential changes to their rewards. We absorbed their reality, so that we in turn could determine the best way to reach them. And to be consistent.

—Mark

4. Set a new voice and tone for employee communication.

Employer brand can make a difference.

And a focus on trust reconfirms why business needs employer brand. It can break the spin cycle by creating a credible communication experience with employees, incorporating a range of media and message.

Employer brand can set a new tone for employee communication in any business by working from the heart of the business. The fact is, employee communicators are *not* reporters. The job is *not* to report the news. Employee communicators are *not* spin doctors. The job is *not* to spin the message. The job *is* to look at your business through the eyes of your employees. That's at the heart of the employer brand and the role of the employee communicator. But it won't happen just because you plant persuasive messages in key communications. It will happen only if you provide evidence for your employees to absorb. And if you trust they will know what to do with the information. If you feed them what they are hungry to hear. As Jeff Swystun and Larry Oakner remark, "aligning the internal brand requires company-wide communications and employee-focused education to help them understand and actualize their valuable roles in expressing the brand and its values through behaviors."[9] To effectively market your employer brand, your communication must begin with what employees want and need.

When welcoming Gillette employees to P&G, the company said, "Our success, both as a company and as individuals, is dependent on the success of everyone who works with and joins P&G. Being able to mine 'the best of the best' is key to achieving greatness. It begins with each of us, through our mindset and the behaviors we practice each and every day." The focus on mindset begins with an admission that, in the past, "P&G was not always fully open to 'outsiders'" with reference to "a sense that 'P&G's arrogance' led us at times to discount the diverse experiences of others." The publication continues with a commitment to valuing diverse thought and taking personal responsibility to embrace other employees, with the acknowledgment "Joining P&G from another company is a significant transition—and one I need to be sensitive to." The publication continues to list specific behaviors for P&G employees to display, including reaching out to make people feel welcome; understand their talents; explain how we work, learn from one another, make connections, and shape the future.[10]

Any communication of employer brand is designed to sustain real change. That won't happen if your business communicates using all of the old words. It's impossible. The communication of the employer brand should use a new manner—set a new tone. It needs to be a voice that reflects the qualities of the brand. And the priorities of the people. Your employer brand can and must create a new language for your business to use to express itself. In fact, it could be said that the only way your business will get maximum return for its investment in employer brand is if the brand leads to the language. Otherwise your business may try to express new ideas with old words. And that's a little like old wine in new bottles.

At the same time, your employer brand, just like your customer brand, extends a promise that the business will offer a specific experience in return for a specific commitment. For a customer, such a promise involves what result a product or service will create for the buyer in return for the purchase. For an

An industrial products company had just been through the wringer. Everything that could go wrong went wrong. Lawsuits. Failed businesses. It was Murphy's Law. But the company had held true to its values, even when it might have been more expedient to abandon them. And that was the story. Well, if the company talked about how great it was because it stuck to its values, it could have come across as a very defensive "aren't we terrific even though we're broke" saga. Instead, we secured outsiders to talk about all the bad luck that had occurred and how the company had responded, with minimal participation from company leaders. The credibility of the third-party observations, as well as the undersell of the message, made it work.

—Mark

employee, such a promise involves how the employee will be rewarded for contributing to the business. Such a "total rewards" package will include elements of pay, benefits, learning, development and career opportunity, and the work environment. And employees want to easily access the details that support any broader messages. On their own time. Just in time. This necessitates a communication infrastructure with simplified online access that enables employees to find what they need when they need it.

5. POSITION THE SENIOR LEADERS AS *THE* MESSAGE.

Your senior leaders must be, essentially, poster children for the behaviors associated with your employer brand. They must live the brand promise. And avoid any say/do gaps that employees will remember and repeat. Their actions must mirror your brand image and promise. And they must be prepared for their actions to be copied throughout a business that will remember, for a long time, *how* they communicate more than *what* they communicate. As Diana Shaheen of P&G observes, "A CEO must demonstrate on-brand behaviors for employees to see as he or she interacts with consumers, customers, shoppers, and employees."

"If you build it, they will come." But online, if you build it, and it doesn't make sense, and people can't find what they want, they get frustrated. A pharma company working on their employer brand talked with employees and learned that the key gap in answering "What's in it for me?" was that people could not find what they needed to know on a very confusing HR intranet site. So we put the site through "web rehab" by using employees to help us redesign the site according to what would be an intuitive way to navigate—the same way external sites work with customers. The outcome? A redesigned, easier-to-navigate site that, through its improved functionality, enables employees to find what they want. And answer the "WIIFM" question."

—**Mark**

Anyone who follows business legends would consider Herb Kelleher a legend. No other business leader, perhaps, has so successfully combined the personality and passion with the common sense and purposeful risk. And he has led a team to create a legendary company by remembering how it started, focusing on the values, and valuing the customer. Our internal freedom at Southwest did not simply happen because we wanted it to happen. We created it over many years, one element at a time, in parallel to the freedom we created for our customers. Herb was at the heart of our declaration of freedom. His laugh. His spirit. His energy. And his generosity in realizing the result of the idea is what matters.

—**Libby and Mark**

6. POSITION AND TRAIN MANAGERS AND SUPERVISORS.

Impressions of senior leaders, though excellent fodder for informal discussion in break rooms or chat rooms, rarely will directly touch where an employee works. And for that immediate work experience—what an employee sees and feels every day—your immediate supervisors will be a window on your business. The employee who simply does not care where your business is going, and may never care, *will* care about how an immediate supervisor treats people in the work area.

At FedEx, managers are trained in the Purple Promise and are clearly told they are at the heart of the company's success. Management understands that their role in motivating employees and recognizing the behavior that makes every FedEx experience outstanding is critical to our success. As Eric Jackson describes it, "Every year we hold a customer summit, to replicate every step of the customer experience, from ordering our service, to tracking a delivery, to filing a claim. We put our senior management through an experience that is typical for our customers. We listen to customers, we gather the customer experiences, the good, the bad and the ugly, and we boil that down to reengineer internal processes and activities to meet those needs, to identify what we need to change to exceed customer expectations."

At Southwest we always said that our managers were the keepers of our culture. That is why we invested in manager and supervisor training. Supervisor training was a three-month program that included one week in the classroom each month for three months and on-the-job assignments called "Quest," with refreshers every couple of years called "Re-Quest." Our premiere training, "MIT," was for managers in training to become our future leadership. The content of the training included all of the usual management topics, with the key cultural messages and emphasis on the type of experience that managers and supervisors provided to their people.

—Libby

7. REINFORCE "WHAT'S IN IT FOR ME?" IN EVERY MESSAGE.

The subtext of every message an employee may receive must be "This is why it makes sense for you to work at this business"—to address the WIIFM issues that employees bring to work. No matter the topic, from the performance of the business to the painting of lines in the parking lot, the underlying message is always one of value—based on the specific direction of the employer brand.

Saying all of this one time, or one time every so often, is not enough. For these key WIIFM messages to stick, they must be repeated over and over, in every possible way, in every possible medium, until they become second nature to employees. And they begin to relate to the messages the same way they do to the cracks in a floor. They feel natural.

For any given period of time—a month, a quarter, a year—identify three key employer brand messages. And include them in every possible communication employees receive. Fact is, if you, as the creator of the message, start to tire of them, that probably is just about when employees will start to pay attention. The *only* way to break through the noise of business today is to repeat. And repeat. And repeat.

One challenge, when communicating employer brand, arises when the company has a whole range of consumer brands that look and feel much different from each other—and in some cases actually represent different businesses whose values may differ from each other, with resulting variations in employer brand. That's when it makes sense to brand at two levels—the larger umbrella brand of the overall company as well as the more specific brand of one particular part of the business.

A hotel chain branded the overall business, with emphasis on what was shared overall, as well as the specific logos, with emphasis on what was specific to that brand. Employees could see "This is my opportunity where I work today" and "This could be the opportunity where I could work tomorrow." A consumer products company, as well, made the overall brand all about the values that bind the various logos, with the message, "No matter where in our world you work, here are the things we stand for. And, sometimes the best way to tell the company story is to tell the story of everything happening around the company without overselling the company point of view."

—Mark

Part of the development of the communication approach is the identification of the key on-brand messages to support the employer brand. We were working with a retail chain, developing employer brand, developing the employer brand messages, and applying them to every story they would tell their employees. We created a new process for them to follow to incorporate the messages and check on the credibility of the messages. But literally every story featured one or more on-brand messages, whether the topic was a new approach to selling shoes or new stripes in the parking lot.

—Mark

8. OFFER SOME PERSONALITY.

The communication of the employer brand is not just about the details. It's about the very aspects of your brand that make it unique. And usually that directly relates to the personality of your business. Employees want the communications to celebrate the characteristics, attributes, and experiences that differentiate the business. So they are happy to say where they work.

As you communicate employer brand, if you try to create a new tone, a new feel, a more emotional approach, stop yourself from retreating to old habits when the topics may return to the more conventional. Your employees are exposed to thousands of messages each day. Advertisers constantly change how they tell their stories, simply because employees become immune to the same old material. Business must do the same. Otherwise, when you reach out to employees, they may be more difficult to find.

With more than thirty thousand employees all over the country, good things happen at Southwest from coast to coast. Many of these things were captured in writing, and sometimes in pictures or on video, by customers and fellow employees. We needed a way to get the word out. In typical Southwest fashion, it didn't have to be fancy or high tech. Our customer relations team just saved the best, most heartwarming customer letters they received each month. They copied them and stapled them together and sent them to all SWA leaders and asked them to read these and pass them on to their teams. Without fail, at least one letter in the packet would bring tears to the readers' eyes. There were stories about little old ladies and children abandoned at the airport, and how employees had helped them. Stories about employees who assisted customers in very embarrassing and sometimes unpleasant situations. Stories about people traveling to aid loved ones who had been injured, or to funerals. The letters not only informed fellow employees how to handle difficult situations in the best possible or most creative manner, but they also created a sense of pride in the organization. Pride generated by the employees who knew their actions were not only commended by a customer or fellow employee, but were now being read and discussed by all.

—Libby

Be careful when you take the employer brand public. Be careful about actually announcing you are taking the employer brand public or that there is an employer brand in the first place. This is a case in which maybe just doing it is a lot smarter than talking about it. That's because employees can be very sensitive about the term *brand*.

A technology company asked us to do some focus groups before addressing employer brand issues. And in these focus groups we showed a bunch of materials the company had produced for employees, all emblazoned with a logo of an internal promotion—an internal brand, if you will. Well, the employees rejected the idea of the brand, and said, "Brands are for selling something, we don't need our company to sell anything to us, we just need them to give us the facts, just the facts." Well, the company did need to market its employer brand, but we turned the tables to launch what we called the "unbrand strategy" (kind of like, remember "7-Up, The Uncola"?) so people would *experience* the brand, not just hear about the brand. We planted the evidence for them to put together.

—Mark

Five Essential Steps

1. Consider your business commitment to transparency in communication with employees—and your willingness to set standards for candor as you communicate the employer brand.
2. Consider if your organization is at all "caught up" in spinning stories for employees—and what it will take to break this pattern.
3. Consider what changes in the behavior of senior leaders may be needed to tighten any say/do gaps that may exist in your organization.
4. Consider what tone of voice—what blend of the personal and the business—is needed in your organization to make the employer brand story credible.
5. Consider what happens in your business during the editing process that makes even the most simple of stories sound very, very complicated. Who is getting their fingers in the pie?

CHAPTER EIGHT

ESSENTIAL #8: NURTURE

OK. You've diagnosed your employer brand, put your team together, developed your employer brand step by step, applied it stage by stage, and marketed it message by message.

So what do you do now? Have a party?

Not yet.

Like any new thing just created, or old thing just rejuvenated, your employer brand must be carefully nurtured if you hope for it to stay alive.

Ultimately, an employer brand is only as successful as the way in which it directs the choices people make every day. After all, that's what a brand is all about. So to keep the employer brand alive, you must focus on that person-by-person commitment. As the brand champion you have a responsibility to live up to all the good work you have put together so far. And you need to be on the lookout for the many things that can push your employer brand off track. Don't want that to happen? Here's a few things you need to do right away. Because it can be *very* easy for your employer brand to get off track.

1. DOCUMENT ALL THE WORK YOU HAVE DONE.

At the end of the day, you need one document that summarizes all of the work you have done to develop the employer brand, as well as how to apply it to the various programs and messages that make up the employee experience.

This "brand guide" will be your ultimate summary of the work you have done. And its contents should capture the substance and nuance of your work to develop your employer brand.

Why your business needs an employer brand. The definitive statement of what role the employer brand will play in the ability of your business to meet its strategic objectives. What difference the employer brand can make to the various stakeholders of your business—especially customers and employees. And how the employer brand can articulate what your business stands for, as a place to buy and a place to work.

What objectives your employer brand will support. The clear declaration of the scope of the employer brand work. If your employer brand will help your business clarify the behavior needed to deliver the brand promise to customers. If your employer brand will be used to help recruit, retain, and engage employees.

What promise your employer brand makes. What the brand promise is to prospective, current, and former employees—how that connects to the brand promise to customers as well as the "big idea" the business stands for. This could be in the form of an employer brand positioning statement to mirror what your marketers may have developed for the external brand.

How your employer brand translates your customer brand. How the attributes of the customer brand translate into the behaviors needed to deliver that promise—as well as the functional and emotional characteristics of your customer brand.

How your employer brand applies to each stage of the employee experience. How, based on the work you completed in Chapter Six, your employer brand is used to frame each stage of the employee experience, from when the employee first hears about the business, through joining, to eventual departure from the business.

What standards your employer brand must follow. Through each program and message, what standards of clarity and consistency your employer brand must adhere to as a discipline for your business, to keep employees (and what they deliver to customers) at the core of how your business works.

How to measure whether your employer brand is working. What specific milestones your employer brand must accomplish for your business to make the necessary contribution—as we'll explore in this chapter.

Now, put all the thinking, and your work through all the steps, into your brand guide.

At Hallmark, for example, this documentation focused on the visual side of the brand. According to Dean Rodenbough,

> Until five years ago, our standards for the visual presentation of the brand centered primarily on the logo, with few guidelines for other presentation elements. Today we have guidelines in place to create a consistent identity. As part of this process, we began with consumer research to better understand how consumers perceived the brand. Then we articulated a brand essence and our creative team developed an aesthetic point of view. First for design standards around the brand logo and color palette, and second for the look and feel of our marketing materials, in-store merchandising, and product packaging. Finally, a brand architecture was established so the company could better manage consistency among more than a dozen subsidiaries and sub-brands.

UPS maintains the UPS Brand Exchange, the official brand resource for its communities, customers, and suppliers. "The web site offers all the tools necessary to effectively communicate the power of the UPS brand," says Tom Pizutti. The organization recognizes the importance of protecting the brand and that "companies with leading brands work hard to ensure that their communications and the experiences they deliver are consistent everywhere they go."

> For any customer brand, a business creates a very detailed set of brand guidelines: the specific rules of how anyone associated with the business can use the brand, from the tone of the voice to the color of the logo. So there's no guesswork. And the brand is kept consistent.
>
> The need is just as great on the inside. Every employer brand, once developed, needs such a set of guidelines. For one technology company, this resides on its intranet, available to anyone preparing to talk about what happens inside the business. There are very specific rules to follow. And the people who monitor the rules are quite willing to issue violation "tickets" to offenders, if needed.
>
> **—Mark**

2. DOCUMENT WHAT YOUR EMPLOYER BRAND MUST MEAN TO EACH OF THE FUNDAMENTAL SYSTEMS THAT SUPPORT YOUR BUSINESS.

Each business has fundamental systems that are essential to its ability to get things done each day.

For the employer brand to "live" in your business, you must specify how it applies to each of these systems.

Recruitment and staffing. How your employer brand will be used as a fundamental message of the employee experience for prospective employees—as well as a key strategic element to achieve staffing objectives. You will want to base recruitment advertising on the employer brand, to keep messaging consistent inside and outside.

Acquisitions. Again, how your employer brand will be used as a key strategy to help onboarding acquired employees—by crystallizing the opportunities and expectations your business carries.

Communications. How your employer brand frames how your business communicates with employees—specifically, in the clarity and relevance of business messages that should resonate with employees. Says Diageo's Yvonne Larkin, "We have an integrated corporate relations function that governs all external and internal messaging. This helps to drive consistency about how we articulate what we stand for."

Marketing. How the external marketing of your business and its brand must consider the promises of the employer brand—to maximize the handoff from the work to market your business to the people who actually deliver to your customers.

Operations. How the employer brand can define what your business must deliver to customers, not just through on-brand behavior, but through the successful delivery of key elements your business must have to get things done, day by day.

Policies. How your employer brand, and what it promises, is carefully considered when developing the specific rules and regulations and guidelines that, when added up, define a great deal of your employee experience.

Leadership. How the employer brand, and the behaviors it requires, influence what your business expects from leaders—and how your leaders can be held accountable for demonstrating such on-brand behaviors.

The key rules of cross-functional teams, as explored in Chapter Four, hold true in keeping the brand alive. Says Linda Boff at GE, "The employer brand works when it is part of the overall marketing and communications rhythm and planning. Our chief marketing officer owns all communications internal and external, all marketing advertising, and our commercial sales efforts. As a result, my colleagues are the people who do advertising, brand, public relations, internet, market research, and if it were not that way it would be a real challenge. The beauty is when they all knit together. The silo'd approach, on the other hand, is less productive."

3. MANAGE YOUR BRAND IMPLEMENTATION AS A CHANGE PROCESS.

Because it *is* a change process.

Your employer brand articulates the promise of an experience, and the results it generates, that ultimately support the business strategy.

The way to tell your brand is alive is when you first begin to notice that it takes on a life of its own. An example of that happened at Southwest. One day I was flying and ordered a beverage. I noticed that one side of the cocktail napkin said "Log on for low fares" and the other side said "We are looking for people, people!" and directed interested candidates to our careers site. I was head of HR and had no idea we had an ad on the back of the napkin. Marketing just did that when they ordered the next set of napkins to promote the web site. They figured if they were going to promote southwest.com, they could also promote that Southwest careers were listed there!

—Libby

It's unlikely, unless your business is fundamentally perfect, that you already do everything that you declare your employer brand must do.

So the effort to move your business and your people from point A to point B—from the current state to the desired end state—is ultimately a change process. And it needs to be planned and managed as a change process.

Now, for those of you who are familiar with textbook approaches to change, the one we're suggesting is a bit more practical and to the point.

In a nutshell, we suggest you follow a five-point change process as you plan how to implement the employer brand—so it sticks with your employees.

Picture the end state—what it will mean for your business, for employees, for customers, for your employer brand to be successfully implemented, for it to "live." What it will mean to your employee experience, stage by stage, as well as to the processes supporting that experience.

Assess the current state—what happens today that will need to change for your business to consistently experience the end state of the employer brand. Specifically, this is a matter of working through each segment of your audience, assessing the potential and risk of that segment to live the brand and their willingness and ability to make the change to the end state experience.

Construct the interventions—what your business needs to stage, in terms of informal and formal experience, indirect and direct communication, to motivate employees to move from the current state to the end state experience of the employer brand. This usually involves a sequence of face-to-face and other types of contact to shift position and persuade employees to jump on the brand bandwagon.

Craft and deliver the story—how your business tells its story, message by message, to all your various stakeholders, to support the effort to move from the current to the end state expe-rience.

Measure the return on investment—how your business estimates its return on this investment in employer brand, based on specific measures outlined at the outset of the change process.

A transportation company based in Asia created a new employer brand as part of a major change in ownership. As part of this change it went through all the diagnostics, thinking, and planning required to brand from inside. But it decided, in a bold, clear move, to refrain from actually talking about its work as its employer brand. It did not want to spoil the essence of the work, which it considered so vital to the long-term health of the business, by affixing a label that employees might or might not understand. So rather than implement "an employer brand," the business designed a change process—with the end result in parallel to the end state of the employer brand (actually following the steps detailed in this book). By implementing a change process rather than the launch of a brand, the business carefully avoided any sense of hype. Instead, the focus was naturally on the end result of employees making, in some cases, significant changes in behavior. And of course, it was on-brand behavior they changed to.

—Mark

4. DEVELOP A SUSTAINED EFFORT TO SUPPORT YOUR EMPLOYER BRAND.

At the same time you are managing the employer brand as a change process, you need to put some fundamental elements of *infrastructure* into place. In fact, the commitment of your business to put the *systems* in place to support the employer brand is as critical to its success as any of the work you have done up to this point.

Basically, you need to implement four fundamental ways to do business—four systematic approaches—to support your employer brand on an ongoing basis.

Coach leaders. Your senior leaders *must* live the attributes of your employer brand. There's no shortcut for this one. They must be the walking examples of what your brand means and what difference your brand can make. They must authentically represent the values your brand articulates. And they can't let up. Your employees, given an inherent cynicism we experience every day, will search for clues to a say/do gap. They will study leaders for evidence of inconsistent action and message.

As brand champion, you must orchestrate how your senior leaders visibly demonstrate that the employer brand is real.

Focus people programs. In Chapter Six you developed your employer brand according to the stages of an employee's relationship with your business. Now, to sustain your employer brand, you must carefully embed the brand into your process to develop, design, and implement *any* and *all* people programs that ultimately define the employee experience. *Every* program or strategy or initiative you begin to develop for your employees *must* begin with a reorientation to the promise of your employer brand. Otherwise the ultimate deliverable will not be consistent. And you may, without intending to, undermine your employer brand.

Shape communications. You developed your employer brand message in Chapter Seven. Now you must embed that message into how you exchange information in your business. On the inside, your employer brand—what it promises and what it stands for—must be at the heart of *every* message and approach you develop to connect with employees. So no matter where they look for messages—from the intranet site they go to every day, to the special communications you develop on specific topics—they experience consistent, clear *on-brand* messages authentic to the business. Such media efforts must be supported behind the scenes as you

A hotel organization was looking for a way to recognize and reward employees who did the right thing. So it put together a program whereby customers could report their positive experiences with employees—perhaps extra service they received, extra effort they noticed. And employees, as notes were written about them, were awarded prizes. Well, the whole thing caught on in a major way, and customers expressed how much they enjoyed being asked to participate in an employee program. The results were positive, too—we found that as we encouraged customers to notice and report positive employee behavior, the behavior continued to strengthen.

—Mark

prepare managers and supervisors to effectively communicate with employees. And this must be supported on the outside by sustained marketing and communication to *tell the story* of the employer brand to customers, prospective employees, and members of the community—to create and maintain the reputation of your business as a place to work and a place to buy. That's the heart of your employer brand.

Involve employees. It's not enough to deliver your employer brand message. Your efforts to sustain the momentum must rely on real-time participation of employees. One way to capitalize on the integrated approach to your employer brand that got you to this point in the first place is to put together a brand advisory group. You may be the champion of the employer brand but, as you learned while developing the employer brand, you simply can't do everything on your own. That multidiscipline approach you followed to develop your employer brand must, in some way, stay together as you manage the employer brand—at least in an advisory capacity. With this as a foundation, your sustained effort must provide opportunities for employees to get involved, from helping you monitor the reactions of customers to participating as buddies with new employees. Only if employees get the chance to *live* the brand can you hope for them to *remember* the brand.

At Hallmark, consumer feedback and stories frequently remind employees at all levels about the power of the brand name. Says Dean Rodenbough,

> For the last three years, the company's public relations team has managed a program known as Writers and Artists on Tour. It involves greeting-card writers and artists traveling back to the cities where they grew up and holding public events to talk about the art of greeting-card writing. We hold events at libraries, community centers, coffee shops, and other venues and invite our consumers and members of the public to learn from the writers and artists and share their own stories and experiences. In each market, the writers and artists do media interviews and talk about the relevance of greeting-card sending today. It's a great forum to promote the brand and our products, as well as to collect amazing consumer experiences. In fact, to date we've created three commercials for the Hallmark Channel from the stories shared during these events. In addition, we also invite consumers to share their card stories and experiences on hallmark.com. The postings are proof points for

our employees to better understand the impact of their work on consumers' lives.

5. COMMIT TO MEASURE THE IMPACT OF YOUR EMPLOYER BRAND.

It all boils down to "Is this effort worth the effort?" And is your business getting a return on its investment in employer brand? That will not be an easy question to answer, simply because, as we have learned throughout this book, employer brand reaches so many facets of a business.

At UPS, the "Employee Relations Index (ERI) is an annual opportunity for all UPS people to express opinions and help make UPS an even better place to be," according to Tom Pizutti, "and we have done the survey each year since 1983. We assess how we are tracking against our commitment to live the values. We benchmark to other organizations. The survey is very visible in terms of its importance to the business. And real action plans come out of the survey results." Diageo's Yvonne Larkin adds, "Our annual Global Values Survey monitors levels of employee engagement and overall progress against the employer brand. As well as analyzing year-on-year changes, we benchmark our performance against other industry leaders."

A department store chain had a very clear sense of its identity, which it used to brand from the inside. And it carried through the implementation of that brand to every fiber of the business. Every policy. Every program. So much so that, in every communication with employees, three on-brand messages were highlighted. Each year the company would go through a planning exercise to select the three brand messages for that year. And by the end of the year they could be certain every employee would remember them, because every employee would hear the key messages over and over. It didn't matter if a communication was about the parking lot or the company picnic, the three key messages to support the employer brand were included. Repeat, repeat, repeat was the approach. And employees certainly did remember.

—Mark

Hallmark's Dean Rodenbough reports, "One category of employee feedback, carefully monitored through a Gallup survey, is 'The mission and purpose of my company makes me feel that my job is important.' In 2005, brand awareness and education efforts were aimed at improving scores in this area. Our employee communications focused on how various employee jobs throughout the company supported the company's mission. As our program evolves, the focus of our brand work is based on what we learn in surveys and focus groups about morale and engagement."

One way to accurately measure the impact of your employer brand is to implement a 360-degree monitoring effort. Call it *full circle feedback* for an employer brand. Let's take a closer look at how this works.

To accurately measure whether your employer brand is working, you need to assess your business as a place to buy (the customer experience) and a place to work (the employee experience). You have to measure both experiences to get the complete picture of the difference your employer brand makes.

Let's look at each one—what you need to measure and how you can get the work done. And keep it going.

A place to buy: The customer experience.
The ultimate result of the employer brand is the difference it makes to the customer—who decides, simply, to buy more. And to tell others.

So your measurement of the employer brand impact on the customer experience must focus on their awareness, choice, use, and loyalty—key parts of the customer experience that your employer brand can influence. This look must include the *functional* reaction of the customer as well as the *emotional* connection to your brand and your business. You need to measure each of the eight elements in Table 8.1.

Measuring each of the eight items will give you a *full circle* view of customer awareness, choice, use, and loyalty. These are key findings to assess the impact of your employer brand.

To get these findings, you need to systematically review information your business likely receives about customers, as well as to periodically invest in some customer research of your own.

Your ideal measurement strategy should include four components.

TABLE 8.1. EIGHT ELEMENTS OF THE CUSTOMER EXPERIENCE.

	Awareness	*Choice*	*Use*	*Loyalty*
Functional	Do customers know the brand, what it stands for, what it promises?	Do customers choose the business because of the reliability of its brand?	Do customers experience the reliability of the brand and the business?	Do customers trust the brand and the business and, as a result, come back for more?
Emotional	Do customers connect with the brand, what it stands for, what it promises?	Do customers choose the business because they connect with the brand?	Do customers engage with the brand as they use products and services?	Do customers advocate for the brand and the business?

Ongoing review of operations data. Any business manages data to measure the effectiveness and efficiency of the operation. You need to monitor this data for clues to what may be going right and what may be going wrong in your day-to-day business. Any breakdowns in service the data reveal may be symptoms of more significant breakdowns in employee engagement that you, as the champion of the employer brand, must in turn address.

Ongoing review of customer letters. As a standard part of doing business for employer brand, collaborate with the appropriate internal departments to regularly review customer letters for clues about how the employer brand is connecting to the customer experience. Specifically, look for any comments, positive or negative, that directly relate to the functional and emotional reactions customers may be having—as well as specific breakdowns in the operations that they may cite. As well, the general tone of customer feedback will help you assess whether the reputation of your business is supporting the natural ups and downs that can occur when a business offers a product or service.

Periodic interviews with customers. At least once each year you need to talk with customers yourself about what they experience. In part because only the more extreme situations may motivate customers to write letters. And also because you simply need to talk with customers directly to clearly learn what impact your employer brand may have. You can't just rely on the data others provide. You know, as the champion of your employer brand, what those customers must experience. So you need to be the one (you or your team, of course) to find out if it's happening.

Ongoing scan of media coverage. For better or for worse, the news media will cover what happens between a business and its customers. And most of those stories will focus on the negative. As the champion of the brand you must carefully monitor what the news media are saying, because all of those reports contribute to the reputation of your business as a place to buy and, as well, as a place to work. As you monitor the news, pay close attention to any phrases reporters use over and over to describe the business, its relationship with customers, and its relationship with employees. Many reporters, once they get a phrase in mind, have a hard time letting go. Depending on what you monitor, part of your ongoing communication strategy should be the proactive effort to educate key people in the news media about what you're doing inside the business to make a difference on the outside.

These facts, from the outside, will help you and your employer brand team develop interventions to strengthen the employee commitment to deliver the brand experience to customers. Only when you base your work on the facts can you hope to sustain levels of commitment and result.

A place to work: The employee experience.
If the ultimate result of your employer brand is the difference it makes to your customer, then what happens on the inside, as we have discussed throughout this book, is the ultimate driver.

As you monitor and measure the customer experience, you must pay close attention to the employee experience and connect what you learn from both perspectives.

Just as you measure the employer brand impact on the *customer* experience, your measurement of the *employee* experience must *also*

A major business had a challenge with a local news reporter. No matter the story, the reporter would use the term *beleaguered* to describe the company. It didn't matter if the news item was a financial report or a charity event, the reference was always to this *beleaguered* organization. Now, this might not concern every organization, but it did concern this one, simply because the notion of it as beleaguered was starting to stick and, most important, starting to influence how potential employees viewed the business as a place to work. So the very strategic communications staff concluded that the only way to get *beleaguered* out of the copy was to get *beleaguered* out of the reporter's mind. So the staff decided to invest substantial time to educate the reporter on all the specific programs and opportunities the company was offering to employees to make a difference in the day-to-day lives of employees. And how that in turn was making a difference to customers and results. Ultimately the reporter changed his wording.

—Mark

focus on their awareness, choice, use, and loyalty—key factors that influence the customer experience. This look needs to include the *functional* reaction of the employee as well as the *emotional* connection to your brand and your business. Again, you need to measure each of the eight items shown in Table 8.2.

Measuring these eight items will, just as on the outside, give you a *full circle* view of the impact of your employer brand.

Just as with customers, to get these findings, you need to systematically review information your business likely collects about employees and periodically invest in some employee research of your own.

Your ideal measurement strategy should include five components:

Ongoing engagement data. Your business may conduct regular surveys of employees to measure their engagement in the business. As brand champion you need to directly connect to this effort so you can influence the content and tone of the questions as well as participate in the review of the findings. Most important, as you interpret the results and apply those findings to the people programs

Table 8.2. Eight Elements of the Employee Experience.

	Awareness	Choice	Use	Loyalty
Functional	Do employees know the employer brand, what it stands for, what it promises?	Do prospective employees choose the business partly because of its reliable reputation as an employer?	Do employees, once they join the business, believe they can get things done?	Do employees trust the employer brand and the business as a place to work?
Emotional	Do employees connect with the employer brand, what it stands for, what it promises?	Do prospective employees choose the business partly because of an emotional connection?	Do employees believe in the inspirational and aspirational qualities of the employer brand?	Do employees advocate for the employer brand and the business?

and communications you design to sustain your employer brand, you can help people inside the business connect the dots.

Pulse surveys. On a regular basis, it makes a lot of sense to ask employees specific questions that directly relate to their perspectives of the customer and employee experiences. If you have an intranet site, check if you have the capability to add a simple "question of the day" with a posting of results. Even a simple question, such as what employees experience and what they observe that customers experience, can reinforce the fundamentals of your employer brand as well as give you specific clues you may need to monitor.

Recruitment surveys. A key reaction to capture is that of the recruit who has just completed the recruitment experience. Those hired and, yes, those who were not hired can provide valuable insight. It's critical to learn how your employer brand did or did not contribute to this experience. And what perception of your business the recruit will carry, regardless of the hiring outcome.

Employee focus groups. Although an ongoing commitment to engagement surveys is an important business tool, the specifics of employer brand demand something more—a qualitative discussion with employees about, simply, what it means to work at your business. This is most effectively handled in a small group discussion. And such discussions should be conducted, on a sample basis at selected locations, at least once a year. The content should focus on the functional as well as the emotional dimensions of your business as a place to work. Specifically, you need to look for employee reaction to the following:

Understand. If your employees understand the promise the brand makes to customers and the role employees must play in delivering that promise.

Believe. If your employees believe in the authenticity of the brand promise to customers based on the authenticity of their experience as employees.

Do. If your employees make the effort, every day, to exceed your customers' expectations to deliver the brand promise.

But that's not enough. You also need to assess how your employees' emotional connection to your business and the brand naturally evolve as the employer brand becomes more a part of the daily experience. Specifically, you need to look for employee reaction to the following:

Appeal. How does your employer brand emotionally appeal to employees?

Connection. How strong is the emotional connection your employees feel to your brand and your business—or is it just a place to work? How does your business nurture that connection?

Aspirational. How does your employer brand help employees picture what working at the business can mean to them—the answer to the WIIFM question.

Inspirational. How your employees identify with and internalize what the business is all about in the first place: why it exists, what it values, what *big idea* it pursues.

Ongoing tools. One attempt to promote the employer brand will not take care of it all. And just as marketers have, at their fingertips, a number of established tools for the customer brand, so must people who focus on your employer brand.

Marketers, for example, can access methodology developed by businesses such as InterBrand and Young and Rubicam to measure the value or equity of brands. Such tools measure, using statistically valid means, the various factors well known to make brands successful. With brand now recognized as one of the most valuable intangible corporate assets, brand metrics are quickly becoming standards on corporate dashboards globally. At the same time, corporate communicators have various indexes to measure corporate reputation and the effectiveness of employee communications.

Valuation methodology for employer brand, on the other hand, has not yet become standardized. In fact, not much has been written on the subject. But that's OK. Because from the start we have believed that employer brand is a means to an end, not an end in itself. And the end to which it works is the performance of your business and the contribution of talent to that performance. Business has many ways to monitor this.

Many of the "best of" business lists include some excellent tools for measuring employer brand. The 100 Best includes a copyrighted trust index that measures how a sample group of employees rates the business on credibility, respect, fairness, pride, and camaraderie.[1] If you participate in the survey, you will have to catalog, through a culture audit, what makes your business special when it comes to benefits and compensation, professional and personal growth opportunities, recognition and rewards, how you treat and value people, communication and information sharing, employee pride, and other things that make your business special. The process includes a survey with a random sample of employees that can show you where you stand.

At the same time, HR can measure the effectiveness of HR programming—taking each program and looking for a quantifiable way to determine if it is delivering value. For example, are incentive plans yielding desired results? Are stated objectives being met? Is there a significant difference between the rewards for your best performers and those for the average workers? Do you have a good way to differentiate? Does base pay attract and retain the right candidates? Do participants in learning and development programs actually deliver at higher performance levels?

What value does your culture contribute? Is your culture a clear competitive advantage in the talent marketplace? Is it healthy? Are your managers and leaders effective? Do they make the right decisions about employees? Do they attract good people and confront difficult issues such as weeding out poor performers? Do they communicate honestly even when messages are difficult?

How does the experience you deliver to employees rate, compared with those delivered by your competitors—those with whom you compete for talent? If you have embarked on process improvement, *has* there been improvement?

A place to lead: The executive experience.

Besides measuring your employer brand, it is also important to measure the reputation of your CEO and leadership teams. How are they viewed by the media and employees? Is the executive team delivering on stated strategies and goals? Is there a robust talent review process to determine how deep the bench of potential leaders is Are your leaders active in recruiting top talent, and do they have an eye for talent?

Again, an approach to measurement should involve a *full circle* of views of the relative contributions of each primary partner in your employer brand, as shown in Table 8.3.

6. USE THE RESULTS OF WHAT YOU MEASURE.

In the end, all the tools in the world won't make a bit of difference if you don't use the results in your ongoing effort to sustain your employer brand.

"Don't expect quick wins," warns Yvonne Larkin at Diageo. "You can't expect results overnight. Be patient. You have to maintain the determination that this is the right thing to do."

The varying dimensions that make an employer brand so powerful—its connection to the outside, its reliance on the inside—make it challenging to sustain. Because so many things can go wrong. Competition can change. The business environment

Table 8.3. Primary Partner Contributions to Employer Brand.

	Awareness	Choice	Use	Loyalty
HR	How does HR build awareness for the employee experience?	How does HR enable employees to choose your business as a place to work?	How does HR enable employees to get things done?	How does HR enable employees to emotionally connect to your business?
Corporate Communications	How does Corporate Communications build awareness of your business as a place to work and buy?	How does Corporate Communications enable employees to choose your business as a place to work?	How does Corporate Communications help employees know how to get things done?	How does Corporate Communications help employees emotionally connect to your business?
Leadership	How does Leadership reinforce your business's reputation as a place to work and buy?	How does Leadership reinforce employee choice of your business as a place to work?	How does Leadership reinforce how employees get things done?	How does Leadership help employees emotionally connect to your business?

can change. Unforeseen disasters can occur. And employees and what they value can change.

So as you look at your role as brand champion, consider four keys to keeping your employer brand alive.

Stop. Every once in awhile, do something outrageous, and stop, think, and wonder. Business runs at such a fast pace there is barely enough time to go to the bathroom, much less collect your thoughts. Real change happens only when we give ourselves a chance to think about what needs to change.

One way Yahoo! differentiates itself from other internet brands is our distinctive personality. We don't want to lose that as we grow. We recently held a meeting with Marketing to discuss how to engage Yahoos worldwide in keeping our personality in every product. One great idea that emerged had to do with how we would send offer letters to new hires. Instead of sending on offer letter in a standard envelope, we ordered purple tubes that Yodeled upon opening and would include a Yahoo pen that Yodels when signing. Before starting work, every new Yahoo will Yodel.

—**Libby**

Listen. And not just to the same people over and over. Walk the halls. Ask people what's happening. If the business is supporting what they are trying to do. If they feel a sense of what's in it for them to work here. If they connect to the brand and the business. In addition to the formal, scheduled ways to measure, seek the informal as well.

Repeat. If you start to tire of your messages, you may be communicating just enough. There is so much noise that your messages must break through to be heard. Once, twice, three times won't do it. Your messages about your employer brand must be constantly repeated in order to simply be received.

Share. This is not a one-person task. Or even the task of your immediate team. For an employer brand to be effectively sustained, it must become the mission of the business. Otherwise it's just words. Perhaps nice words. But just words.

In the end, the employer brand will live only if dedicated, committed people maintain the focus.

You started this employer brand effort with the building of a business case that will remain your ultimate way to measure and nurture your employer brand.

Just don't try to do it all yourself.

Five Essential Steps

1. Now that you have gone through the steps to develop your employer brand, take the extra step to document your work in a set of clear guidelines, much as a business does for its external brand.

2. As you consider ways to implement the employer brand, look at its becoming a natural part of life in the business by creating an actual change process, to focus on the end state behaviors that will make the difference to the business.

3. Acknowledge that an employer brand takes just as much effort to keep alive as to initially build. Businesses change. And the brand must change right along.

4. Plan for specific steps to take on a regular basis to keep the brand alive, including work with leaders and employees—in fact, your holistic employer brand champion team members may be seeing each other for quite some time.

5. Develop and implement ways to collect meaningful feedback on the impact of the employer brand. This is not about how people feel— it's about what people do in their jobs day to day, and the perceptions that motivate those actions, positive or negative.

PART FOUR

WHAT IT MEANS FOR YOU

Chapter Nine

You and Employer Brand

So now you're ready.

You are all set to build your employer brand *from the inside*.

Throughout this book we have talked about what this will mean to your business.

So as we wind up, the question is, what can this mean to you? And what can employer brand mean to your career as an HR, corporate communications, or marketing professional?

Well, the way we see it, there's no more important issue for you to command today. Period.

Let's face it—what CEO or senior executive team would not want to have leagues of champions spreading the word that their business is a wonderful place to work? That the products are the best out there? And that the service levels inside the business are as high for employees as they are on the outside for customers? What employee wouldn't want to go to a cocktail party, PTA meeting, or soccer match and proudly announce, "I work for [fill in the blank], the best branded employer in the universe"?

And how easy would it be for you to find the right talent if those employee champions were encouraging the sharpest people they meet in these social situations to send a resume or meet for lunch to discuss opportunities and sample the legendary employer brand first hand?

If you succeed in building your employer brand from the inside, what customer won't want to connect with your business, knowing every point of contact will be consistent with your highest standards for the brand? By just doing business with you, they will feel and sense your values, and they will know what you stand for.

How will it feel to work in an atmosphere without silos? With your partners in HR, Corporate Communications, Marketing, and every other function or business unit working in a holistic way to create a legendary brand? With a brand that starts inside the business and is based on values, vision, and mission; a brand that communicates what you stand for and creates a stellar corporate reputation; and a brand that acts as a magnet for consumers?

What will your CFO think if she can ascribe a significant amount of market value to the brand equity built by you and your colleagues?

By looking at how you brand from the inside, as we have described, you will absorb your overall vision, mission, and strategy, your products and services, your customers and marketplaces; your people, communications, and culture; your behavior, how you get stuff done, and your creative design—all under one brand.

If you are in HR, you will be recognized for crafting an HR agenda that fosters a best employer brand. You may wake up one day to find yourself the people leader of one of the top businesses in your city, America, or the world. Your employees will be engaged and productive, your retention will be high, the best talent will find you, your job will be easier, and you will be acclaimed as an HR star. Your CEO won't ever think of having a meeting whose outcome could affect employees without you at the table. You will become a respected strategic advisor and counselor to the top leaders and the board, and a thought leader. You will be sought after as a speaker, quoted in the media, and considered for the best career opportunities within and outside of your organization. You might be one of the first of a new generation of HR leaders who move into CEO or board positions.

As a communicator, you'll find the media flocking to your door. The halo effect will create a rosy lens through which everything you do will be viewed. Even a misstep will be reported as an abnormality, not an irrevocable mistake. If *60 Minutes* shows up to do an interview, it will be about your business's legendary employer brand, undisputed market value, and differentiated products and services. You will become a Wall Street darling, and the likes of Jim Cramer will be shouting "Buy, buy, buy" on CNBC. Your bookshelves will be overloaded with Gold Quill awards. And your chairman and your CEO will never consider uttering a world without your advice and counsel. You might be considered as a potential successor for the CEO.

As a marketer, your brand valuation scores and brand equity will be climbing high, high, high. Your marketing budget will be plentiful, not only because the organization recognizes the ROI, but also because you won't need to spend as much to raise brand awareness—buzz will carry the brand. You will be honored by the CMO council as CMO of the year, and you will be sought after by the media and for plumb career opportunities and overwhelmed with honors and awards. You will be oft quoted and asked to speak at the best conferences; every agency will want to partner with you. You may even be considered as a potential successor for the CEO.

No matter what role you play in making the brand as relevant to employees as it is to customers, if you succeed, everybody wins. Your shareholders will see a return on investment. Your customers will be loyal, as they develop a life-long relationship with your brand. Your management team will enjoy the pride, success, and rewards of being part of a winning, well-respected organization. Your employees will enjoy opportunities for learning and growth, intrinsic and extrinsic rewards, and a higher degree of engagement.

Is this nirvana? Maybe. So few organizations have been able to achieve such a holistic approach to brand. So few organizations have been admired so much. So few have stood the test of time. But it can be done, through the power of a brand that is owned by everyone associated with the business.

So head out the office door and start to brand within—who knows what will happen?

We'll be with you every step of the way.

Because employer brand is a mission, not just a strategy; a cause, not just an approach; a purpose, not simply a task.

Our best of luck to you.

Notes

Chapter One

1. www.pg.com
2. Conversation with Diana Shaheen, Procter & Gamble.
3. www.kraft.com
4. www.anheuser-busch.com
5. Materials provided to authors by Hallmark.
6. Material provided to authors by UPS.
7. Conversation with Tom Pizutti, UPS.
8. Materials provided to authors by Hallmark.
9. www.disney.com
10. www.thebodyshop.com
11. www.colgate.com
12. www.pfizer.com
13. www.wrigley.com
14. Marc Gobé, *Emotional Branding: The New Paradigm for Connecting Brands to People* (New York: Allworth, 2001), p. 62.
15. www.kelloggs.com
16. Gobé, p. 62.
17. Materials provided to authors by Hallmark.
18. Gobé, p. xiv.
19. www.hallmark.com
20. www.harley-davidson.com
21. Jeff Swystun and Larry Oakner, "Deliver Your Brand's Promise," *Marketing,* 109:38 (November 22, 2004), p. 37.
22. www.esteelauder.com
23. Carl Sewell and Paul B. Brown, *Customers for Life: How to Turn That One-Time Buyer into a Lifetime Customer* (New York: Random House, 2002).
24. www.krispykreme.com
25. www.wamu.com
26. www.gap.com
27. www.ikea.com
28. www.pepsico.com
29. Gobé, p. xiv.
30. www.kashi.com
31. www.intel.com
32. www.mcdonalds.com
33. Pam Danzinger, "Luxury Brand Connects Corporate Strategy with Consumer Psychology, According to Unity Marketing; Brand Loyalty Is Scorecard to Measure Success," *Business Wire* (June 15, 2004), p. 5066.
34. Material provided to authors by FedEx.
35. Material provided to authors by UPS.

36. "Best Global Brands," *Business Week* (July 2005).

37. Material provided to authors by Hallmark.

38. Clare Dowdy, "Internal Branding," *Financial Times* (November 6, 2001), p. 4.

39. www.restorationhardware.com

40. www.thebodyshop.com

41. Chuck Brymer, "What Makes Brands Great," *Marketing* (January 15, 2004), p. 20.

42. Material provided to authors by Hallmark.

43. Deborah Kania, *Branding.Com: Online Branding for Marketing Success* (New York: McGraw-Hill, 2001), p. 12.

44. Brymer.

45. Yahoo! Hot Jobs poll of online users, 2005.

46. Material provided to authors by UPS.

47. Conversation with Linda Boff, GE.

48. Conversation with Eric Jackson, FedEx.

49. www.bmw.com

50. www.dell.com

Chapter Two

1. Conversation with Linda Boff, GE.

2. Conversation with Linda Clark-Santos, Washington Mutual.

3. Conversation with Annette Browdy, Hodes Research, 2005.

4. Yahoo! Hot Jobs.

5. Conversation with Yvonne Larkin, Diageo.

6. Jeff Swystun and Larry Oakner, "Deliver Your Brand's Promise," *Marketing* (November 22, 2004), p. 37.

7. Conversation with Dean Rodenbough, Hallmark.

8. James Trusty, "Give Your Workforce a (Basic) Instinct," *Brand Week* (February 24, 2003).

9. Material provided to authors by FedEx.

10. Conversation with Libby Hutchison, Washington Mutual.

11. Swystun and Oakner.

12. Brymer.

13. Material provided to authors by FedEx.

14. Trusty.

15. Brymer.

16. Allan Steinmetz, *B to B* (September 3, 2004), p. 9.

17. Material provided to authors by FedEx.

18. www.jetblue.com

19. www.intel.com

20. www.nike.com

21. www.gap.com

22. www.coca-cola.com

23. www.mbusa.com

24. www.nike.com

25. Swystun and Oakner.

26. www.ebay.com

27. www.diageo.com

28. Ruth Mortimer, *Brand Strategy* (April 2002), p. 20.

Chapter Three

1. Peter Cappelli, *Organizational Dynamics* (Riverwoods, Ill.: CCH Inc., 2003), p. 95.

2. John Sullivan, *Rethinking Strategic HR* (Riverwoods, Ill.: CCH Inc., 2003), p. 291.

Chapter Four

1. Jim Collins, *Good to Great* (New York: HarperCollins, 2001), p. 21.
2. Libby Sartain, "Getting Extraordinary Results from Ordinary People: Human Resources in the 21st Century," in *Human Resources in the 21st Century*, edited by Marc Effron, Robert Gandossy, and Marshall Goldsmith (New York: Wiley, 2003), p. 6.
3. *Fortune*, "The 100 Best Companies to Work for in America" (1993), p. xiii.
4. Tom Gibbon, quoted in *On Staffing: Advice and Perspectives from HR Leaders*, edited by Nicholas C. Burkholder, Preston J. Edwards, and Libby Sartain (New York: Wiley, 2003), p. 46.
5. Ruth Mortimer, *Brand Strategy* (April 2002), p. 20.
6. Jon R. Katzenbach, *Why Pride Matters More Than Money* (New York: Random House, 2003), p. 32.

Chapter Five

1. Many thanks to Tim Sanders, an author and professional speaker (and irrepressible advocate for good values in the business world) for sharing this story. Tim is the author of the best sellers *Love Is the Killer App* and *The Likeability Factor*. Thanks, Tim.
2. www.hp.com
3. www.harley-davidson.com
4. www.heinz.com
5. www.pbg.com
6. www.ebay.com
7. www.anheuser-busch.com
8. www.amazon.com
9. www.dell.com
10. www.motorola.com
11. www.generalmills.com
12. www.kraft.com
13. www.coach.com
14. www.ritzcarlton.com
15. www.bp.com
16. www.williams-sonoma.com
17. www.pfizer.com
18. www.intel.com
19. www.coca-cola.com
20. www.nokia.com
21. Material provided to authors by Hallmark.
22. www.porsche.com
23. www.jnj.com
24. www.boeing.com
25. www.bp.com
26. www.shell.com
27. www.gm.com
28. www.wholefoodsmarket.com
29. www.ikea.com
30. www.heineken.com
31. www.starbucks.com
32. www.kelloggs.com
33. www.gap.com
34. www.ikea.com
35. www.containerstore.com
36. www.wholefoodsmarket.com
37. www.nordstrom.com
38. www.americanexpress.com
39. www.pizzahut.com
40. www.ebay.com

41. www.gillette.com
42. www.americanapparel.net
43. www.heineken.com
44. www.tiffany.com
45. www.jnj.com
46. www.williams-sonoma.com
47. www.porsche.com
48. www.pfizer.com
49. www.merck.com
50. www.restorationhardware.com
51. www.pfizer.com
52. www.merck.com
53. www.ikea.com
54. www.apple.com
55. www.americanapparel.net
56. www.ebay.com
57. www.amazon.com
58. www.starbucks.com
59. www.williams-sonoma.com
60. www.wholefoodsmarket.com
61. www.sap.com
62. www.gap.com
63. www.tiffany.com
64. www.gillette.com
65. www.nordstrom.com
66. www.boeing.com
67. www.diageo.com
68. www.intel.com
69. www.kelloggs.com
70. www.nike.com
71. www.jetblue.com
72. www.anheuser-busch.com
73. www.amazon.com
74. www.starbucks.com
75. www.containerstore.com
76. www.coach.com
77. www.pfizer.com
78. www.kelloggs.com
79. www.heinz.com
80. www.pizzahut.com
81. www.boeing.com
82. www.diageo.com
83. www.pfizer.com
84. www.nike.com
85. www.merck.com
86. www.hsbc.com
87. www.kelloggs.com
88. www.gap.com
89. www.heinz.com
90. www.jetblue.com
91. www.anheuser-busch.com
92. www.dell.com
93. www.shell.com
94. www.containerstore.com
95. www.ups.com
96. www.generalmills.com
97. www.jnj.com
98. www.ge.com
99. www.merck.com
100. www.sap.com
101. www.kelloggs.com
102. www.toyota.com
103. www.heinz.com
104. www.citibank.com
105. www.americanexpress.com
106. www.gillette.com
107. www.americanapparel.net
108. www.heineken.com
109. www.anheuser-busch.com
110. www.wholefoodsmarket.com
111. www.halfpricebooks.com
112. www.coca-cola.com
113. www.hp.com
114. www.amazon.com
115. www.generalmills.com
116. www.boeing.com

Chapter Six
1. Tom Gibbon, "Employer Branding: The Last Legal Advantage in Winning the War for Talent," Chapter 6, *On Staffing: Advice and Perspectives from HR Leaders*, edited by

Nicholas C. Burkholder, Preston J. Edwards, and Libby Sartain (New York: Wiley, 2003), pp. 36–37.

2. Interview with Gerry Crispin, June 23, 2005.

3. Interview with Mukund Ramachadran, senior product marketing manager for Yahoo! Hot Jobs, June 24, 2005.

4. Keith H. Hammonds, "Why We Hate HR," *Fast Company* (August 2005), p. 43.

5. Ron Lieber, "Wired for Hiring: Microsoft's Slick Recruitment Machine," *Fortune* (February 2, 1996), http://money.cnn.com/magazines/fortune/fortune_archive/1996/02/05/207333/index.htm.

6. Jon R. Katzenbach, *Peak Performance: Aligning Hearts and Minds of Your Employees* (Watertown, Mass.: Harvard Business School Publishing, 2000), p. 186.

Chapter Seven

1. www.porsche.com

2. www.diageo.com

3. www.jnj.com

4. www.wholefoodsmarket.com

5. www.boeing.com

6. www.motorola.com

7. www.porsche.com

8. *Is It Time to Take the "Spin" Out of Employee Communication?* Towers Perrin study (2004).

9. Swystun and Oakner, "Deliver Your Brand's Promise."

10. Material provided to authors by P&G.

Chapter Eight

1. Great Places to Work Institute: www.greatplacestowork.com

ACKNOWLEDGMENTS

A book like this is more than words on paper; it is a way to thank so many people who have made a difference to our work over all these years.

Together, we sincerely thank people with whom we shared fabulous experiences at Southwest, especially Phyllis Adams and Ralph Kimmich, among many others; and Kevin McDermott at Towers Perrin.

Together, we sincerely thank people with whom we have shared more recent efforts at Yahoo!—Loree Farrar, Heidi Burgett, Barbara Oshima, Cheryl Van, Carol Mahoney, Chris Castro, Cammie Dunaway, Murray Gaylord, Kiersten Hollars, Joanna Stevens, and the creative team at Soho Square.

From Libby, special thanks go to Jack Bruner and Gary Mitchner, who brought the concept of internal branding to Southwest Airlines in the mid-nineties, and Martha Finney, who taught the process of writing and publishing a book.

From Mark, special thanks go to people who shared the essence of effective employee engagement through communication over the years, from Larry Bishop and Pat Milligan to Kevin Chapman, Brad Breininger, Katherine Woodall, and Bill Greene.

From both of us, we thank our research and editorial assistant, Jonathan Schumann, who introduced us to many new companies and connected us to the online work of so many well-branded organizations.

We thank Yahoo! Hot Jobs for conducting a compelling poll of people looking for jobs, and the Bernard Hodes Group for giving us an early glimpse of the results from their global employer branding survey.

A special thanks to our marvelous copyeditor, Kristi Hein, who brought such clarity to our thinking.

And we thank our colleagues from the many well-known brands mentioned in this book, who willingly shared their experiences, observations, and work products for this book. It's clear the community of people who believe in employer brand is wide. Thank you for adding to its richness.

Libby and Mark

THE AUTHORS

LIBBY SARTAIN, senior vice president of human resources and chief people Yahoo, is responsible for leading Yahoo! Inc.'s global human resources efforts and for managing and developing the human resources team, focusing on attracting, retaining, and developing Yahoo!'s employees, who promote and strengthen the company culture as well as represent the powerful Yahoo! brand. Prior to joining Yahoo! in August 2001, Libby was "vice president of people" at Southwest Airlines, where she led all human resources functions including employment, training, benefits, and compensation. She also played a key role in developing an employment brand strategy, which helped double employee growth in six years and fostered the company reputation as a leading employer of choice. Libby also served as chairman of the Society for Human Resource Management in 2001 and was named a fellow of the National Academy of Human Resources in 1998. She holds an MBA from the University of North Texas and a BBA from Southern Methodist University.

Libby coauthored *HR from the Heart: Inspiring Stories and Strategies for Building the People Side of Great Business* (AMACOM, 2003). She has authored numerous book chapters and articles on human resource management.

Libby currently divides her time between San Carlos, California, and her ranch near Bastrop, Texas. She is married and has a grown daughter.

MARK SCHUMANN, ABC, is the former global communication practice leader for the consulting firm Towers Perrin. As a consultant, Mark specializes in helping businesses use communication, change management, and measurement approaches to engage and motivate employees to commit—as well as help employees see "what's in it for them" to contribute to the business. During his more than twenty-five years of doing this work, Mark has counseled leaders of dozens of major businesses around the world during many challenging situations of defining change. For his work, Mark is the winner of thirteen Gold Quill Awards of Excellence from the International Association of Business Communicators (IABC) as well as the recipient of thirty-four Silver and Bronze Quill awards from IABC. He has won ten awards of excellence in employee communications from Business Insurance Magazine, and films he created were twice named "Best Picture of the Year" at the U.S. International Film Festival. Mark was also named Communicator of the Year of Houston in 1988 and Communicator of the Year of Dallas in 1990 by IABC. He is an accredited business communicator of IABC and a member of the IABC executive board of directors. Mark holds a bachelor's degree from Austin College, Sherman, Texas, and a master's degree from the University of Denver. He and his wife, Leann, are the parents of three sons.

INDEX